Peirce on Signs

■   ■   ■

Charles Sanders Peirce about 1860.
By permission of the Houghton Library, Harvard University

Peirce

ON

SIGNS

■   ■   ■

Writings on Semiotic by

Charles Sanders Peirce

Edited by James Hoopes

The University of North Carolina Press

Chapel Hill and London

Library of Congress Cataloging-in-Publication Data
Peirce, Charles S. (Charles Sanders), 1839–1914.
    Peirce on signs: writings on semiotic/by Charles Sanders
Peirce; edited by James Hoopes.
        p.   cm.
    Includes bibliographical references and index.
    ISBN 0-8078-1992-1 (alk. paper).—ISBN 0-8078-4342-3
(pbk.: alk. paper)
    1. Peirce, Charles S. (Charles Sanders), 1839–1914—
Contributions in semiotics.   2. Semiotics.   I. Hoopes,
James, 1944–   .   II. Title.
P85.P38P44 1991
121'.68—dc20   91-50253
                                                        C I P

The paper in this book meets the guidelines for perma-
nence and durability of the Committee on Production
Guidelines for Book Longevity of the Council on Library
Resources.

Manufactured in the United States of America
95   94   93   92   91   5   4   3   2   1

This volume's first ten selections are reprinted with per-
mission of Indiana University Press from volumes 1–3 of
*The Writings of Charles S. Peirce: A Chronological Edi-
tion*, edited by Edward C. Moore, Max H. Fisch, Christian
J. W. Kloesel et al. Copyright © 1982 by Peirce Edition
Project.

Contents

■   ■   ■

Acknowledgments

■　■　■

Christian J. W. Kloesel and other staff members at the Peirce Edition Project in Indianapolis have been generous and supportive to a newcomer to the work of editing Peirce. Not only their personal generosity but their superb multi-volume edition *Writings of Charles S. Peirce: A Chronological Edition* have been important in completing this much smaller project, as is indicated in the source attributions preceding many of the selections below.

When I began this project, it was my understanding that no other Peirce anthologies were imminent. As matters now stand, however, Indiana University Press will be publishing a Peirce anthology at about the same time as this one is published. In light of that fact, I am grateful to Indiana University Press for granting, in this one instance and in return for a fee, permission to reproduce this volume's first ten selections from volumes 1–3 of *The Writings of Charles S. Peirce: A Chronological Edition* edited by Edward C. Moore, Max H. Fisch, Christian J. W. Kloesel et al. Material from Peirce's manuscripts is published by permission of the Department of Philosophy of Harvard University. The manuscripts themselves are located in the Charles S. Peirce Papers at the Houghton Library at Harvard.

Albert Anderson, Vincent Colapietro, George Cotkin, David Hollinger, Christopher Hookway, and Bruce Kuklick kindly offered comments, either on the manuscript or on my initial proposal for this book. Christian J. W. Kloesel read both the proposal and the manuscript. I alone, of course, am responsible for the final result.

A generous stipend from the Babson College Board of Research enabled me to begin the project in the summer of 1989. Most of the work was done in congenial circumstances at the University of Manchester during the 1989–90 academic year, thanks to the members of the American studies department there and also to Graham Bird of the philosophy department. For making possible the year at Manchester I am grateful to Robert Burchell, to the Fulbright Commission in London, and to the Council for the International Exchange of Scholars. I am grateful to Diane Collins for preparing the line drawings.

As always, the love and patience of Carol, Johanna, and Benjamin Hoopes were essential.

Peirce on Signs

■　■　■

The Peirce Geodetic Monument in Indianapolis,
Indiana, is used as a marker in satellite surveys
conducted by the National Oceanic and Atmospheric
Administration. Employed for much of his adult life
by NOAA's ancestor organization, the U.S. Coast
and Geodetic Survey, Peirce was one of the
foremost geodesists of his day. (Courtesy of the
Dean of the School of Liberal Arts at Indiana
University–Purdue University at Indianapolis.)

Introduction

■ ■ ■

Charles Sanders Peirce (1839–1914) was born and raised in the most intellectually advantageous circumstances offered by nineteenth-century America. Benjamin Peirce, his father, was professor of mathematics and astronomy at Harvard and a preeminent American scientist who served many years with the United States Coast and Geodetic Survey. The talented parent recognized his son's great gifts and devoted many hours to training Charles's mental facility and powers of concentration. After Charles's graduation from Harvard, Benjamin arranged for his Coast Survey employment, which lasted for thirty years. Charles probably also owed to his father an assistantship at the Harvard Observatory from 1869 to 1872, which resulted in his only book published in his lifetime, *Photometric Researches* (1878). In these positions Charles not only made lasting, internationally recognized contributions to geodesy and astronomy but gained the closest practical familiarity with scientific method of any American philosopher.

As with Peirce's science, so too did his philosophy owe something to his father's early assistance. Charles recalled in old age that "before I came to man's estate, being greatly impressed with Kant's *Critic of Pure Reason*, my father . . . pointed out to me lacunæ in Kant's reasoning which I should probably not otherwise have discovered."[1] At least partly owing to his father's influence, Peirce's "New List of Categories" (1867) revised Kant's categories and, in doing so, first opened the way, as Max Fisch has observed, "to making the general theory of signs fundamental in logic, epistemology, and metaphysics."[2] The "New List," together with the related Cognition Series of 1868–69—"Questions concerning Certain Faculties Claimed for Man,"

1. *Collected Papers of Charles Sanders Peirce*, 8 vols., edited by Charles Hartshorne and Paul Weiss (vols. 1–6) and by Arthur Burks (vols. 7–8) (Cambridge: Harvard University Press, 1931–58), 1:299.

2. Max Fisch, Introduction to *Writings of Charles S. Peirce: A Chronological Edition*, 5 vols. to date (Bloomington: Indiana University Press, 1982–), 1:xxvi.

"Consequences of Four Incapacities," and "Grounds of Validity of the Laws of Logic"—and his 1871 review of Fraser's edition of *The Works of George Berkeley*, was one of the most important and thorough challenges to the Cartesian tradition since it came to dominate Western philosophy in the seventeenth century.

That a life begun so well should end in poverty and ruin is tragic, but it also lends poignancy to one of the basic thrusts of Peirce's semiotic—that self-knowledge is no easy affair. By comparison with other nineteenth-century intellectuals, Peirce married early, at twenty-three, to Zina Fay, the daughter of the Episcopal bishop of Vermont. The marriage was unhappy. In 1875, when Peirce was in the middle of a scientifically successful but financially disastrous year of gravitational work in Europe, Zina sailed home alone, and they eventually divorced. Unaccompanied when he next visited Europe in 1877, Peirce occupied himself during the voyage by writing the first of his famous *Popular Science* essays on the logic of science. That essay, "The Fixation of Belief," concluded that "the genius of a man's logical method should be loved and reverenced as his bride" (159). The series's second essay, "How to Make Our Ideas Clear," pointedly likened an obscure idea mistakenly cherished to the fabulous German "Melusina" (164)—Zina's given name.

Divorce itself was a large stigma to bear in respectable American society, but Peirce compounded his problems with further affronts to middle-class sensibilities. At Johns Hopkins, where he was appointed part-time lecturer in logic in 1879, there was a mistaken impression that he was an agnostic. Moreover, he became embroiled in unpleasant disputes with other members of the Hopkins faculty. Although he fell short of the needed standard of diplomacy in such controversies, the surviving documents do not suggest that he alone was at fault for the bad feelings. The final blow, however, was the discovery by the university's trustees that Peirce had shared accommodations with a mysterious French woman, Juliette Pourtalai, before marrying her in 1883.[3] His appointment, which he had expected to be made permanent, was terminated. Seven years later, in 1891, he reluctantly resigned from the Coast Survey after lengthy disputes with its officials.

Peirce's fortunes spiraled downward. Squandering his inheritance on a grand house in the small resort town of Milford, Pennsylvania, he mixed with the monied high society that congregated there and indulged in grandiose

3. Nathan Houser, Introduction to *Writings of Charles S. Peirce*, 4:lii–lxv.

plans for making a fortune. Not all of his money-making schemes were unrealistic in themselves, but they were unrealizable by Peirce, with his impulsive character and damaged reputation. By writing dictionary definitions, assisting with engineering calculations, and lecturing occasionally, he was able to support himself for a time, but he ended his days living on the charity of relatives and friends such as William James.

Three-quarters of a century after Peirce's death, his philosophy is beginning to receive the attention it deserves. The fact that Peirce left his system incomplete seems less and less to obscure the equally important fact that few philosophers have accomplished so much so well. Although there has always been a small group of philosophers knowledgeable and appreciative of Peirce, there has recently been a rapid and remarkable surge of interest among scholars in a wide variety of disciplines. This interest extends far beyond Peirce's native United States. The sesquicentennial of his birth was commemorated in September 1989 by an international congress at Harvard with more than four hundred scholars in attendance.

Humanist scholars, more or less independently of Peirce, have been coming round to something like his description of language and thought as processes of sign interpretation, but they badly need his chastening realism. The last twenty-five years have brought many new methodologies. Among these are deconstruction and poststructuralism. Although there are important differences between them and although their adherents sometimes quite ardently oppose each other, these methodologies may be conveniently grouped under a broad rubric—the interpretive revolution. The spokespersons for these methodologies attribute an extraordinary degree of either freedom or transitoriness to human thought, language, and interpretation—with little explanation of how such a universe is possible or of how reasonably honest and thoughtful people could have so wrongly overestimated the constraints within which human beings live. These methodological radicals would do well to consider Peirce's semiotic realism, according to which interpretation proceeds under the weight of many natural, logical limits. Both the 1868–69 Cognition Series and the better-known *Popular Science* essays of 1877–78 culminate in defenses of logic as objective and natural, making clear that the goal of Peirce's semiotic was constructive rather than deconstructive. Not the arbitrariness of meaning but the objective validity of logical truth was his cherished object. Yet contemporary methodological radicals, in rejecting simplistic empiricism as a model of humanity's relationship to the natural world, have helped to prepare an audience for Peirce.

At the same time, Peirce scholars have corrected the once-conventional opinion that Peirce was a failed genius, thwarted by his difficult personality and his tormented personal life. He has been most widely remembered as the man generously credited by William James with the founding of pragmatism but who otherwise accomplished little because he did not hold a permanent university appointment. After he died in poverty in 1914, it was commonly said that he had published little. Actually, during his lifetime Peirce published more than ten thousand pages in scholarly journals and popular periodicals, in scientific annuals, and in dictionaries and encyclopedias—an amount equal to twenty books of five hundred pages each.[4] He contributed to mathematics and to many sciences—chemistry, geodesy, astronomy, and experimental psychology—as well as to philosophy, where his chief contributions were in logic and metaphysics. In short, Peirce was a polymath whose published writings have lain scattered in so many different places that it has been difficult to estimate them justly.

Indiana University Press is correcting this situation with a thirty-volume collection entitled *Writings of Charles S. Peirce*, begun under the leadership of Max Fisch and the general editorship of Edward C. Moore. This new edition will supersede what was previously the standard published source, the eight-volume *Collected Papers of Charles Sanders Peirce*, of which the last two volumes (1958) were edited by Arthur W. Burks and the first six (1931–35) by Charles Hartshorne and Paul Weiss. To these scholars, especially Hartshorne and Weiss, whose work was for half a century the only published source for many important papers, all Peirce students must be grateful. But the new edition of *Writings*, which now goes forward under the direction of Christian J. W. Kloesel, will be an immense improvement in its chronological arrangement, in its comprehensiveness, and in its editorial thoroughness. As this introduction is written, the fourth volume has recently been published, and it is hoped that the entire edition will be complete shortly after the end of this century. By then it is possible that Peirce will be generally recognized as the greatest American philosopher and perhaps even, as Sir Karl Popper said, "one of the greatest philosophers of all time."[5]

Meanwhile, the present selection is aimed at filling the need for a one-

4. Christian J. W. Kloesel, "Editing Peirce," unpublished essay.
5. Karl Popper, *Objective Knowledge: An Evolutionary Approach* (Oxford: Clarendon Press, 1972), p. 212.

volume collection to make Peirce's writings on semiotic accessible to students and to scholars in disciplines other than philosophy. While there are other Peirce collections in print, they date from a time when there was not much general interest in semiotic. This is the first single-volume collection offering a general introduction to Peirce's semiotic and aimed at showing that semiotic was at the heart of his philosophy. Much of the material printed here has appeared in no other single-volume edition, and the rest had been divided among collections with no special focus on semiotic. The semiotic aspect of even this previously anthologized material should therefore be more easily comprehended here.

An additional objective of this edition is to publish accurate texts. Obvious errors in punctuation, spelling, or typography have been silently corrected, and in a few instances words have been added in brackets [ ] for clarity. Translations are also provided within brackets following foreign language passages when the context does not indicate their meaning, and I have used the translations given in the Indiana edition. With these exceptions, the following selections are faithful to the sources identified after the headnotes. Inconsistent but not obviously erroneous spelling, punctuation, and word usage have been retained in order to present the texts to the reader as Peirce himself intended. Nearly all of the essays included here that were published in Peirce's lifetime are printed uncut, in the form in which he intended to present them to the reader. All footnotes are Peirce's, but full bibliographic information has been added in brackets where his citations are incomplete. All other editorial annotation has been foregone in order to allow space for as comprehensive a selection of Peirce's semiotic writings as possible in a single, compact volume. Excellent editorial notes may be found in the present and forthcoming volumes of the *Writings*.

Readers well acquainted with Peirce's writings on signs will recognize how limited in scope this edition is. But no single volume could provide an entirely comprehensive survey of Peirce's intricate analyses of the various types and divisions of signs. The object of this volume is to offer a general overview of his semiotic theory. Those inspired to seek a deeper acquaintance with Peirce should turn to the *Collected Papers* and, better yet, to the *Writings* as those volumes become available.

Peirce's semeiotic, as he preferred to spell it, is best understood as a stage in the history of philosophy of mind and especially as a rejection of Western philosophy's traditional problem of knowledge as it was defined in the seventeenth century by René Descartes and John Locke. Descartes divided the created universe into two substances, matter and mind. The essence of matter was extension. The essence of mind was thought. External objects were represented subjectively in the human mind by "ideas." Locke extended Descartes's system of ideas into an argument for empiricism, a description of every idea as either a copy of a sensation or a reflection upon the mind's operations. It is well known that Locke's system had skeptical implications. If our ideas are internal experience, we have no way of knowing whether our ideas completely or accurately represent their external objects. Many histories of eighteenth- and early-nineteenth-century philosophy are therefore organized around the various materialist, idealist, commonsense, and transcendentalist responses to the epistemological skepticism that Locke's system helped to provoke.

These well-known facts must be contrasted with a much less well noticed tendency in Descartes's and Locke's views. They affirmed and inspired confidence in one form of knowledge—self-knowledge, or knowledge of one's own thoughts. Even if "I imagine a . . . chimera," said Descartes, "it is not less true that I imagine [it]."[6] Whether the mind's ideas are true or false, the mind accurately and completely perceives the ideas as in themselves they really are. "For let any Idea be as it will," said Locke, the idea "can be no other but such as the Mind perceives it to be."[7] Although Locke proposed a science of signs in a famous passage of the *Essay concerning Human Understanding*, he meant by "signs" not thoughts but words and other devices for representing thought externally and communicating it to others. As far as our selves are concerned, there is no need for our thoughts to be represented in signs, according to Locke, for they are present and immediately known to us.

This notion that human beings possess infallible knowledge of their thoughts exercised a profound influence in modern history. Confidence in self-knowledge underlay much of eighteenth- and early-nineteenth-century Western culture. The free-market ideology depended on a new confidence that human beings, tempered by the "moral sense" propounded by Francis Hutcheson and Adam Smith, were capable of discerning their self-interest.

6. René Descartes, *Meditations on First Philosophy*, in René Descartes, *Philosophical Works*, translated by Elizabeth S. Haldane and G. R. T. Ross, 2 vols. (Cambridge: Cambridge University Press, 1931), 1:159.

7. John Locke, *An Essay concerning Human Understanding*, edited by Peter H. Nidditch (Oxford: Oxford University Press, 1975), p. 364.

Conversely, if people with immediate knowledge of their mental processes feel free, they possess seemingly empirical evidence for free will. The emphasis on individual autonomy in republican political theory, education reform, feminism, abolitionism, and humanitarian movements of all sorts rested on such arguments.

To the degree that eighteenth- and early-nineteenth-century faith in individualism, democracy, and freedom rested on confidence in the immediate availability of self-knowledge, it rested on what now seems to have been a great mistake. Much twentieth-century psychology rejects Locke's notion that self-knowledge is immediately available to the conscious mind. So too did much Western psychology before Locke deny that humanity was capable of immediate self-knowledge and self-control. Western intellectual history since the middle of the nineteenth century might well be written around the theme of the long, slow, reluctant, and far-from-complete disengagement from the belief that self-knowledge requires only an inward glance.

But one nineteenth-century American quickly and completely abandoned belief in introspective self-knowledge. As early as 1867, when he was twenty-seven years old, Peirce rejected both Cartesian dualism and the Lockean description of all thought as the experience or internal perception of ideas.

The difference between an "idea" and a "sign" is at the heart of Peirce's semiotic. An idea may supposedly occur, in Descartes's terminology, "clearly and distinctly" in the mind.[8] Because the idea is perceived introspectively in the mind, its meaning is intuited, or immediately known. A "sign," as Peirce employed the term, is also a thought, but it differs from an "idea" in that its meaning is not self-evident. A sign receives its meaning by being interpreted by a subsequent thought or action. A stop sign at a street corner, for example, is first perceived as an octagonal shape bearing the letters *S-T-O-P*. It is only in relation to a subsequent thought—what Peirce called an interpretant—that the sign attains meaning. The meaning lies not in the perception but in the interpretation of the perception as a signal to stop or, better still, in the act of stopping. Peirce held that, like the perception of the stop sign, every thought is a sign without meaning until interpreted by a subsequent thought, an interpretant. Thus the meaning of every thought is established by a triadic relation, an *interpretation* of the thought as a *sign* of a determining *object*. Consequently, there is no such thing as a Lockean idea whose meaning is immediately, intuitively known or experienced.

8. Descartes, *Meditations*, p. 190.

Of course people feel that they have immediate knowledge of many of their thoughts, but Peirce pointed out that that feeling "has not prevented men from disputing very warmly as to which cognitions are intuitive" (36). Many beliefs once thought to be intuitive have turned out to be inferential in origin. Prior to Berkeley's book on vision, for example, nothing seemed more self-evident than that the third dimension of space is intuited, but Berkeley showed it to be inferred. Since the feeling that some knowledge is intuitive has often been mistaken and since the feeling is the only evidence for intuition, there is no ground for belief in intuition. "Only by external facts can thought be known at all," and thus follows the revolutionary conclusion that "all thought, therefore, must necessarily be in signs" (49). Thought is not immediate perception or undeniable experience of ideas within a self. Thought is in signs that attain meaning through the triadic relation:

OBJECT SIGN INTERPRETANT

According to Peirce, the triadic nature of thinking is exemplified in the process through which the concept of the self is, itself, created. An infant, inferring no self, knows no distinction between its body and the body of a hot stove. The child may therefore touch the stove. From the resulting feeling (sign), the child arrives at the conclusion (interpretant) that there is such a thing as error and that it inheres in its self (object).

Moreover, every thought, regardless of its object, is, according to Peirce, a feeling that semiotically manifests the self: "When we think, then, we our selves, as we are at that moment, appear as a sign" (67). The relation of object and interpretant through the sign or feeling is therefore also "a phenomenal manifestation of ourselves . . . , just as a rainbow is at once a manifestation both of the sun and of the rain" (67). Like the rainbow, the self is manifested in a sign relation; indeed, the self *is* the sign relation, since feeling is meaningless unless it is interpreted as the sign of an object.

To describe thinking as an interpretive process seems to open the door to just the sort of epistemological doubt that Peirce's philosophy was meant to avoid, but he believed that his views were grounds less for skepticism than for faith. Peirce refused to address Kant's "critical" question *whether* thought can truthfully signify reality because he believed on faith that it can do so. But he followed Kant's method of analyzing conceptions in order to explain *why* truth is attainable by thinking. From Kant, Peirce had learned that "every cognition contains a sensual element" (17). Truth being the agreement of a sign with its object, Peirce held that an entirely true thought cannot *become* true but must be true even the first time it is thought. Since "derivation not in time is the relation of accident to substance" (21) and since the sign is thought, the object is thought. This constitution of the known universe in thought was Peirce's "idealism," as it is sometimes called, but it is more accurately described as semiotic realism. For it is based on a commonsense acceptance of the world as it is apprehended and holds that the world is thus accurately represented to us because the very thoughts or signs in which we conceive of the world share a monistic or substantial identity with it.

Humanities scholars and social scientists may find Peirce's monism and semiotic realism useful as a model for relating mind to body, thought to action, and culture to society. Many of the methodological disagreements within and between disciplines are owing to the Cartesian dualism that still dominates much scholarship in the humanities and social sciences. Many of us tend to subscribe unquestioningly to two propositions that actually contradict each other: (1) external "reality" can be experienced in thought, even though (2) thought is supposed to be internal, or subjective, and therefore entirely distinct from external reality. By describing thought as bodily feeling or action, Peirce's semiotic realism avoids this contradiction and cuts through many of the resulting snarls that befoul contemporary discussion of the relation of thought to behavior.

Thinking, in Peirce's view, is not something that must be somehow related to behavior. Thinking *is* behavior. Thinking is action just as real, just as historical, just as behavioral as operating a machine, fighting a war, or eating a meal. Peirce's model of thought as feeling or action corrects the assumption of some "hard" social scientists that thinking is not as "real" and potentially influential as other, seemingly more tangible, elements in human life and society. Similarly, it corrects the view of some humanists that thinking is an utterly free process, unfettered from the relations in the natural world that constrain other kinds of human activity. These unrealistic methodological biases are, at bottom, derived from either materialist or idealist rebellions against Cartesian dualism. Peirce's semiotic offers a middle ground, a rejection of dualism that nevertheless avoids the excesses of either materialism or idealism.

Even though he viewed what is commonly called matter as thought, he was no traditional idealist, for thought, according to Peirce, does not occur as ideas immediately perceived "in" a self or soul or mind. In the eighteenth century, Bishop Berkeley had responded to the problem of epistemological skepticism with an idealism that interpreted material objects as perceptions or ideas *in* the mind of human beings and, ultimately, God. Peirce, on the other hand, described thought as a relation of signs possessing a material quality. He was therefore willing to describe human thought in physiological terms. For Peirce, then, human thought is, among other things, a brain process—a view probably congenial even to many who do not otherwise agree with his metaphysics.

Yet if Peirce allowed for a material quality in thought, he also believed that materialism provides no more accurate a description of intelligence than does idealism. The universe, he insisted, could not be satisfactorily described in terms of mechanical force, or what he called secondness—the process of action and reaction when one object strikes a second. Besides material force or secondness, there is another kind of real relation that Peirce called thirdness and that we call intelligence—the representation of one object to a second by a third, which is the essence of his semiotic. A thought may be a feeling in an organic body or brain, but a feeling in and of itself is meaningless. A feeling is a mere sign, awaiting interpretation in its relation with a subsequent thought or feeling before it can have meaning. Peirce was quite willing to agree with materialists that intelligence is not immediate knowledge of ideas inside a mind or soul. But he did not agree with materialists that intelligence could therefore be reduced to mechanical force or dyadic relations between material objects. Since intelligence involves meaning or interpretation, it cannot be described in terms of mere secondness, mere mechanics or brute force. Intelligence is a triadic, representational relation in which one object is represented to a second by a third, a sign.

All three categories are objectively real. Firstness is the sheer thisness, or existence, of things. Secondness is dyadic, or reactive, relations between things. And thirdness is triadic, or representational, relations among things.

Since thirdness, or intelligence, is objectively real, thought cannot be discounted as a general force in the universe, as Peirce believed most modern scientists had done. This is yet another realist dimension of semiotic realism; the sign relation is real, and therefore scholastic realists were right about universals. Deploring the nominalist tendency of modern science to affirm the reality of only individual facts and dyadic relations between them, Peirce held that "general principles are really operative in nature" (244). Denial of the real force of thirdness, or thought, in the world was attributable either to madness or blind loyalty to materialist theory, the weakness to which Peirce attributed the implicit nominalism of his scientific colleagues.

Seen against the background of Peirce's view of thought as objectively real and not bodilessly confined within a subjective self, the recent interest by literary theorists in "self-fashioning" and in "decentering" the self appears less radical than it is usually supposed to be. These theorists see the self as a cultural "construct" or "artifact" but offer no explanation of how it is constructed beyond assertions of a constitutive power in language. Perhaps they mean to suggest a semiotic realism similar to Peirce's. But they are unclear, and it is more likely that they have not thought the matter through and mean only that it is *subjective* identity that is fashioned by and in some transcendental self. As Vincent Colapietro has said, "Surely textualism is simply the most recent variety of the idealistic ideology."[9]

Although some passages in Peirce suggest a similar failure to escape subjectivity, he went far beyond any concept of the self as ideal or subjective. Sometimes he reads like a harbinger of the most recent motif of literary theory: "Men and words reciprocally educate each other" (84). But words, for Peirce, were thoughts, and he carried his description of thinking as a process of objective, interpretive relation to its logical conclusion: if the self did not contain thought, thought contained the self. As a young man he philosophized that "just as we say that a body is in motion, and not that motion is in a body we ought to say that we are in thought, and not that thoughts are in us" (71). This was an opinion he never abandoned, despite changes in his metaphysics, and in old age he advised William James that "one must not take a nominalistic view of Thought as if it were something that a man had in his consciousness. . . . It is we that are in it, rather than it in any of us."[10]

Why is Peirce's assertion of the constitutive power of thought better than a similar claim for language by some literary theorists? The answer is that the literary theorists derive their semiotic from French linguistics, especially Ferdinand de Saussure's emphasis on the supposedly arbitrary relations between the *signifié* (interpretant, in Peirce's terminology) and *signifiant* (sign). While words may be arbitrary in some respects, verbal language is far too narrow a field from which to construct a general theory of signs, as becomes evident from the arbitrariness posited of the social world by those who suppose that it is constituted in language. Peirce's theory, based on an analysis of thought rather than language (in the narrow, verbal sense), posits within the signifying

9. Vincent M. Colapietro, *Peirce's Approach to the Self: A Semiotic Perspective on Human Subjectivity* (Albany: State University of New York Press, 1989), p. 48.

10. Peirce to James, November 25, 1902, in Peirce, *Collected Papers*, 8:189.

process not only an object and its sign but also a third element, the interpretant, or thought, to which the sign gives rise. The meaning of the sign is not necessarily arbitrary but may be as logical as the thought that interprets it. While some contemporary literary theorists tell us that signs are arbitrary, verbal representations of their objects and as free to depart from them as "rose" from its flower, Peirce pointed out that many interpretants predicate real relations between signs and their objects. He called such signs indices, and one of his favorite examples was the interpretation of a weathercock as accurately signifying the direction of the wind because of its having a real relation with the wind. Moreover, even arbitrary symbols such as the stop sign are nevertheless not arbitrarily interpreted. A stop sign might just as well be triangular in shape if that were the arbitrarily chosen convention, but its interpretant would still be the thought of stopping. A driver might of course arbitrarily interpret the stop sign to mean "floor it!" In doing so, however, he would put himself at *real* risk.

Peirce's semiotic therefore allows for realistic recognition that human life and society are to a significant degree a matter not only of freedom but also of constraint, a matter of people being shoved this way or that by bullets and ballots, a surplus or shortage of land, the rise and fall of technologies and industries, and so on. On the other hand, Peirce's monism and semiotic realism allow for some freedom or, rather, a role for thought. By explaining how thought is action, Peirce's semiotic makes it possible to understand why thinking, language, and culture are *real* historical forces.

Semiotic is no magic wand that lets us avoid the hard work of thinking, but by adopting the viewpoint of Peirce's semiotic, it is possible to avoid either gnawing the old bone of the relation of thought to behavior or else isolating intellectual activity from society. Once intellectual activity is understood to be "real" behavior, its possible importance can be weighed fairly against other "real" elements in society. Conversely, social institutions such as government, political parties, corporations, labor unions, voluntary associations, and so on may be regarded as thought, once a thought is understood to be, not an idea known immediately within a mind, but rather, an interpretive relation. Once thought is understood as a process of sign interpretation, a great range of social phenomena too large to be comprehended within any individual mind may nevertheless be best understood as the result of a process of intelligence. Institutions and organizations are semiotic syntheses, so to speak, of the thoughts of a great many people. In this way, society may be understood as a human process even when study is not focused narrowly on the local and particular, as has been the fashion, for example, among social historians in the past quarter century. The superiority of Peirce's semiotic to Cartesian dualism is that it allows the study of society to be an objective science but not a strictly physical or material science. On the other hand, while thought is admitted into the real world, it is denied its traditional idealistic privileges, denied its absolute freedom, so to speak, from natural constraints.

Although Peirce has great relevance for the current emphasis on scholarly synthesis and interdisciplinary methodology, his semiotic would nevertheless allow for the usefulness of much specialized scholarship in the traditional disciplines. The situation might be compared to that in the physical sciences during Peirce's own lifetime. He regretted that the increasingly materialist assumptions and biases of nineteenth-century scientists tended to isolate the sciences, denying them integration with mental phenomena—the universe of thirdness. Yet many findings in these sciences were nonetheless useful and valid. Similarly, the adoption now of a Peircean perspective would not require the wholesale dismantling of the traditional humanistic disciplines and social sciences that seems to be called for by some other, methodologically more radical semiotics (and with nothing like Peirce's attempt to explain rather than merely to assert why our old assumptions are invalid and need to be discarded). Yet even while allowing for the usefulness of much past, traditional scholarship, Peirce's semiotic points to a new use for that scholarship by thinking about thinking in a way that does not divorce it from the natural world.

1

. . .

An Essay on the Limits of

Religious Thought Written to

Prove That We Can Reason

upon the Nature of God

The following is from the first of a group of brief essays, written in the summer of 1859 and unpublished in Peirce's lifetime. Here he argues that though some notions, such as the idea of God, are literally unthinkable and cannot be immediately present in the mind, they can nevertheless be represented and can therefore be thought of. While this view was not radical, the assertion that thinking can be done in signs was a step along the path to Peirce's eventual conclusion that all thinking is in signs.

Source: *Writings of Charles S. Peirce*, 1:37.

What can we discuss? Can we discuss nothing we do not comprehend? Can we not even discuss that which has no existence in nature or the imagination? We can discuss whatever we can syllogise upon. We can syllogize upon whatever we can define. And strange as it is we can give intelligible comprehensible definitions of many things which can never be themselves comprehended.

I will give two instances of this; one simple and the other practical. Suppose somebody should talk about an OG and when you asked him what he meant he should say it was a four-sided triangle. You would proceed to show that he had no such conception that nobody had. You would reason upon that which you could not conceive of. This instance is too elementary. Suppose someone should tell me he could imagine two persons interchanging identities. I should proceed to reason on the pretended imagination and show that it was inconceivable.

2

■ ■ ■

[A Treatise on Metaphysics]

If the mind immediately perceives ideas but the ideas are representatives of things without, then the truth of those representative ideas is in doubt. Immanuel Kant had addressed himself to demonstrating, within limits, the truth of perception in his *Critic of Pure Reason*. Peirce as a teenager had studied Kant assiduously and then, in his early twenties, rejected Kant's critical transcendentalism as an unwitting return to faith. Peirce preferred to base philosophy on a frank acknowledgment that knowledge always contains an element of faith, an undemonstrable but necessary belief that "the normal representations of truth within us are really correct," as he says in the following extract from a projected book of which he wrote ten thousand words in 1861. In the three sorts of representation that the youthful Peirce here identifies—*copy, sign,* and *type*—he adumbrates his eventual general typology of signs as *icon, index,* and *symbol.*

Source: *Writings of Charles S. Peirce*, 1:72–83.

Introduction

Chapter III
On the Uselessness of Transcendentalism

§1. *The Stand-point of the Transcendentalist*

When the view that metaphysics is the study of the human consciousness is carried out in a one-sided way, in forgetfulness that it is as truly Philosophy and also the Analysis of Conceptions, it produces Transcendentalism (better named Criticism), which is the system of investigation which thinks necessary to prove that the normal representations of truth within us are really correct. . . .

§3. *On Faith*

A. Need of It

I shall show

α. that the Transcendentalists conclude with a return to Faith.

β. that the use they make of it in their own procedure is the source of all that is valuable in their investigations.

γ. that while their own faith is necessarily blind, their reasoning is not so close as to leave no room for demonstrably trustworthy faith.

I. *Kant's Work*

An inference is involved in every cognition.

Proof. Relative cognition is the recognition of our relations to things.

All cognition of objects is relative, that is we know things only in their relations to us.

Every cognition must have an object (the subject of the proposition). The faculties whereby we become conscious of our relation to things are known as perceptions or sense.

∴Every cognition contains a sensual element.

Now the information of mere sensation is a chaotic manifold, while every cognition must be brought into the unity of one thought.

∴Every cognition involves an operation on the data.

An operation upon data resulting in cognition is an inference. ∴&c.

This demonstration is extracted from Kant. It does not extend to the cognition "*I think*."

Nothing is certain except what rests on the combined testimony of the senses and *I think*.

Proof. All knowledge, as we have just seen, is an inference from sensual minor premises. In metaphysics, all inferences have major premises. All knowledge is inferential except the *I think*. No cognition is certain which rests only on what is inferential. ∴&c.

Such is Kant's reasoning. He then proceeds to test all our Conceptions as to objective validity by finding whether they are anything but particular expressions of the *I think* or of sensuousness. The following he makes objectively valid:—

The Form of the External Sense—Space
The Form of the Internal Sense—Time

The Conceptions of the Understanding

I	II
Of Quantity	*Of Quality*
Unity	Reality
Plurality	Negation
Totality	Limitation

III	IV
Of Relation	*Of Modality*
Substantia et Accidens	Possibility–Impossibility
Causality	Existence–Non-existence
Action and Reaction	Necessity–Contingency

The following can never enter into any certain thought:—

The Ideas of Reason.

1. The Immateriality, Incorruptibility, Personality, Animality[1] of the Soul.

2. The Nature of the World as to
$$\left\{ \begin{array}{l} \text{Limitation} \\ \text{Compositeness} \\ \text{Fate} \\ \text{Createdness.} \end{array} \right.$$

3. God.

α. Though Kant cannot demonstrate the validity of the Ideas of pure reason, yet he chooses to believe it. Although there is not to him one whit more probability that they are true than that they are false, still he *trusts* in them,—he has Faith.

β. He also takes the validity of sensibility and of the *I think* for granted. Yet only by doing so has he made any solid work.

γ. A part of his argument is that nothing which rests only on what is inferential can be certain. This is not axiomatic nor demonstrable. It therefore leaves hope of proving the contrary which establishes the validity of faith. . . .

1. Animality = existence as a principle of life in matter.

B. Reason of Faith

Unfaith is either total or partial scepticism.

The different faculties have different realms by which they are distinguished. No faculty is to be trusted out of its own realm. ∴Hence no faculty can derive any support from another but each must stand upon its own credibility. No one faculty has more inherent credibility than another. ∴Partial scepticism is inconsistent. Total scepticism condemns itself. ∴Faith is the only consistent course.

The argument has the following advantages.

1. It puts faith on the same ground as all certitude.

2. It does not make it so sure that it is no longer faith.

3. By showing that faith is inherent in the very idea of the attainment of truth, it makes its acceptance *axiomatic*, and thus explains how we were already sure before we had reasoned about Faith.

C. Nature of Faith

I. What Faith is Not

1. It is not a purely intellectual principle; it is an unaccountable impulse to confide in certain truths.

This is forgotten by those who are over-anxious about the details of evidence in religion. They forget that with the highest certitude of inspiration and of history, belief still depends on an internal impulse. For, some things we should not believe though the angel Gabriel told us, while true religion is instinctively accepted by the ingenuous mind.

2. Faith is not peculiar to or more needed in one province of thought than in another. For every premiss we require faith and nowhere else is there any room for it.

This is overlooked by Kant and others who draw a distinction between *knowledge* and *faith*. Wherever there is knowledge there is Faith. Wherever there is Faith (properly speaking) there is knowledge.

3. There is no such thing as having immediate faith in the statements of others, be they men or angels or what. For whenever we believe statements, it is either *because* there is something in the fact itself which makes it credible or *because* we know something of the character of the witness. In either case there is a because whose major premiss is some principle concerning general characters of credibility. To believe without any such 'because' is mere credulity.

II. What Faith is

1. It is the recognition by consciousness of itself. It is the strength of that faculty by which abstractions are conceived.

2. It is the hearing of the testimony of consciousness, which developes into trust in every man till there is reason for distrust and a spirit of obedience to the Law of God.

3. It is the vigour of that part of the mind which is in communication with the eternal verities. By this, mountains are moved.

III. Effect of faith on Transcendentalism

1. *Criticism* is entirely swept away as useless.

2. *Transcendentalism* as a study of the out-reaching of the human mind retains its full value.

3. This study of consciousness is the examination of abstractions by analysis of conceptions.

BOOK I.
PRINCIPLES OF METAPHYSICAL INVESTIGATION

Chapter I. *Man the Measure of Things*

In the Introduction we have considered the Nature of Metaphysics, and have rejected certain false notions of its procedure.

In our investigations, metaphysics is to be taken as the analysis of Conceptions.

We need not ask the critical question; but still there is a question of uncritical transcendentalism with which every method of philosophy must open. It is, How should the conceptions which spring up freely in our minds by virtue of the constitution thereof be true for the outward world?

In this question we detect three leading conceptions *Truth, the Innateness of Ideas, Externality*. Let us analyze each of these.

§1. Of Truth

True is an adjective applicable solely to representations and things considered as representations. It implies the agreement of the representation with its object.

A. The simplest kind of agreement of truth is a resemblance between the representation and its object. I call this *verisimilitude*, and the representation a *copy*.

Resemblance consists in a likeness, which is a sameness of predicates. Carried to the highest point, it would destroy itself by becoming identity. All real resemblance, therefore, has a limit. Beyond the limits of resemblance, verisimilitude ceases. ∴Verisimilitude is partial truth.

Whatever claims to be a representation (a portrait for example) is a representation. Truth is that which, claiming to be a representation, is a representation. ∴Truth has no absolute antithesis.

> Falsehood also claims to be a representation
> It is an imperfect *copy* of truth
> ∴Verisimilitude is falsehood.

From Chapter III of the Introduction, it follows that there is no falsehood in our conceptions.

∴The truth of conceptions is not *verisimilitude*.

B. A representation agreeing with its object, without essential resemblance thereto, is a sign. The truth of a sign, I denominate *veracity*.

Veracity consists in a constant connection between the sign and the thing; for if the sign sometimes goes without the thing, then it may speak falsely, and if the thing goes without the sign, it may be belied in negative cases. Moreover a sign cannot exist as such the first time it is presented, because it must *become* a sign.

Conceptions claim as much truth the first time they are presented as they ever do.

∴The truth of conceptions is not *veracity*.

C. The objection to verisimilitude's being the truth of conceptions is its limitation as to completeness; the objection to veracity's is its limitation in beginning. Neither is open to the objection against the other. But veracity was called that kind of truth which was not verisimilitude.

Conceive, however, veracity to be perfect—to be founded not upon convention but upon the very nature of things and what have we?

1. The nature of a thing is that which it derives from its origin. Derivation not in time is the relation of accident to substance. Hence, an invariable connection in the nature of things is unity of substance.

2. The qualities of things are founded in the nature of things; hence, unity of substance implies perfect correspondence of qualities.

3. Hence perfect veracity is of a distinct character from cognizable veracity and it approaches quite as nearly perfection of verisimilitude. I will call it *verity*, and the representation a *type*.

4. Since conceptions perfectly correspond with qualities and since they have a connection therewith in the nature of things, they are *types* of things.

3

■ ■ ■

On a New List of Categories

Not long before Peirce presented the following paper to the American Academy of Arts and Sciences on May 14, 1867, he wrote in a private notebook that his new list of the fundamental categories of thought was "the gift I make to the world. That is my child. In it I shall live when oblivion has me—my body," and thirty-eight years later he referred to the paper as "my one contribution to philosophy" (quoted by Max H. Fisch in the Introduction to *Writings of Charles S. Peirce*, 1:xxvi). Time has vindicated these sentiments. Although he modified his categories throughout his career, this listing of Representation as the category closest to Substance made possible Peirce's general theory of signs. Eventually, he dispensed with Substance and Being, and he generalized "representation" into the metaphysical category of thirdness, or triadic relations. (For a succinct and accessible description of the categories as Peirce developed them in maturity, see "A Guess at the Riddle," selection 12 in this volume.) But he remained loyal to this paper's typology of "representamens" (subsequently, signs): likeness (subsequently, icon), index, and symbol.

Source: *Writings of Charles S. Peirce*, 2:49–59. Originally published in *Proceedings of the American Academy of Arts and Sciences* 7 (May 1867): 287–98.

§1. This paper is based upon the theory already established, that the function of conceptions is to reduce the manifold of sensuous impressions to unity, and that the validity of a conception consists in the impossibility of reducing the content of consciousness to unity without the introduction of it.

§2. This theory gives rise to a conception of gradation among those conceptions which are universal. For one such conception may unite the manifold of sense and yet another may be required to unite the conception and the manifold to which it is applied; and so on.

§3. That universal conception which is nearest to sense is that of *the present, in general*. This is a conception, because it is universal. But as the act of *attention* has no connotation at all, but is the pure denotative power of the mind, that is to say, the power which directs the mind to an object, in contradistinction to the power of thinking any predicate of that object,—so the conception of *what is present in general*, which is nothing but the general recognition of what is contained in attention, has no connotation, and therefore no proper unity. This conception of the present in general, or IT in general, is rendered in philosophical language by the word "substance" in one of its meanings. Before any comparison or discrimination can be made between what is present, what is present must have been recognized as such, as *it*, and subsequently the metaphysical parts which are recognized by abstraction are attributed to this *it*, but the *it* cannot itself be made a predicate. This *it* is thus neither predicated of a subject, nor in a subject, and accordingly is identical with the conception of substance.

§4. The unity to which the understanding reduces impressions is the unity of a proposition. This unity consists in the connection of the predicate with the subject; and, therefore, that which is implied in the copula, or the conception of *being*, is that which completes the work of conceptions of reducing the manifold to unity. The copula (or rather the verb which is copula in one of its senses) means either *actually is* or *would be*, as in the two propositions, "There *is* no griffin," and "A griffin *is* a winged quadruped." The conception of *being* contains only that junction of predicate to subject wherein these two verbs agree. The conception of being, therefore, plainly has no content.

If we say "The stove is black," the stove is the *substance*, from which its blackness has not been differentiated, and the *is*, while it leaves the substance just as it was seen, explains its confusedness, by the application to it of *blackness* as a predicate.

Though *being* does not affect the subject, it implies an indefinite determinability of the predicate. For if one could know the copula and predicate of any proposition, as " . . . is a tailed-man," he would know the predicate to be applicable to something supposable, at least. Accordingly, we have propositions whose subjects are entirely indefinite, as "There is a beautiful ellipse," where the subject is merely *something actual or potential*; but we have no propositions whose predicate is entirely indeterminate, for it would be quite senseless to say, "*A* has the common characters of all things," inasmuch as there are no such common characters.

Thus substance and being are the beginning and end of all conception. Substance is inapplicable to a predicate, and being is equally so to a subject.

§5. The terms "prescision" and "abstraction," which were formerly applied to every kind of separation, are now limited, not merely to mental separation, but to that which arises from *attention to* one element and *neglect of* the other. Exclusive attention consists in a definite conception or *supposition* of one part of an object, without any supposition of the other. Abstraction or prescision ought to be carefully distinguished from two other modes of mental separation, which may be termed *discrimination* and *dissociation*. Discrimination has to do merely with the essences of terms, and only draws a distinction in meaning. Dissociation is that separation which, in the absence of a constant association, is permitted by the law of association of images. It is the consciousness of one thing, without the necessary simultaneous consciousness of the other. Abstraction or prescision, therefore, supposes a greater separation than discrimination, but a less separation than dissociation. Thus I can discriminate red from blue, space from color, and color from space, but not red from color. I can prescind red from blue, and space from color (as is manifest from the fact that I actually believe there is an uncolored space between my face and the wall); but I cannot prescind color from space, nor red from color. I can dissociate red from blue, but not space from color, color from space, nor red from color.

Prescision is not a reciprocal process. It is frequently the case, that, while *A* cannot be prescinded from *B*, *B* can be prescinded from *A*. This circumstance is accounted for as follows. Elementary conceptions only arise upon the occasion of experience; that is, they are produced for the first time according to a general law, the condition of which is the existence of certain impressions. Now if a conception does not reduce the impressions upon which it follows to unity, it is a mere arbitrary addition to these latter; and elementary conceptions do not arise thus arbitrarily. But if the impressions could be definitely comprehended without the conception, this latter would not reduce them to unity. Hence, the impressions (or more immediate conceptions) cannot be definitely conceived or attended to, to the neglect of an elementary conception which reduces them to unity. On the other hand, when such a conception has once been obtained, there is, in general, no reason why the premises which have occasioned it should not be neglected, and therefore the explaining conception may frequently be prescinded from the more immediate ones and from the impressions.

§6. The facts now collected afford the basis for a systematic method of searching out whatever universal elementary conceptions there may be intermediate between the manifold of substance and the unity of being. It has been shown that the occasion of the introduction of a universal elementary conception is either the reduction of the manifold of substance to unity, or else the conjunction to substance of another conception. And it has further been shown that the elements conjoined cannot be supposed without the conception, whereas the conception can generally be supposed without these elements. Now, empirical psychology discovers the occasion of the introduction of a conception, and we have only to ascertain what conception already lies in the data which is united to that of substance by the first conception, but which cannot be supposed without this first conception, to have the next conception in order in passing from being to substance.

It may be noticed that, throughout this process, *introspection* is not resorted to. Nothing is assumed respecting the subjective elements of consciousness which cannot be securely inferred from the objective elements.

§7. The conception of *being* arises upon the formation of a proposition. A proposition always has, besides a term to express the substance, another to express the quality of that substance; and the function of the conception of being is to unite the quality to the substance. Quality, therefore, in its very widest sense, is the first conception in order in passing from being to substance.

Quality seems at first sight to be given in the impression. Such results of introspection are untrustworthy. A proposition asserts the applicability of a mediate conception to a more immediate one. Since this is *asserted*, the more mediate conception is clearly regarded independently of this circumstance, for otherwise the two conceptions would not be distinguished, but one would be thought through the other, without this latter being an object of thought, at all. The mediate conception, then, in order to be *asserted* to be applicable to the other, must first be considered without regard to this circumstance, and taken immediately. But, taken immediately, it transcends what is given (the more immediate conception), and its applicability to the latter is hypothetical. Take, for example, the proposition, "This stove is black." Here the conception of *this stove* is the more immediate, that of *black* the more mediate, which latter, to be predicated of the former, must be discriminated from it and considered *in itself*, not as applied to an object, but simply as embodying a quality, *blackness*. Now this *blackness* is a pure species or abstraction, and its application to *this stove* is entirely hypothetical. The same thing is meant by "the stove is black," as by "there is blackness in the stove." *Embodying blackness* is the equivalent of *black*.[1] The proof is this. These conceptions are applied indifferently to precisely the same facts. If, therefore, they were different, the one which was first applied would fulfil every function of the other; so that one of them would be superfluous. Now a superfluous conception is an arbitrary fiction, whereas elementary conceptions arise only upon the requirement of experience; so that a superfluous elementary conception is impossible. Moreover, the conception of a pure abstraction is indispensable, because we cannot comprehend an agreement of two things, except as an agreement in some *respect*, and this respect is such a pure abstraction as blackness. Such a pure abstraction, reference to which constitutes a *quality* or general attribute, may be termed a *ground*.

Reference to a ground cannot be prescinded from being, but being can be prescinded from it.

§8. Empirical psychology has established the fact that we can know a quality only by means of its contrast with or similarity to another. By contrast and agreement a thing is referred to a correlate, if this term may be used in a wider sense than usual. The occasion of the introduction of the conception of reference to a ground is the reference to a correlate, and this is, therefore, the next conception in order.

Reference to a correlate cannot be prescinded from reference to a ground; but reference to a ground may be prescinded from reference to a correlate.

§9. The occasion of reference to a correlate is obviously by comparison. This act has not been sufficiently studied by the psychologists, and it will, therefore, be necessary to adduce some examples to show in what it consists. Suppose we wish to compare the letters p and b. We may imagine one of them to be turned over on the line of writing as an axis, then laid upon the other, and finally to become transparent so that the other can be seen through it. In this way we shall form a new image which mediates between the images of the two letters, inasmuch as it represents one of them to be (when turned over) the likeness of the other. Again, suppose we think of a murderer as being in relation to a murdered person; in this case we conceive the act of the murder,

---

1. This agrees with the author of *De Generibus et Speciebus, Ouvrages Inédits d'Abélard* [*Sancti Anselmi Contuariensis opuscula philosophico-theologica selecta*, edited by Carolus Haas (Tübingen, 1863)], p. 528.

and in this conception it is represented that corresponding to every murderer (as well as to every murder) there is a murdered person; and thus we resort again to a mediating representation which represents the relate as standing for a correlate with which the mediating representation is itself in relation. Again, suppose we look up the word *homme* in a French dictionary; we shall find opposite to it the word *man*, which, so placed, represents *homme* as representing the same two-legged creature which *man* itself represents. By a further accumulation of instances, it would be found that every comparison requires, besides the related thing, the ground, and the correlate, also a *mediating representation which represents the relate to be a representation of the same correlate which this mediating representation itself represents.* Such a mediating representation may be termed an *interpretant*, because it fulfils the office of an interpreter, who says that a foreigner says the same thing which he himself says. The term "representation" is here to be understood in a very extended sense, which can be explained by instances better than by a definition. In this sense, a word represents a thing to the conception in the mind of the hearer, a portrait represents the person for whom it is intended to the conception of recognition, a weathercock represents the direction of the wind to the conception of him who understands it, a barrister represents his client to the judge and jury whom he influences.

Every reference to a correlate, then, conjoins to the substance the conception of a reference to an interpretant; and this is, therefore, the next conception in order in passing from being to substance.

Reference to an interpretant cannot be prescinded from reference to a correlate; but the latter can be prescinded from the former.

§10. Reference to an interpretant is rendered possible and justified by that which renders possible and justifies comparison. But that is clearly the diversity of impressions. If we had but one impression, it would not require to be reduced to unity, and would therefore not need to be thought of as referred to an interpretant, and the conception of reference to an interpretant would not arise. But since there is a manifold of impressions, we have a feeling of complication or confusion, which leads us to differentiate this impression from that, and then, having been differentiated, they require to be brought to unity. Now they are not brought to unity until we conceive them together as being *ours*, that is, until we refer them to a conception as their interpretant. Thus, the reference to an interpretant arises upon the holding together of diverse impressions, and therefore it does not join a conception to the substance, as the other two references do, but unites directly the manifold of the substance itself. It is, therefore, the last conception in order in passing from being to substance.

§11. The five conceptions thus obtained, for reasons which will be sufficiently obvious, may be termed *categories*. That is,

BEING,
    Quality (Reference to a Ground),
    Relation (Reference to a Correlate),
    Representation (Reference to an Interpretant),
SUBSTANCE.

The three intermediate conceptions may be termed accidents.

§12. This passage from the many to the one is numerical. The conception of a *third* is that of an object which is so related to two others, that one of these must be related to the other in the same way in which the third is related to that other. Now this coincides with the conception of an interpretant. An *other* is plainly equivalent to a *correlate*. The conception of second differs from that of other, in implying the possibility of a third. In the same way, the conception of *self* implies the possibility of an *other*. The *Ground* is the self abstracted from the concreteness which implies the possibility of an other.

§13. Since no one of the categories can be prescinded from those above it, the list of supposable objects which they afford is,

What is.
    Quale—that which refers to a ground,
    Relate—that which refers to ground and correlate,
    Representamen—that which refers to ground, correlate, and
        interpretant.
It.

§14. A quality may have a special determination which prevents its being prescinded from reference to a correlate. Hence there are two kinds of relation.

1st. That of relates whose reference to a ground is a prescindible or internal quality.

2d. That of relates whose reference to a ground is an unprescindible or relative quality.

In the former case, the relation is a mere *concurrence* of the correlates in one character, and the relate and correlate are not distinguished. In the latter case the correlate is set over against the relate, and there is in some sense an *opposition*.

Relates of the first kind are brought into relation simply by their agreement. But mere disagreement (unrecognized) does not constitute relation, and therefore relates of the second kind are only brought into relation by correspondence in fact.

A reference to a ground may also be such that it cannot be prescinded from a reference to an interpretant. In this case it may be termed an *imputed* quality. If the reference of a relate to its ground can be prescinded from reference to an interpretant, its relation to its correlate is a mere concurrence or community in the possession of a quality, and therefore the reference to a correlate can be prescinded from reference to an interpretant. It follows that there are three kinds of representations.

1st. Those whose relation to their objects is a mere community in some quality, and these representations may be termed *Likenesses*.

2d. Those whose relation to their objects consists in a correspondence in fact, and these may be termed *Indices* or *Signs*.

3d. Those the ground of whose relation to their objects is an imputed character, which are the same as *general signs*, and these may be termed *Symbols*.

§15. I shall now show how the three conceptions of reference to a ground, reference to an object, and reference to an interpretant are the fundamental ones of at least one universal science, that of logic. Logic is said to treat of second intentions as applied to first. It would lead me too far away from the matter in hand to discuss the truth of this statement; I shall simply adopt it as one which seems to me to afford a good definition of the subject-genus of this science. Now, second intentions are the objects of the understanding considered as representations, and the first intentions to which they apply are the objects of those representations. The objects of the understanding, considered as representations, are symbols, that is, signs which are at least potentially general. But the rules of logic hold good of any symbols, of those which are written or spoken as well as of those which are thought. They have no immediate application to likenesses or indices, because no arguments can be constructed of these alone, but do apply to all symbols. All symbols, indeed, are in one sense relative to the understanding, but only in the sense in which also all things are relative to the understanding. On this account, therefore, the relation to the understanding need not be expressed in the definition of the sphere of logic, since it determines no limitation of that sphere. But a distinction can be made between concepts which are supposed to have no existence except so far as they are actually present to the understanding, and external symbols which still retain their character of symbols so long as they are only *capable* of being understood. And as the rules of logic apply to these latter as much as to the former (and though only through the former, yet this character, since it belongs to all things, is no limitation), it follows that logic has for its subject-genus all symbols and not merely concepts.[2] We come, therefore, to this, that logic treats of the reference of symbols in general to their objects. In this view it is one of a trivium of conceivable sciences. The first would treat of the formal conditions of symbols having meaning, that is of the reference of symbols in general to their grounds or imputed characters, and this might be called formal grammar; the second, logic, would treat of the formal conditions of the truth of symbols; and the third would treat of the formal conditions of the force of symbols, or their power of appealing to a mind, that is, of their reference in general to interpretants, and this might be called formal rhetoric.

There would be a general division of symbols, common to all these sciences; namely, into,

1°: Symbols which directly determine only their *grounds* or imputed qualities, and are thus but sums of marks or *terms*;

2°: Symbols which also independently determine their *objects* by means of other term or terms, and thus, expressing their own objective validity, become capable of truth or falsehood, that is, are *propositions*; and,

3°: Symbols which also independently determine their *interpretants*, and thus the minds to which they appeal, by premising a proposition or propositions which such a mind is to admit. These are *arguments*.

2. Herbart says: "Unsre sämmtlichen Gedanken lassen sich von zwei Seiten betrachten; theils als Thätigkeiten unseres Geistes, theils in Hinsicht dessen, *was* durch sie gedacht wird. In letzterer Beziehung heissen sie *Begriffe*, welches Wort, indem es das *Begriffene* bezeichnet, zu abstrahiren gebietet von der Art und Weise, wie wir den Gedanken empfangen, produciren, oder reproduciren mögen." ["All our thoughts may be considered from two points of view; partly as activities of our mind, partly in relation to what is thought through them. In the latter respect they are called *concepts*, which term, by signifying *what is conceived*, requires us to abstract from the mode and manner in which we might receive, produce, or reproduce the thought." Johann Friedrich Herbart, *Lehrbuch zur Einleitung in die Philosophie*, vol. 1 of *Sämmtliche Werke*, edited by G. Hartenstein (Leipzig: Leopold Voss, 1850).] But the whole difference between a concept and an external sign lies in these respects which logic ought, according to Herbart, to abstract from.

And it is remarkable that, among all the definitions of the proposition, for example, as the *oratio indicativa*, as the subsumption of an object under a concept, as the expression of the relation of two concepts, and as the indication of the mutable ground of appearance, there is, perhaps, not one in which the conception of reference to an object or correlate is not the important one. In the same way, the conception of reference to an interpretant or third, is always prominent in the definitions of argument.

In a proposition, the term which separately indicates the object of the symbol is termed the subject, and that which indicates the ground is termed the predicate. The objects indicated by the subject (which are always potentially a plurality,—at least, of phases or appearances) are therefore stated by the proposition to be related to one another on the ground of the character indicated by the predicate. Now this relation may be either a concurrence or an opposition. Propositions of concurrence are those which are usually considered in logic; but I have shown in a paper upon the classification of arguments that it is also necessary to consider separately propositions of opposition, if we are to take account of such arguments as the following:—

Whatever is the half of anything is less than that of which it is the half;

$$A \text{ is half of } B:$$
$$\therefore A \text{ is less than } B.$$

The subject of such a proposition is separated into two terms, a "subject nominative" and an "object accusative."

In an argument, the premises form a representation of the conclusion, because they indicate the interpretant of the argument, or representation representing it to represent its object. The premises may afford a likeness, index, or symbol of the conclusion. In deductive argument, the conclusion is represented by the premises as by a general sign under which it is contained. In hypotheses, something *like* the conclusion is proved, that is, the premises form a likeness of the conclusion. Take, for example, the following argument:—

$$M \text{ is, for instance, } P', P'', P''', \text{ and } P^{iv};$$
$$S \text{ is } P', P'', P''', \text{ and } P^{iv}:$$
$$\therefore S \text{ is } M.$$

Here the first premise amounts to this, that "P', P'', P''', and P^{iv}" is a likeness of M, and thus the premises are or represent a likeness of the conclusion. That it is different with induction another example will show.

S', S'', S''', and S^{iv} are taken as samples of the collection M;
S', S'', S''', and S^{iv} are P:
∴ All M is P.

Hence the first premise amounts to saying that "S', S'', S''', and S^{iv}" is an index of M. Hence the premises are an index of the conclusion.

The other divisions of terms, propositions, and arguments arise from the distinction of extension and comprehension. I propose to treat this subject in a subsequent paper. But I will so far anticipate that, as to say that there is, first, the direct reference of a symbol to its objects, or its denotation; second, the reference of the symbol to its ground, through its object, that is, its reference to the common characters of its objects, or its connotation; and third, its reference to its interpretants through its object, that is, its reference to all the synthetical propositions in which its objects in common are subject or predicate, and this I term the information it embodies. And as every addition to what it denotes, or to what it connotes, is effected by means of a distinct proposition of this kind, it follows that the extension and comprehension of a term are in an inverse relation, as long as the information remains the same, and that every increase of information is accompanied by an increase of one or other of these two quantities. It may be observed that extension and comprehension are very often taken in other senses in which this last proposition is not true.

This is an imperfect view of the application which the conceptions which, according to our analysis, are the most fundamental ones find in the sphere of logic. It is believed, however, that it is sufficient to show that at least something may be usefully suggested by considering this science in this light.

4

■ ■ ■

Questions concerning Certain
Faculties Claimed for Man

This essay and the following two constitute what is often referred to as Peirce's Cognition Series.

In the previous essay, "On a New List of Categories," Peirce had called attention to the fact that his argument did not rely on introspection. He probably had already arrived at the negative answer he gave to Question 4 below, in which he denied that human beings possessed the power of introspection—that is, the supposed power of immediate, or direct (unrepresented), knowledge of their thoughts. The denial of introspection opens the way to the claim, in the answer to Question 5, that all thought is in signs that have no immediate content but require a subsequent thought, an interpretant, to give them meaning by interpreting them as representations.

It may aid comprehension of Peirce's declaration that a human being is a sign, in the essay following this one, if his negative answer to Question 2 below is studied carefully. Peirce was denying neither that human beings are real nor that there is a sense in which they may be said to be self-conscious. Rather, he was asserting that the sense of self, the individual's awareness of being distinct from the rest of the universe, is not an immediately known "idea" (in the Lockean sense) but is an inference, an interpretation of signs.

Source: *Writings of Charles S. Peirce*, 2:193–211.
Originally published in *Journal of Speculative Philosophy* 2
(1868): 103–14.

QUESTION 1. *Whether by the simple contemplation of a cognition, independently of any previous knowledge and without reasoning from signs, we are enabled rightly to judge whether that cognition has been determined by a previous cognition or whether it refers immediately to its object.*

Throughout this paper, the term *intuition* will be taken as signifying a cognition not determined by a previous cognition of the same object, and therefore so determined by something out of the consciousness.[1] Let me request the reader to note this. *Intuition* here will be nearly the same as "premise not itself a conclusion"; the only difference being that premises and conclusions are judgments, whereas an intuition may, as far as its definition states, be any kind of cognition whatever. But just as a conclusion (good or bad) is determined in the mind of the reasoner by its premise, so cognitions not judgments may be determined by previous cognitions; and a cognition not so determined, and therefore determined directly by the transcendental object, is to be termed an *intuition*.

Now, it is plainly one thing to have an intuition and another to know intuitively that it is an intuition, and the question is whether these two things, distinguishable in thought, are, in fact, invariably connected, so that we can always intuitively distinguish between an intuition and a cognition determined by another. Every cognition, as something present, is, of course, an intuition of itself. But the determination of a cognition by another cognition or by a

---

1. The word *intuitus* first occurs as a technical term in St. Anselm's *Monologium* [*Sancti Anselmi Contuariensis opuscula philosophico-theologica selecta*, edited by Carolus Haas (Tübingen, 1863), 1:89–90, 95]. He wished to distinguish between our knowledge of God and our knowledge of finite things (and, in the next world, of God, also); and thinking of the saying of St. Paul, *Videmus nunc per speculum in aenigmate: tunc autem facie ad faciem* ["For now we see in a mirror, darkly; but then face to face" (1 Cor. 13:12)], he called the former *speculation* and the latter *intuition*. This use of "speculation" did not take root, because that word already had another exact and widely different meaning. In the middle ages, the term "intuitive cognition" had two principal senses, 1st, as opposed to abstractive cognition, it meant the knowledge of the present as present, and this is its meaning in Anselm; but 2d, as no intuitive cognition was allowed to be determined by a previous cognition, it came to be used as the opposite of discursive cognition (see Scotus, *In sententias* [*Scriptum in quatuor libros Sententiarum*, 2 vols. (Venice, 1477)], lib. 2, dist. 3, qu. 9), and this is nearly the sense in which I employ it. This is also nearly the sense in which Kant uses it, the former distinction being expressed by his *sensuous* and *non-sensuous*. (See *Werke*, herausg. Rosenkrantz [*Immanuel Kant's sämmtliche Werke*, edited by Karl Rosenkranz and Friedrich Wilhelm Schubert (Leipzig: Leopold Voss, 1838–42)], Thl. 2, S. 713, 31, 41, 100, u. s. w.) An enumeration of six meanings of intuition may be found in Hamilton's *Reid* [*The Works of Thomas Reid*, 5th ed., edited by William Hamilton (Edinburgh: Maclachlan and Stewart, 1858)], p. 759.

transcendental object is not, at least so far as appears obviously at first, a part of the immediate content of that cognition, although it would appear to be an element of the action or passion of the transcendental *ego*, which is not, perhaps, in consciousness immediately; and yet this transcendental action or passion may invariably determine a cognition of itself, so that, in fact, the determination or non-determination of the cognition by another may be a part of the cognition. In this case, I should say that we had an intuitive power of distinguishing an intuition from another cognition.

There is no evidence that we have this faculty, except that we seem to *feel* that we have it. But the weight of that testimony depends entirely on our being supposed to have the power of distinguishing in this feeling whether the feeling be the result of education, old associations, etc., or whether it is an intuitive cognition; or, in other words, it depends on presupposing the very matter testified to. Is this feeling infallible? And is this judgment concerning it infallible and so on, *ad infinitum*? Supposing that a man really could shut himself up in such a faith, he would be, of course, impervious to the truth, "evidence-proof."

But let us compare the theory with the historic facts. The power of intuitively distinguishing intuitions from other cognitions has not prevented men from disputing very warmly as to which cognitions are intuitive. In the middle ages, reason and external authority were regarded as two coördinate sources of knowledge, just as reason and the authority of intuition are now; only the happy device of considering the enunciations of authority to be essentially indemonstrable had not yet been hit upon. All authorities were not considered as infallible, any more than all reasons; but when Berengarius said that the authoritativeness of any particular authority must rest upon reason, the proposition was scouted as opinionated, impious, and absurd. Thus, the credibility of authority was regarded by men of that time simply as an ultimate premise, as a cognition not determined by a previous cognition of the same object, or, in our terms, as an intuition. It is strange that they should have thought so, if, as the theory now under discussion supposes, by merely contemplating the credibility of the authority, as a Fakir does his God, they could have seen that it was not an ultimate premise! Now, what if our *internal* authority should meet the same fate, in the history of opinions, as that external authority has met? Can that be said to be absolutely certain which many sane, well-informed, and thoughtful men already doubt?[2]

2. The proposition of Berengarius is contained in the following quotation from his *De Sacra Cœna*: "*Maximi plane cordis est, per omnia ad dialecticam confugere, quia*

Every lawyer knows how difficult it is for witnesses to distinguish between what they have seen and what they have inferred. This is particularly noticeable in the case of a person who is describing the performances of a spiritual

---

confugere ad eam ad rationem est confugere, quo qui non confugit, cum secundum rationem sit factus ad imaginem dei, suum honorem reliquit, nec potest renovari de die in diem ad imaginem dei." ["Clearly it is characteristic of a great soul to take refuge in dialectic in all circumstances, because to take refuge in it is to take refuge in reason, and whoever does not take refuge there, since it is in respect of reason that he is made in the image of God, gives up his honor; nor can he be renewed from day to day in the image of God." Peirce's source for this quotation from Berengarius was Carl Prantl, *Geschichte der Logik im Abendlande*, 3 vols. (Leipzig: S. Hirzel, 1855–67), 2:72–75.] The most striking characteristic of medieval reasoning, in general, is the perpetual resort to authority. When Fredegisus and others wish to prove that darkness is a thing, although they have evidently derived the opinion from nominalistic-Platonistic meditations, they argue the matter thus: "God called the darkness, night" [quoted in Prantl, *Geschichte*, 2:17–19]; then, certainly, it is a thing, for otherwise before it had a name, there would have been nothing, not even a fiction to name. Abelard thinks it worth while to cite Boëthius, when he says that space has three dimensions, and when he says that an individual cannot be in two places at once [*Ouvrages inédits d'Abélard pour servir à l'histoire de la philosophie scholastique en France*, edited by Victor Cousin (Paris: Imprimerie Royale, 1836), p. 179]. The author of *De Generibus et Speciebus*, a work of a superior order, in arguing against a Platonic doctrine, says that if whatever is universal is eternal, the *form* and matter of Socrates, being severally universal, are both eternal, and that, therefore, Socrates was not created by God, but only put together, "*quod quantum a vero deviet, palam est.*" The authority is the final court of appeal. The same author, where in one place he doubts a statement of *Boëthius*, finds it necessary to assign a special reason why in this case it is not absurd to do so. *Exceptio probat regulam in casibus non exceptis* [*Ouvrages inédits d'Abélard*, pp. 528, 517, 535]. Recognized authorities were certainly sometimes disputed in the twelfth century; their mutual contradictions insured that; and the authority of philosophers was regarded as inferior to that of theologians. Still, it would be impossible to find a passage where the authority of Aristotle is directly denied upon any logical question. "*Sunt et multi errores eius,*" says John of Salisbury, "*qui in scripturis tam Ethnicis, quam fidelibus poterunt inveniri: verum in logica parem habuisse non legitur.*" ["Although there are many mistakes in Aristotle, as is evident from the writings of Christians and pagans alike, his equal in logic has yet to be found."] "*Sed nihil adversus Aristotelem*" ["But nothing against Aristotle," *Ouvrages inédits*, p. 293], says Abelard, and in another place, "*Sed si Aristotelem Peripateticorum principem culpare possumus, quam amplius in hac arte recepimus?*" ["But if we can find fault with Aristotle, the prince of the Peripatetics, what *can* we trust in this art?," *Ouvrages inédits*, p. 204.] The idea of going without an authority, or of subordinating authority to reason, does not occur to him.

medium or of a professed juggler. The difficulty is so great that the juggler himself is often astonished at the discrepancy between the actual facts and the statement of an intelligent witness who has not understood the trick. A part of the very complicated trick of the Chinese rings consists in taking two solid rings linked together, talking about them as though they were separate—taking it for granted, as it were—then pretending to put them together, and handing them immediately to the spectator that he may see that they are solid. The art of this consists in raising, at first, the strong suspicion that one is broken. I have seen McAlister do this with such success, that a person sitting close to him, with all his faculties straining to detect the illusion, would have been ready to swear that he saw the rings put together, and, perhaps, if the juggler had not professedly practised deception, would have considered a doubt of it as a doubt of his own veracity. This certainly seems to show that it is not always very easy to distinguish between a premise and a conclusion, that we have no infallible power of doing so, and that in fact our only security in difficult cases is in some signs from which we can infer that a given fact must have been seen or must have been inferred. In trying to give an account of a dream, every accurate person must often have felt that it was a hopeless undertaking to attempt to disentangle waking interpretations and fillings out from the fragmentary images of the dream itself.

The mention of dreams suggests another argument. A dream, as far as its own content goes, is exactly like an actual experience. It is mistaken for one. And yet all the world believes that dreams are determined, according to the laws of the association of ideas, &c., by previous cognitions. If it be said that the faculty of intuitively recognizing intuitions is asleep, I reply that this is a mere supposition, without other support. Besides, even when we wake up, we do not find that the dream differed from reality, except by certain *marks*, darkness and fragmentariness. Not unfrequently a dream is so vivid that the memory of it is mistaken for the memory of an actual occurrence.

A child has, as far as we know, all the perceptive powers of a man. Yet question him a little as to *how* he knows what he does. In many cases, he will tell you that he never learned his mother-tongue; he always knew it, or he knew it as soon as he came to have sense. It appears, then, that *he* does not possess the faculty of distinguishing, by simple contemplation, between an intuition and a cognition determined by others.

There can be no doubt that before the publication of Berkeley's book on Vision, it had generally been believed that the third dimension of space was immediately intuited, although, at present, nearly all admit that it is known by inference. We had been *contemplating* the object since the very creation of man, but this discovery was not made until we began to *reason* about it.

Does the reader know of the blind spot on the retina? Take a number of this journal, turn over the cover so as to expose the white paper, lay it sideways upon the table before which you must sit, and put two cents upon it, one near the left-hand edge, and the other to the right. Put your left hand over your left eye, and with the right eye look *steadily* at the left-hand cent. Then, with your right hand, move the right-hand cent (which is now plainly seen) *towards* the left hand. When it comes to a place near the middle of the page it will disappear—you cannot see it without turning your eye. Bring it nearer to the other cent, or carry it further away, and it will reappear; but at that particular spot it cannot be seen. Thus it appears that there is a blind spot nearly in the middle of the retina; and this is confirmed by anatomy. It follows that the space we immediately see (when one eye is closed) is not, as we had imagined, a continuous oval, but is a ring, the filling up of which must be the work of the intellect. What more striking example could be desired of the impossibility of distinguishing intellectual results from intuitional data, by mere contemplation?

A man can distinguish different textures of cloth by feeling; but not immediately, for he requires to move his fingers over the cloth, which shows that he is obliged to compare the sensations of one instant with those of another.

The pitch of a tone depends upon the rapidity of the succession of the vibrations which reach the ear. Each of those vibrations produces an impulse upon the ear. Let a single such impulse be made upon the ear, and we know, experimentally, that it is perceived. There is, therefore, good reason to believe that each of the impulses forming a tone is perceived. Nor is there any reason to the contrary. So that this is the only admissible supposition. Therefore, the pitch of a tone depends upon the rapidity with which certain impressions are successively conveyed to the mind. These impressions must exist previously to any tone; hence, the sensation of pitch is determined by previous cognitions. Nevertheless, this would never have been discovered by the mere contemplation of that feeling.

A similar argument may be urged in reference to the perception of two dimensions of space. This appears to be an immediate intuition. But if we were to *see* immediately an extended surface, our retinas must be spread out in an extended surface. Instead of that, the retina consists of innumerable needles pointing towards the light, and whose distances from one another are decidedly greater than the *minimum visible*. Suppose each of those nerve-points conveys the sensation of a little colored surface. Still, what we immediately see must even then be, not a continuous surface, but a collection of spots. Who could discover this by mere intuition? But all the analogies of the nervous system are against the supposition that the excitation of a single nerve can produce an idea as complicated as that of a space, however small. If the excitation of no one of these nerve-points can immediately convey the impression of space, the excitation of all cannot do so. For, the excitation of each produces some impression (according to the analogies of the nervous system), hence, the sum of these impressions is a necessary condition of any perception produced by the excitation of all; or, in other terms, a perception produced by the excitation of all is determined by the mental impressions produced by the excitation of every one. This argument is confirmed by the fact that the existence of the perception of space can be fully accounted for by the action of faculties known to exist, without supposing it to be an immediate impression. For this purpose, we must bear in mind the following facts of physio-psychology: 1. The excitation of a nerve does not of itself inform us where the extremity of it is situated. If, by a surgical operation, certain nerves are displaced, our sensations from those nerves do not inform us of the displacement. 2. A single sensation does not inform us how many nerves or nerve-points are excited. 3. We can distinguish between the impressions produced by the excitations of different nerve-points. 4. The differences of impressions produced by different excitations of similar nerve-points are similar. Let a momentary image be made upon the retina. By No. 2, the impression thereby produced will be indistinguishable from what might be produced by the excitation of some conceivable single nerve. It is not conceivable that the momentary excitation of a single nerve should give the sensation of space. Therefore, the momentary excitation of all the nerve-points of the retina cannot, immediately or mediately, produce the sensation of space. The same argument would apply to any unchanging image on the retina. Suppose, however, that the image moves over the retina. Then the peculiar excitation which at one instant affects one nerve-point, at a later instant will affect another. These will convey impressions which are very similar by 4, and yet which are distinguishable by 3. Hence, the conditions for the recognition of a relation between these impressions are present. There being, however, a very great number of nerve-points affected by a very great number of successive excitations, the relations of the resulting impressions will be almost inconceivably complicated. Now, it is a known law of mind, that when phenomena of an extreme complexity are presented, which yet would be reduced to *order* or mediate simplicity by the application of a certain conception, that conception sooner or later arises in application to those phenomena. In the case under consideration, the conception of extension would reduce the phenomena to unity, and, therefore, its genesis is fully accounted for. It remains only to explain why the previous cognitions which determine it are not more clearly apprehended. For this explanation, I shall refer to a paper upon a new list of categories, §5,[3] merely adding that just as we are able to recognize our friends by certain appearances, although we cannot possibly say what those appearances are and are quite unconscious of any process of reasoning, so in any case when the reasoning is easy and natural to us, however complex may be the premises, they sink into insignificance and oblivion proportionately to the satisfactoriness of the theory based upon them. This theory of space is confirmed by the circumstance that an exactly similar theory is imperatively demanded by the facts in reference to time. That the course of time should be immediately felt is obviously impossible. For, in that case, there must be an element of this feeling at each instant. But in an instant there is no duration and hence no immediate feeling of duration. Hence, no one of these elementary feelings is an immediate feeling of duration; and, hence the sum of all is not. On the other hand, the impressions of any moment are very complicated,—containing all the images (or the elements of the images) of sense and memory, which complexity is reducible to mediate simplicity by means of the conception of time.[4]

3. *Proceedings of the American Academy*, May 14, 1867.

4. The above theory of space and time does not conflict with that of Kant so much as it appears to do. They are in fact the solutions of different questions. Kant, it is true, makes space and time intuitions, or rather forms of intuition, but it is not essential to his theory that intuition should mean more than "individual representation." The apprehension of space and time results, according to him, from a mental *process*,—the "Synthesis der Apprehension in der Anschauung." (See *Critik d. reinen Vernunft*. Ed. 1781, pp. 98 *et seq.*) My theory is merely an account of this synthesis.

The gist of Kant's "Transcendental Æsthetic" is contained in two principles. First, that universal and necessary propositions are not given in experience. Second, that universal and necessary facts are determined by the conditions of experience in general. By a universal proposition is meant merely, one which asserts something of *all* of a sphere,—not necessarily one which all men believe. By a necessary proposition,

We have, therefore, a variety of facts, all of which are most readily explained on the supposition that we have no intuitive faculty of distinguishing intuitive from mediate cognitions. Some arbitrary hypothesis may otherwise explain any one of these facts; this is the only theory which brings them to support one another. Moreover, no facts require the supposition of the faculty in question. Whoever has studied the nature of proof will see, then, that there are here very strong reasons for disbelieving the existence of this faculty. These will become still stronger when the consequences of rejecting it have, in this paper and in a following one, been more fully traced out.

---

is meant one which asserts what it does, not merely of the actual condition of things, but of every possible state of things; it is not meant that the proposition is one which we cannot help believing. Experience, in Kant's first principle, cannot be used for a product of the objective understanding, but must be taken for the first impressions of sense with consciousness conjoined and worked up by the imagination into images, together with all which is logically deducible therefrom. In this sense, it may be admitted that universal and necessary propositions are not given in experience. But, in that case, neither are any inductive conclusions which might be drawn from experience, given in it. In fact, it is the peculiar function of induction to produce universal and necessary propositions. Kant points out, indeed, that the universality and necessity of scientific inductions are but the analogues of philosophic universality and necessity; and this is true, in so far as it is never allowable to accept a scientific conclusion without a certain indefinite drawback. But this is owing to the insufficiency in the number of the instances; and whenever instances may be had in as large numbers as we please, *ad infinitum*, a truly universal and necessary proposition is inferable. As for Kant's second principle, that the truth of universal and necessary propositions is dependent upon the conditions of the general experience, it is no more nor less than the principle of Induction. I go to a fair and draw from the "grab-bag" twelve packages. Upon opening them, I find that every one contains a red ball. Here is a universal fact. It depends, then, on the condition of the experience. What is the condition of the experience? It is solely that the balls are the contents of packages drawn from that bag, that is, the only thing which determined the experience, was the drawing from the bag. I infer, then, according to the principle of Kant, that what is drawn from the bag will contain a red ball. This is induction. Apply induction not to any limited experience but to all human experience and you have the Kantian philosophy, so far as it is correctly developed.

Kant's successors, however, have not been content with his doctrine. Nor ought they to have been. For, there is this third principle: "Absolutely universal propositions must be analytic." For whatever is absolutely universal is devoid of all content or determination, for all determination is by negation. The problem, therefore, is not how universal propositions can be synthetical, but how universal propositions appearing to be synthetical can be evolved by thought alone from the purely indeterminate.

QUESTION 2. *Whether we have an intuitive self-consciousness.*

Self-consciousness, as the term is here used, is to be distinguished both from consciousness generally, from the internal sense, and from pure apperception. Any cognition is a consciousness of the object as represented; by self-consciousness is meant a knowledge of ourselves. Not a mere feeling of subjective conditions of consciousness, but of our personal selves. Pure apperception is the self-assertion of THE *ego*; the self-consciousness here meant is the recognition of my *private* self. I know that *I* (not merely *the* I) exist. The question is, how do I know it; by a special intuitive faculty, or is it determined by previous cognitions?

Now, it is not self-evident that we have such an intuitive faculty, for it has just been shown that we have no intuitive power of distinguishing an intuition from a cognition determined by others. Therefore, the existence or nonexistence of this power is to be determined upon evidence, and the question is whether self-consciousness can be explained by the action of known faculties under conditions known to exist, or whether it is necessary to suppose an unknown cause for this cognition, and, in the latter case, whether an intuitive faculty of self-consciousness is the most probable cause which can be supposed.

It is first to be observed that there is no known self-consciousness to be accounted for in extremely young children. It has already been pointed out by Kant[5] that the late use of the very common word "I" with children indicates an imperfect self-consciousness in them, and that, therefore, so far as it is admissible for us to draw any conclusion in regard to the mental state of those who are still younger, it must be against the existence of any self-consciousness in them.

On the other hand, children manifest powers of thought much earlier. Indeed, it is almost impossible to assign a period at which children do not already exhibit decided intellectual activity in directions in which thought is indispensable to their well-being. The complicated trigonometry of vision, and the delicate adjustments of coördinated movement, are plainly mastered very early. There is no reason to question a similar degree of thought in reference to themselves.

A very young child may always be observed to watch its own body with great attention. There is every reason why this should be so, for from the child's point of view this body is the most important thing in the universe.

5. *Werke*, vii (2), 11.

Only what it touches has any actual and present feeling; only what it faces has any actual color; only what is on its tongue has any actual taste.

No one questions that, when a sound is heard by a child, he thinks, not of himself as hearing, but of the bell or other object as sounding. How when he wills to move a table? Does he then think of himself as desiring, or only of the table as fit to be moved? That he has the latter thought, is beyond question; that he has the former, must, until the existence of an intuitive self-consciousness is proved, remain an arbitrary and baseless supposition. There is no good reason for thinking that he is less ignorant of his own peculiar condition than the angry adult who denies that he is in a passion.

The child, however, must soon discover by observation that things which are thus fit to be changed are apt actually to undergo this change, after a contact with that peculiarly important body called Willy or Johnny. This consideration makes this body still more important and central, since it establishes a connection between the fitness of a thing to be changed and a tendency in this body to touch it before it is changed.

The child learns to understand the language; that is to say, a connection between certain sounds and certain facts becomes established in his mind. He has previously noticed the connection between these sounds and the motions of the lips of bodies somewhat similar to the central one, and has tried the experiment of putting his hand on those lips and has found the sound in that case to be smothered. He thus connects that language with bodies somewhat similar to the central one. By efforts, so unenergetic that they should be called rather instinctive, perhaps, than tentative, he learns to produce those sounds. So he begins to converse.

It must be about this time that he begins to find that what these people about him say is the very best evidence of fact. So much so, that testimony is even a stronger mark of fact than *the facts themselves*, or rather than what must now be thought of as the *appearances* themselves. (I may remark, by the way, that this remains so through life; testimony will convince a man that he himself is mad.) A child hears it said that the stove is hot. But it is not, he says; and, indeed, that central body is not touching it, and only what that touches is hot or cold. But he touches it, and finds the testimony confirmed in a striking way. Thus, he becomes aware of ignorance, and it is necessary to suppose a *self* in which this ignorance can inhere. So testimony gives the first dawning of self-consciousness.

But, further, although usually appearances are either only confirmed or merely supplemented by testimony, yet there is a certain remarkable class of appearances which are continually contradicted by testimony. These are those predicates which *we* know to be emotional, but which *he* distinguishes by their connection with the movements of that central person, himself (that the table wants moving, etc.). These judgments are generally denied by others. Moreover, he has reason to think that others, also, have such judgments which are quite denied by all the rest. Thus, he adds to the conception of appearance as the actualization of fact, the conception of it as something *private* and valid only for one body. In short, *error* appears, and it can be explained only by supposing a *self* which is fallible.

Ignorance and error are all that distinguish our private selves from the absolute *ego* of pure apperception.

Now, the theory which, for the sake of perspicuity, has thus been stated in a specific form, may be summed up as follows: At the age at which we know children to be self-conscious, we know that they have been made aware of ignorance and error; and we know them to possess at that age powers of understanding sufficient to enable them to infer from ignorance and error their own existence. Thus we find that known faculties, acting under conditions known to exist, would rise to self-consciousness. The only essential defect in this account of the matter is, that while we know that children exercise *as much* understanding as is here supposed, we do not know that they exercise it in precisely this way. Still the supposition that they do so is infinitely more supported by facts, than the supposition of a wholly peculiar faculty of the mind.

The only argument worth noticing for the existence of an intuitive self-consciousness is this. We are more certain of our own existence than of any other fact; a premise cannot determine a conclusion to be more certain than it is itself; hence, our own existence cannot have been inferred from any other fact. The first premise must be admitted, but the second premise is founded on an exploded theory of logic. A conclusion cannot be more certain than that some one of the facts which support it is true, but it may easily be more certain than any one of those facts. Let us suppose, for example, that a dozen witnesses testify to an occurrence. Then my belief in that occurrence rests on the belief that each of those men is generally to be believed upon oath. Yet the fact testified to is made more certain than that any one of those men is generally to be believed. In the same way, to the developed mind of man, his own existence is supported by *every other fact*, and is, therefore, incomparably more certain than any one of these facts. But it cannot be said to be more certain than that there is another fact, since there is no doubt perceptible in either case.

It is to be concluded, then, that there is no necessity of supposing an intuitive self-consciousness, since self-consciousness may easily be the result of inference.

QUESTION 3. *Whether we have an intuitive power of distinguishing between the subjective elements of different kinds of cognitions.*

Every cognition involves something represented, or that of which we are conscious, and some action or passion of the self whereby it becomes represented. The former shall be termed the objective, the latter the subjective, element of the cognition. The cognition itself is an intuition of its objective element, which may therefore be called, also, the immediate object. The subjective element is not necessarily immediately known, but it is possible that such an intuition of the subjective element of a cognition of its character, whether that of dreaming, imagining, conceiving, believing, etc., should accompany every cognition. The question is whether this is so.

It would appear, at first sight, that there is an overwhelming array of evidence in favor of the existence of such a power. The difference between seeing a color and imagining it is immense. There is a vast difference between the most vivid dream and reality. And if we had no intuitive power of distinguishing between what we believe and what we merely conceive, we never, it would seem, could in any way distinguish them; since if we did so by reasoning, the question would arise whether the argument itself was believed or conceived, and this must be answered before the conclusion could have any force. And thus there would be a *regressus ad infinitum*. Besides, if we do not know that we believe, then, from the nature of the case, we do not believe.

But be it noted that we do not intuitively know the existence of this faculty. For it is an intuitive one, and we cannot intuitively know that a cognition is intuitive. The question is, therefore, whether it is necessary to suppose the existence of this faculty, or whether then the facts can be explained without this supposition.

In the first place, then, the difference between what is imagined or dreamed and what is actually experienced, is no argument in favor of the existence of such a faculty. For it is not questioned that there are distinctions in what is present to the mind, but the question is, whether independently of any such distinctions in the immediate *objects* of consciousness, we have any immediate power of distinguishing different modes of consciousness. Now, the very fact of the immense difference in the immediate objects of sense and imagination, sufficiently accounts for our distinguishing those faculties; and instead of being an argument in favor of the existence of an intuitive power of distinguishing the subjective elements of consciousness, it is a powerful reply to any such argument, so far as the distinction of sense and imagination is concerned.

Passing to the distinction of belief and conception, we meet the statement that the knowledge of belief is essential to its existence. Now, we can unquestionably distinguish a belief from a conception, in most cases, by means of a peculiar feeling of conviction; and it is a mere question of words whether we define belief as that judgment which is accompanied by this feeling, or as that judgment from which a man will act. We may conveniently call the former *sensational*, the latter *active* belief. That neither of these necessarily involves the other, will surely be admitted without any recital of facts. Taking belief in the sensational sense, the intuitive power of reorganizing it will amount simply to the capacity for the sensation which accompanies the judgment. This sensation, like any other, is an object of consciousness; and therefore the capacity for it implies no intuitive recognition of subjective elements of consciousness. If belief is taken in the active sense, it may be discovered by the observation of external facts and by inference from the sensation of conviction which usually accompanies it.

Thus, the arguments in favor of this peculiar power of consciousness disappear, and the presumption is again against such a hypothesis. Moreover, as the immediate objects of any two faculties must be admitted to be different, the facts do not render such a supposition in any degree necessary.

QUESTION 4. *Whether we have any power of introspection, or whether our whole knowledge of the internal world is derived from the observation of external facts.*

It is not intended here to assume the reality of the external world. Only, there is a certain set of facts which are ordinarily regarded as external, while others are regarded as internal. The question is whether the latter are known otherwise than by inference from the former. By introspection, I mean a direct perception of the internal world, but not necessarily a perception of it *as* internal. Nor do I mean to limit the signification of the word to intuition, but would extend it to any knowledge of the internal world not derived from external observation.

There is one sense in which any perception has an internal object, namely, that every sensation is partly determined by internal conditions. Thus, the sensation of redness is as it is, owing to the constitution of the mind; and in this sense it is a sensation of something internal. Hence, we may derive a knowledge of the mind from a consideration of this sensation, but that knowledge would, in fact, be an inference from redness as a predicate of something external. On the other hand, there are certain other feelings—the emotions, for example—which appear to arise in the first place, not as predicates at all, and to be referable to the mind alone. It would seem, then, that by means of these, a knowledge of the mind may be obtained, which is not inferred from any character of outward things. The question is whether this is really so.

Although introspection is not necessarily intuitive, it is not self-evident that we possess this capacity; for we have no intuitive faculty of distinguishing different subjective modes of consciousness. The power, if it exists, must be known by the circumstance that the facts cannot be explained without it.

In reference to the above argument from the emotions, it must be admitted that if a man is angry, his anger implies, in general, no determinate and constant character in its object. But, on the other hand, it can hardly be questioned that there is some relative character in the outward thing which makes him angry, and a little reflection will serve to show that his anger consists in his saying to himself, "this thing is vile, abominable, etc.," and that it is rather a mark of returning reason to say, "I am angry." In the same way any emotion is a predication concerning some object, and the chief difference between this and an objective intellectual judgment is that while the latter is relative to human nature or to mind in general, the former is relative to the particular circumstances and disposition of a particular man at a particular time. What is here said of emotions in general, is true in particular of the sense of beauty and of the moral sense. Good and bad are feelings which first arise as predicates, and therefore are either predicates of the not-I, or are determined by previous cognitions (there being no intuitive power of distinguishing subjective elements of consciousness).

It remains, then, only to inquire whether it is necessary to suppose a particular power of introspection for the sake of accounting for the sense of willing. Now, volition, as distinguished from desire, is nothing but the power of concentrating the attention, of abstracting. Hence, the knowledge of the power of abstracting may be inferred from abstract objects, just as the knowledge of the power of seeing is inferred from colored objects.

It appears, therefore, that there is no reason for supposing a power of introspection; and, consequently, the only way of investigating a psychological question is by inference from external facts.

QUESTION 5. *Whether we can think without signs.*

This is a familiar question, but there is, to this day, no better argument in the affirmative than that thought must precede every sign. This assumes the impossibility of an infinite series. But Achilles, as a fact, will overtake the tortoise. *How* this happens, is a question not necessary to be answered at present, as long as it certainly does happen.

If we seek the light of external facts, the only cases of thought which we can find are of thought in signs. Plainly, no other thought can be evidenced by external facts. But we have seen that only by external facts can thought be known at all. The only thought, then, which can possibly be cognized is thought in signs. But thought which cannot be cognized does not exist. All thought, therefore, must necessarily be in signs.

A man says to himself, "Aristotle is a man; *therefore*, he is fallible." Has he not, then, thought what he has not said to himself, that all men are fallible? The answer is, that he has done so, so far as this is said in his *therefore*. According to this, our question does not relate to *fact*, but is a mere asking for distinctness of thought.

From the proposition that every thought is a sign, it follows that every thought must address itself to some other, must determine some other, since that is the essence of a sign. This, after all, is but another form of the familiar axiom, that in intuition, i.e. in the immediate present, there is no thought, or, that all which is reflected upon has past. *Hinc loquor inde est*. That, since any thought, there must have been a thought, has its analogue in the fact that, since any past time, there must have been an infinite series of times. To say, therefore, that thought cannot happen in an instant, but requires a time, is but another way of saying that every thought must be interpreted in another, or that all thought is in signs.

QUESTION 6. *Whether a sign can have any meaning, if by its definition it is the sign of something absolutely incognizable.*

It would seem that it can, and that universal and hypothetical propositions are instances of it. Thus, the universal proposition, "all ruminants are clovenhoofed," speaks of a possible infinity of animals, and no matter how many ruminants may have been examined, the possibility must remain that there are others which have not been examined. In the case of a hypothetical proposition, the same thing is still more manifest; for such a proposition speaks not merely of the actual state of things, but of every possible state of things, all of which are not knowable, inasmuch as only one can so much as exist.

On the other hand, all our conceptions are obtained by abstractions and combinations of cognitions first occurring in judgments of experience. Accordingly, there can be no conception of the absolutely incognizable, since nothing of that sort occurs in experience. But the meaning of a term is the conception which it conveys. Hence, a term can have no such meaning.

If it be said that the incognizable is a concept compounded of the concept *not* and *cognizable*, it may be replied that *not* is a mere syncategorematic term and not a concept by itself.

If I think "white," I will not go so far as Berkeley and say that I think of a person seeing, but I will say that what I think is of the nature of a cognition, and so of anything else which can be experienced. Consequently, the highest concept which can be reached by abstractions from judgments of experience—and therefore, the highest concept which can be reached at all—is the concept of something of the nature of a cognition. *Not*, then, or *what is other than*, if a concept, is a concept of the cognizable. Hence, not-cognizable, if a concept, is a concept of the form "*A*, not-*A*," and is, at least, self-contradictory. Thus, ignorance and error can only be conceived as correlative to a real knowledge and truth, which latter are of the nature of cognitions. Over against any cognition, there is an unknown but knowable reality; but over against all possible cognition, there is only the self-contradictory. In short, *cognizability* (in its widest sense) and *being* are not merely metaphysically the same, but are synonymous terms.

To the argument from universal and hypothetical propositions, the reply is, that though their truth cannot be cognized with absolute certainty, it may be probably known by induction.

QUESTION 7. *Whether there is any cognition not determined by a previous cognition.*

It would seem that there is or has been; for since we are in possession of cognitions, which are all determined by previous ones, and these by cognitions earlier still, there must have been a *first* in this series or else our state of cognition at any time is completely determined, according to logical laws, by our state at any previous time. But there are many facts against the last supposition, and therefore in favor of intuitive cognitions.

On the other hand, since it is impossible to know intuitively that a given cognition is not determined by a previous one, the only way in which this can be known is by hypothetic inference from observed facts. But to adduce the cognition by which a given cognition has been determined is to explain the determinations of that cognition. And it is the only way of explaining them. For something entirely out of consciousness which may be supposed to determine it, can, as such, only be known and only adduced in the determinate cognition in question. So, that to suppose that a cognition is determined solely by something absolutely external, is to suppose its determinations incapable of explanation. Now, this is a hypothesis which is warranted under no circumstances, inasmuch as the only possible justification for a hypothesis is that it explains the facts, and to say that they are explained and at the same time to suppose them inexplicable is self-contradictory.

If it be objected that the peculiar character of *red* is not determined by any previous cognition, I reply that that character is not a character of red as a cognition; for if there be a man to whom red things look as blue ones do to me and *vice versa*, that man's eyes teach him the same facts that they would if he were like me.

Moreover, we know of no power by which an intuition could be known. For, as the cognition is beginning, and therefore in a state of change, at only the first instant would it be intuition. And, therefore, the apprehension of it must take place in no time and be an event occupying no time.[6] Besides, all the cognitive faculties we know of are relative, and consequently their products are relations. But the cognition of a relation is determined by previous cognitions. No cognition not determined by a previous cognition, then, can be known. It does not exist, then, first, because it is absolutely incognizable, and second, because a cognition only exists so far as it is known.

The reply to the argument that there must be a first is as follows: In retracing our way from conclusions to premises, or from determined cognitions to those which determine them, we finally reach, in all cases, a point beyond which the consciousness in the determined cognition is more lively than in the cognition which determines it. We have a less lively consciousness in the cognition which determines our cognition of the third dimension than in the latter cognition itself; a less lively consciousness in the cognition which determines our cognition of a continuous surface (without a blind spot) than in

---

6. This argument, however, only covers a part of the question. It does not go to show that there is no cognition undetermined except by another like it.

this latter cognition itself; and a less lively consciousness of the impressions which determine the sensation of tone than of that sensation itself. Indeed, when we get near enough to the external this is the universal rule. Now let any horizontal line represent a cognition, and let the length of the line serve to measure (so to speak) the liveliness of consciousness in that cognition. A point, having no length, will, on this principle, represent an object quite out of consciousness. Let one horizontal line below another represent a cognition which determines the cognition represented by that other and which has the same object as the latter. Let the finite distance between two such lines represent that they are two different cognitions. With this aid to thinking, let us see whether "there must be a first." Suppose an inverted triangle ∇ to be gradually dipped into water. At any date or instant, the surface of the water makes a horizontal line across that triangle. This line represents a cognition. At a subsequent date, there is a sectional line so made, higher upon the triangle. This represents another cognition of the same object determined by the former, and having a livelier consciousness. The apex of the triangle represents the object external to the mind which determines both these cognitions. The state of the triangle before it reaches the water, represents a state of cognition which contains nothing which determines these subsequent cognitions. To say, then, that if there be a state of cognition by which all subsequent cognitions of a certain object are not determined, there must subsequently be some cognition of that object not determined by previous cognitions of the same object, is to say that when that triangle is dipped into the water there must be a sectional line made by the surface of the water lower than which no surface line had been made in that way. But draw the horizontal line where you will, as many horizontal lines as you please can be assigned at finite distances below it and below one another. For any such section is at some distance above the apex, otherwise it is not a line. Let this distance be a. Then there have been similar sections at the distances $\frac{1}{2}a$, $\frac{1}{4}a$, $\frac{1}{8}a$, $\frac{1}{16}a$, above the apex, and so on as far as you please. So that it is not true that there must be a first. Explicate the logical difficulties of this paradox (they are identical with those of the Achilles) in whatever way you may. I am content with the result, as long as your principles are fully applied to the particular case of cognitions determining one another. Deny motion, if it seems proper to do so; only then deny the process of determination of one cognition by another. Say that instants and lines are fictions; only say, also, that states of cognition and judgments are fictions. The point here insisted on is not this or that logical solution of the difficulty, but merely that cognition arises by a *process* of beginning, as any other change comes to pass.

In a subsequent paper, I shall trace the consequences of these principles, in reference to the questions of reality, of individuality, and of the validity of the laws of logic.

5

■ ■ ■

Some Consequences of
Four Incapacities

Having argued in the first essay of the Cognition Series that all thinking is inferential interpretation of signs, Peirce now turns to the consequences of his denial
of the Cartesian model of thinking as immediate perception of ideas within the
mind or soul. If thinking is not an immaterial perception in a mind or spirit, the
question arises, Of what is thought constituted? Peirce here answers—and it is
an answer that he never repudiated—that thought has a material quality. Human thought is a bodily, or physiological, process.

One stumbling block to an understanding of Peirce is this question: If thought
is in signs, how are signs grasped by the self, or mind? The premise of the
question is mistaken. A thought or sign does not have to be grasped, for it *is* a
physiological or bodily state. That is why Peirce can here declare that "the
Immediate . . . runs in a continuous stream through our lives." Yet even if the
sign is an immediate bodily state, its meaning as thought can be known only
mediately, through an act of interpretation. A thought is a feeling, but the feeling has no meaning until it is interpreted as a sign of an object, as Peirce shows
here in his discussion of emotion.

In this physiological context, there is nothing ethereal about either Peirce's
description of the self as a sign or his statement in footnote 4 that the self does
not contain thought but, rather, the self is contained in thought. The self sign is,
among other things, a material quality or organic bodily state interpreted as
constituting one's self.

The fact that a thought or feeling is meaningless until interpreted as standing
for something means that, contrary to philosophical convention in Peirce's time,
"the very highest and most metaphysical conceptions" are complex. They have
the form of the triadic relation—object, sign, interpretant. The description of

the highest metaphysical conceptions as relations of signs is the basis for Peirce's attack near the end of this essay on the nominalist belief that everything real is singular. Peirce maintains instead that the true conception of reality is general and implies the existence of a community of inquirers.

The bracketed words on page 77 belong to Peirce.

Source: *Writings of Charles S. Peirce*, 2:211–42.
Originally published in *Journal of Speculative Philosophy* 2
(1868): 140–57.

Descartes is the father of modern philosophy, and the spirit of Cartesianism—that which principally distinguishes it from the scholasticism which it displaced—may be compendiously stated as follows:

1. It teaches that philosophy must begin with universal doubt; whereas scholasticism had never questioned fundamentals.

2. It teaches that the ultimate test of certainty is to be found in the individual consciousness; whereas scholasticism had rested on the testimony of sages and of the Catholic Church.

3. The multiform argumentation of the middle ages is replaced by a single thread of inference depending often upon inconspicuous premises.

4. Scholasticism had its mysteries of faith, but undertook to explain all created things. But there are many facts which Cartesianism not only does not explain, but renders absolutely inexplicable, unless to say that "God makes them so" is to be regarded as an explanation.

In some, or all of these respects, most modern philosophers have been, in effect, Cartesians. Now without wishing to return to scholasticism, it seems to me that modern science and modern logic require us to stand upon a very different platform from this.

1. We cannot begin with complete doubt. We must begin with all the prejudices which we actually have when we enter upon the study of philosophy. These prejudices are not to be dispelled by a maxim, for they are things which it does not occur to us *can* be questioned. Hence this initial skepticism will be a mere self-deception, and not real doubt; and no one who follows the Cartesian method will ever be satisfied until he has formally recovered all those beliefs which in form he has given up. It is, therefore, as useless a preliminary as going to the North Pole would be in order to get to Constantinople by coming down regularly upon a meridian. A person may, it is true, in the course of his studies, find reason to doubt what he began by believing;

but in that case he doubts because he has a positive reason for it, and not on account of the Cartesian maxim. Let us not pretend to doubt in philosophy what we do not doubt in our hearts.

2. The same formalism appears in the Cartesian criterion, which amounts to this: "Whatever I am clearly convinced of, is true." If I were really convinced, I should have done with reasoning, and should require no test of certainty. But thus to make single individuals absolute judges of truth is most pernicious. The result is that metaphysicians will all agree that metaphysics has reached a pitch of certainty far beyond that of the physical sciences;—only they can agree upon nothing else. In sciences in which men come to agreement, when a theory has been broached, it is considered to be on probation until this agreement is reached. After it is reached, the question of certainty becomes an idle one, because there is no one left who doubts it. We individually cannot reasonably hope to attain the ultimate philosophy which we pursue; we can only seek it, therefore, for the *community* of philosophers. Hence, if disciplined and candid minds carefully examine a theory and refuse to accept it, this ought to create doubts in the mind of the author of the theory himself.

3. Philosophy ought to imitate the successful sciences in its methods, so far as to proceed only from tangible premises which can be subjected to careful scrutiny, and to trust rather to the multitude and variety of its arguments than to the conclusiveness of any one. Its reasoning should not form a chain which is no stronger than its weakest link, but a cable whose fibers may be ever so slender, provided they are sufficiently numerous and intimately connected.

4. Every unidealistic philosophy supposes some absolutely inexplicable, unanalyzable ultimate; in short, something resulting from mediation itself not susceptible of mediation. Now that anything *is* thus inexplicable can only be known by reasoning from signs. But the only justification of an inference from signs is that the conclusion explains the fact. To suppose the fact absolutely inexplicable, is not to explain it, and hence this supposition is never allowable.

In the last number of this journal will be found a piece entitled "Questions concerning Certain Faculties Claimed for Man," which has been written in this spirit of opposition to Cartesianism. That criticism of certain faculties resulted in four denials, which for convenience may here be repeated:

1. We have no power of Introspection, but all knowledge of the internal

world is derived by hypothetical reasoning from our knowledge of external facts.

2. We have no power of Intuition, but every cognition is determined logically by previous cognitions.

3. We have no power of thinking without signs.

4. We have no conception of the absolutely incognizable.

These propositions cannot be regarded as certain; and, in order to bring them to a further test, it is now proposed to trace them out to their consequences. We may first consider the first alone; then trace the consequences of the first and second; then see what else will result from assuming the third also; and, finally, add the fourth to our hypothetical premises.

In accepting the first proposition, we must put aside all prejudices derived from a philosophy which bases our knowledge of the external world on our self-consciousness. We can admit no statement concerning what passes within us except as a hypothesis necessary to explain what takes place in what we commonly call the external world. Moreover when we have upon such grounds assumed one faculty or mode of action of the mind, we cannot, of course, adopt any other hypothesis for the purpose of explaining any fact which can be explained by our first supposition, but must carry the latter as far as it will go. In other words, we must, as far as we can do so without additional hypotheses, reduce all kinds of mental action to one general type.

The class of modifications of consciousness with which we must commence our inquiry must be one whose existence is indubitable, and whose laws are best known, and, therefore (since this knowledge comes from the outside), which most closely follows external facts; that is, it must be some kind of cognition. Here we may hypothetically admit the second proposition of the former paper, according to which there is no absolutely first cognition of any object, but cognition arises by a continuous process. We must begin, then, with a *process* of cognition, and with that process whose laws are best understood and most closely follow external facts. This is no other than the process of valid inference, which proceeds from its premise, *A*, to its conclusion, *B*, only if, as a matter of fact, such a proposition as *B* is always or usually true when such a proposition as *A* is true. It is a consequence, then, of the first two principles whose results we are to trace out, that we must, as far as we can, without any other supposition than that the mind reasons, reduce all mental action to the formula of valid reasoning.

But does the mind in fact go through the syllogistic process? It is certainly very doubtful whether a conclusion—as something existing in the mind independently, like an image—suddenly displaces two premises existing in the mind in a similar way. But it is a matter of constant experience, that if a man is made to believe in the premises, in the sense that he will act from them and will say that they are true, under favorable conditions he will also be ready to act from the conclusion and to say that that is true. Something, therefore, takes place within the organism which is equivalent to the syllogistic process.

A valid inference is either *complete* or *incomplete*. An incomplete inference is one whose validity depends upon some matter of fact not contained in the premises. This implied fact might have been stated as a premise, and its relation to the conclusion is the same whether it is explicitly posited or not, since it is at least virtually taken for granted; so that every valid incomplete argument is virtually complete. Complete arguments are divided into *simple* and *complex*. A complex argument is one which from three or more premises concludes what might have been concluded by successive steps in reasonings each of which is simple. Thus, a complex inference comes to the same thing in the end as a succession of simple inferences.

A complete, simple, and valid argument, or syllogism, is either *apodictic* or *probable*. An apodictic or deductive syllogism is one whose validity depends unconditionally upon the relation of the fact inferred to the facts posited in the premises. A syllogism whose validity should depend not merely upon its premises, but upon the existence of some other knowledge, would be impossible; for either this other knowledge would be posited, in which case it would be a part of the premises, or it would be implicitly assumed, in which case the inference would be incomplete. But a syllogism whose validity depends partly upon the *non-existence* of some other knowledge, is a *probable* syllogism.

A few examples will render this plain. The two following arguments are apodictic or deductive:

1. No series of days of which the first and last are different days of the week exceeds by one a multiple of seven days; now the first and last days of any leap-year are different days of the week, and therefore no leap-year consists of a number of days one greater than a multiple of seven.

2. Among the vowels there are no double letters; but one of the double letters (*w*) is compounded of two vowels: hence, a letter compounded of two vowels is not necessarily itself a vowel.

In both these cases, it is plain that as long as the premises are true, however other facts may be, the conclusions will be true. On the other hand, suppose that we reason as follows: "A certain man had the Asiatic cholera. He was in a state of collapse, livid, quite cold, and without perceptible pulse. He was bled copiously. During the process he came out of collapse, and the next morning was well enough to be about. Therefore, bleeding tends to cure the cholera." This is a fair probable inference, provided that the premises represent our whole knowledge of the matter. But if we knew, for example, that recoveries from cholera were apt to be sudden, and that the physician who had reported this case had known of a hundred other trials of the remedy without communicating the result, then the inference would lose all its validity.

The absence of knowledge which is essential to the validity of any probable argument relates to some question which is determined by the argument itself. This question, like every other, is whether certain objects have certain characters. Hence, the absence of knowledge is either whether besides the objects which, according to the premises, possess certain characters, any other objects possess them; or, whether besides the characters which, according to the premises, belong to certain objects, any other characters not necessarily involved in these belong to the same objects. In the former case, the reasoning proceeds as though all the objects which have certain characters were known, and this is *induction*; in the latter case, the inference proceeds as though all the characters requisite to the determination of a certain object or class were known, and this is *hypothesis*. This distinction, also, may be made more plain by examples.

Suppose we count the number of occurrences of the different letters in a certain English book, which we may call A. Of course, every new letter which we add to our count will alter the relative number of occurrences of the different letters; but as we proceed with our counting, this change will be less and less. Suppose that we find that as we increase the number of letters counted, the relative number of e's approaches nearly $11\frac{1}{4}$ *per cent* of the whole, that of the t's $8\frac{1}{2}$ *per cent*, that of the a's 8 *per cent*, that of the s's $7\frac{1}{2}$ *per cent*, &c. Suppose we repeat the same observations with half a dozen other English writings (which we may designate as B, C, D, E, F, G) with the like result. Then we may infer that in every English writing of some length, the different letters occur with nearly those relative frequencies.

Now this argument depends for its validity upon our *not* knowing the proportion of letters in any English writing besides A, B, C, D, E, F, and G. For if we know it in respect to H, and it is not nearly the same as in the others, our conclusion is destroyed at once; if it is the same, then the legitimate inference is from *A, B, C, D, E, F, G*, and *H*, and not from the first seven alone. This, therefore, is an *induction*.

Suppose, next, that a piece of writing in cypher is presented to us, without the key. Suppose we find that it contains something less than 26 characters, one of which occurs about 11 *per cent* of all the times, another $8\frac{1}{2}$ *per cent*, another 8 *per cent*, and another $7\frac{1}{2}$ *per cent*. Suppose that when we substitute for these *e, t, a,* and *s,* respectively, we are able to see how single letters may be substituted for each of the other characters so as to make sense in English, provided, however, that we allow the spelling to be wrong in some cases. If the writing is of any considerable length, we may infer with great probability that this is the meaning of the cipher.

The validity of this argument depends upon there being no other known characters of the writing in cipher which would have any weight in the matter; for if there are—if we know, for example, whether or not there is any other solution of it—this must be allowed its effect in supporting or weakening the conclusion. This, then, is *hypothesis*.

All valid reasoning is either deductive, inductive, or hypothetic; or else it combines two or more of these characters. Deduction is pretty well treated in most logical text-books; but it will be necessary to say a few words about induction and hypothesis in order to render what follows more intelligible.

Induction may be defined as an argument which proceeds upon the assumption that all the members of a class or aggregate have all the characters which are common to all those members of this class concerning which it is known, whether they have these characters or not; or, in other words, which assumes that that is true of a whole collection which is true of a number of instances taken from it at random. This might be called statistical argument. In the long run, it must generally afford pretty correct conclusions from true premises. If we have a bag of beans partly black and partly white, by counting the relative proportions of the two colors in several different handfuls, we can approximate more or less to the relative proportions in the whole bag, since a sufficient number of handfuls would constitute all the beans in the bag. The central characteristic and key to induction is, that by taking the conclusion so reached as major premise of a syllogism, and the proposition stating that such and such objects are taken from the class in question as the minor premise, the other premise of the induction will follow from them deductively. Thus, in the above example we concluded that all books in English have about $11\frac{1}{4}$ *per cent* of their letters *e*'s. From that as major premise, together with the proposition that *A, B, C, D, E, F,* and *G* are books in English, it follows deductively that *A, B, C, D, E, F,* and *G* have about $11\frac{1}{4}$ *per cent* of their letters *e*'s. Accordingly, induction has been defined by Aristotle as the inference of the major premise of a syllogism from its minor premise and conclusion. The function of an induction is to substitute for a series of many subjects, a single one which embraces them and an indefinite number of others. Thus it is a species of "reduction of the manifold to unity."

Hypothesis may be defined as an argument which proceeds upon the assumption that a character which is known necessarily to involve a certain number of others, may be probably predicated of any object which has all the characters which this character is known to involve. Just as induction may be regarded as the inference of the major premise of a syllogism, so hypothesis may be regarded as the inference of the minor premise, from the other two propositions. Thus, the example taken above consists of two such inferences of the minor premises of the following syllogisms:

1. Every English writing of some length in which such and such characters denote *e, t, a,* and *s,* has about $11\frac{1}{4}$ *per cent* of the first sort of marks, $8\frac{1}{2}$ of the second, 8 of the third, and $7\frac{1}{2}$ of the fourth;
This secret writing is an English writing of some length, in which such and such characters denote *e, t, a,* and *s,* respectively:
∴ This secret writing has about $11\frac{1}{4}$ *per cent* of its characters of the first kind, $8\frac{1}{2}$ of the second, 8 of the third, and $7\frac{1}{2}$ of the fourth.
2. A passage written with such an alphabet makes sense when such and such letters are severally substituted for such and such characters.
This secret writing is written with such an alphabet.
∴ This secret writing makes sense when such and such substitutions are made.

The function of hypothesis is to substitute for a great series of predicates forming no unity in themselves, a single one (or small number) which involves them all, together (perhaps) with an indefinite number of others. It is, therefore, also a reduction of a manifold to unity.[1] Every deductive syllogism may be put into the form

If *A,* then *B*;

But *A*:

∴ *B*.

1. Several persons versed in logic have objected that I have here quite misapplied the term *hypothesis*, and that what I so designate is an argument from *analogy*. It is a

And as the minor premise in this form appears as antecedent or reason of a hypothetical proposition, hypothetic inference may be called reasoning from consequent to antecedent.

The argument from analogy, which a popular writer upon logic calls reasoning from particulars to particulars, derives its validity from its combining

---

sufficient reply to say that the example of the cipher has been given as an apt illustration of hypothesis by Descartes (Rule 10 Œuvres choisies: Paris, 1865, page 334), by Leibniz (Nouveaux Essais [Opera philosophica quae exstant latina gallica germanica omnia (Berlin: G. Eichler, 1840)], lib. 4, ch. 12, §13, Ed. [Johannes Eduard] Erdmann, p. 383 b), and (as I learn from D. Stewart; Works [The Collected Works of Dugald Stewart, edited by William Hamilton (Edinburgh: Thomas Constable, 1854)], vol. 3, pp. 305 et seqq.) by Gravesande, Boscovich, Hartley, and G. L. Le Sage. The term Hypothesis has been used in the following senses:—1. For the theme or proposition forming the subject of discourse. 2. For an assumption. Aristotle divides theses or propositions adopted without any reason into definitions and hypotheses. The latter are propositions stating the existence of something. Thus the geometer says, "Let there be a triangle." 3. For a condition in a general sense. We are said to seek other things than happiness ἐξ ὑποθέσεως, conditionally. The best republic is the ideally perfect, the second the best on earth, the third the best ἐξ ὑποθέσεως, under the circumstances. Freedom is the ὑπόθεσις or condition of democracy. 4. For the antecedent of a hypothetical proposition. 5. For an oratorical question which assumes facts. 6. In the Synopsis of Psellus, for the reference of a subject to the things it denotes. 7. Most commonly in modern times, for the conclusion of an argument from consequence and consequent to antecedent. This is my use of the term. 8. For such a conclusion when too weak to be a theory accepted into the body of a science.

I give a few authorities to support the seventh use:

Chauvin.—Lexicon Rationale, 1st Ed. [Etienne Chauvin, Lexicon rationale sive thesaurus philosophicus (Rotterdam: Petrus vander Slaart, 1692)]—"Hypothesis est propositio, quæ assumitur ad probanda aliam veritatem incognitam. Requirunt multi, ut hæc hypothesis vera esse cognoscatur, etiam antequam appareat, an alia ex eâ deduci possint. Verum aiunt alii, hoc unum desiderari, ut hypothesis pro vera admittatur, quod nempe ex hac talia deducitur, quæ respondent phænomenis, et satisfaciunt omnibus difficultatibus, quæ hac parte in re, et in iis quæ de ea apparent, occurrebant."

["A hypothesis is a proposition that is assumed in order to test the truth of what is not yet known to be true. Many demand that for a hypothesis to be identified as being true, no matter how true it appears before, other things must be deducible from it. But others say that for a hypothesis to be true, this one thing is required; namely that such things must be deducible from it as correspond to phenomena and as satisfy all the difficulties encountered, on the one hand, in the thing itself and, on the other, in such as arise from it."]

Newton.—"Hactenus phænomena cœlorum et maris nostri per vim gravitatis exposui, sed causam gravitatis nondum assignavi. . . . Rationem vero harum gravitatis the characters of induction and hypothesis, being analyzable either into a deduction or an induction, or a deduction and a hypothesis.

But though inference is thus of three essentially different species, it also belongs to one genus. We have seen that no conclusion can be legitimately derived which could not have been reached by successions of arguments having two premises each, and implying no fact not asserted.

---

proprietatum ex phænomenis nondum potui deducere, et hypotheses non fingo. Quicquid enim ex phænomenis non deducitur, *hypothesis* vocanda est. . . . In hâc Philosophiâ Propositiones deducuntur ex phænomenis, et redduntur generales per inductionem." *Principia. Ad fin.* ["I have thus far explained the phenomena of the heavens and sea by the force of gravity, but have not yet assigned the cause of gravity. . . . I have not yet been able to deduce from the phenomena the reason for these properties of gravity, and I do not invent hypotheses. Whatever cannot be deduced from the phenomena should be called a *hypothesis.* . . . In this philosophy, propositions are deduced from phenomena and are rendered general by induction." Isaac Newton, *Philosophiae naturalis principia mathematica*, 2 vols., edited by Thomas Le Seur and Franciscus Jacquier (Glasgow: T. T. and J. Tegg, 1833), 2:201–2.]

Sir Wm. Hamilton.—"*Hypotheses*, that is, propositions which are assumed with probability, in order to explain or prove something else which cannot otherwise be explained or proved."—*Lectures on Logic* (Am. Ed.) [edited by Henry L. Mansel and John Veitch (Boston: Gould and Lincoln, 1859)], p. 188.

"The name of *hypothesis* is more emphatically given to provisory suppositions, which serve to explain the phenomena in so far as observed, but which are only asserted to be true, if ultimately confirmed by a complete induction."—Ibid., p. 364.

"When a phenomenon is presented which can be explained by no principle afforded through experience, we feel discontented and uneasy; and there arises an effort to discover some cause which may, at least provisionally, account for the outstanding phenomenon; and this cause is finally recognized as valid and true, if, through it, the given phenomenon is found to obtain a full and perfect explanation. The judgment in which a phenomenon is referred to such a problematic cause, is called a *Hypothesis.*"—Ibid., pp. 449, 450. See also *Lectures on Metaphysics* [edited by Henry L. Mansel and John Veitch (Boston: Gould and Lincoln, 1859)], p. 117.

J. S. Mill.—"An hypothesis is any supposition which we make (either without actual evidence, or on evidence avowedly insufficient), in order to endeavor to deduce from it conclusions in accordance with facts which are known to be real; under the idea that if the conclusions to which the hypothesis leads are known truths, the hypothesis itself either must be, or at least is likely to be true."—*Logic* [*A System of Logic, Ratiocinative and Inductive: Being a Connected View of the Principles of Evidence, and the Methods of Scientific Investigation*, 2 vols. (London: Longmans, Green, 1865)] (6th Ed.), vol. 2, p. 8.

Kant.—"*If all the consequents of a cognition are true, the cognition itself is true.* . . . It is allowable, therefore, to conclude from consequent to *a* reason, but

Either of these premises is a proposition asserting that certain objects have certain characters. Every term of such a proposition stands either for certain objects or for certain characters. The conclusion may be regarded as a proposition substituted in place of either premise, the substitution being justified by the fact stated in the other premise. The conclusion is accordingly derived from either premise by substituting either a new subject for the subject of the premise, or a new predicate for the predicate of the premise, or by both substitutions. Now the substitution of one term for another can be justified only so far as the term substituted represents only what is represented in the term replaced. If, therefore, the conclusion be denoted by the formula,

$$S \text{ is } P;$$

and this conclusion be derived, by a change of subject, from a premise which may on this account be expressed by the formula,

$$M \text{ is } P,$$

then the other premise must assert that whatever thing is represented by S is represented by M, or that

$$\text{Every } S \text{ is an } M;$$

---

without being able to determine this reason. From the complexus of all consequents alone can we conclude the truth of a determinate reason. . . . The difficulty with this *positive* and *direct* mode of inference (*modus ponens*) is that the totality of the consequents cannot be apodeictically recognized, and that we are therefore led by this mode of inference only to a probable and *hypothetically* true cognition (*Hypotheses*)."—*Logik* [edited] by [Gottlieb Benjamin] Jäsche; *Werke*, ed. Rosenkranz and Schubert [*Immanuel Kant's sämmtliche Werke*, 12 parts in 14 vols., edited by Karl Rosenkranz and Friedrich Wilhelm Schubert (Leipzig: Leopold Voss, 1838–42)], vol. 3, p. 221.

"A hypothesis is the judgment of the truth of a reason on account of the sufficiency of the consequents."—Ibid., p. 262.

Herbart.—"We can make hypotheses, thence deduce consequents, and afterwards see whether the latter accord with experience. Such suppositions are termed hypotheses."—*Einleitung*; *Werke* [Johann Friedrich Herbart, *Lehrbuch zur Einleitung in die Philosophie*, in *Sämmtliche Werke*, edited by G. Hartenstein (Leipzig: Leopold Voss, 1850)], vol. 1, p. 53.

Beneke.—"Affirmative inferences from consequent to antecedent, or hypotheses."—*System der Logik* [Friedrich Eduard Beneke, *System der Logik als Kunstlehre des Denken*, 2 vols. (Berlin: Ferdinand Dümmler, 1842)], vol. 2, p. 103.

There would be no difficulty in greatly multiplying these citations.

while, if the conclusion, S is P, is derived from either premise by a change of predicate, that premise may be written

$$S \text{ is } M;$$

and the other premise must assert that whatever characters are implied in P are implied in M, or that

$$\text{Whatever is } M \text{ is } P.$$

In either case, therefore, the syllogism must be capable of expression in the form,

$$S \text{ is } M; M \text{ is } P:$$
$$\therefore S \text{ is } P.$$

Finally, if the conclusion differs from either of its premises, both in subject and predicate, the form of statement of conclusion and premise may be so altered that they shall have a common term. This can always be done, for if P is the premise and C the conclusion, they may be stated thus:

$$\text{The state of things represented in } P \text{ is real,}$$
$$\text{and}$$
$$\text{The state of things represented in } C \text{ is real.}$$

In this case the other premise must in some form virtually assert that every state of things such as is represented by C is the state of things represented in P.

All valid reasoning, therefore, is of one general form; and in seeking to reduce all mental action to the formulæ of valid inference, we seek to reduce it to one single type.

An apparent obstacle to the reduction of all mental action to the type of valid inferences is the existence of fallacious reasoning. Every argument implies the truth of a general principle of inferential procedure (whether involving some matter of fact concerning the subject of argument, or merely a maxim relating to a system of signs), according to which it is a valid argument. If this principle is false, the argument is a fallacy; but neither a valid argument from false premises, nor an exceedingly weak, but not altogether illegitimate, induction or hypothesis, however its force may be overestimated, however false its conclusion, is a fallacy.

Now words, taken just as they stand, if in the form of an argument, thereby do imply whatever fact may be necessary to make the argument conclusive;

so that to the formal logician, who has to do only with the meaning of the words according to the proper principles of interpretation, and not with the intention of the speaker as guessed at from other indications, the only fallacies should be such as are simply absurd and contradictory, either because their conclusions are absolutely inconsistent with their premises, or because they connect propositions by a species of illative conjunction, by which they cannot under any circumstances be validly connected.

But to the psychologist an argument is valid only if the premises from which the mental conclusion is derived would be sufficient, if true, to justify it, either by themselves, or by the aid of other propositions which had previously been held for true. But it is easy to show that all inferences made by man, which are not valid in this sense, belong to four classes, viz.: 1. Those whose premises are false; 2. Those which have some little force, though only a little; 3. Those which result from confusion of one proposition with another; 4. Those which result from the indistinct apprehension, wrong application, or falsity, of a rule of inference. For, if a man were to commit a fallacy not of either of these classes, he would, from true premises conceived with perfect distinctness, without being led astray by any prejudice or other judgment serving as a rule of inference, draw a conclusion which had really not the least relevancy. If this could happen, calm consideration and care could be of little use in thinking, for caution only serves to insure our taking all the facts into account, and to make those which we do take account of, distinct; nor can coolness do anything more than to enable us to be cautious, and also to prevent our being affected by a passion in inferring that to be true which we wish were true, or which we fear may be true, or in following some other wrong rule of inference. But experience shows that the calm and careful consideration of the same distinctly conceived premises (including prejudices) will insure the pronouncement of the same judgment by all men. Now if a fallacy belongs to the first of these four classes and its premises are false, it is to be presumed that the procedure of the mind from these premises to the conclusion is either correct, or errs in one of the other three ways; for it cannot be supposed that the mere falsity of the premises should affect the procedure of reason when that falsity is not known to reason. If the fallacy belongs to the second class and has some force, however little, it is a legitimate probable argument, and belongs to the type of valid inference. If it is of the third class and results from the confusion of one proposition with another, this confusion must be owing to a resemblance between the two propositions; that is to say, the person reasoning, seeing that one proposition has some of the characters which belong to the other, concludes that it has all the essential characters of the other, and is equivalent to it. Now this is a hypothetic inference, which though it may be weak, and though its conclusion happens to be false, belongs to the type of valid inferences; and, therefore, as the *nodus* of the fallacy lies in this confusion, the procedure of the mind in these fallacies of the third class conforms to the formula of valid inference. If the fallacy belongs to the fourth class, it either results from wrongly applying or misapprehending a rule of inference, and so is a fallacy of confusion, or it results from adopting a wrong rule of inference. In this latter case, this rule is in fact taken as a premise, and therefore the false conclusion is owing merely to the falsity of a premise. In every fallacy, therefore, possible to the mind of man, the procedure of the mind conforms to the formula of valid inference.

The third principle whose consequences we have to deduce is, that, whenever we think, we have present to the consciousness some feeling, image, conception, or other representation, which serves as a sign. But it follows from our own existence (which is proved by the occurrence of ignorance and error) that everything which is present to us is a phenomenal manifestation of ourselves. This does not prevent its being a phenomenon of something without us, just as a rainbow is at once a manifestation both of the sun and of the rain. When we think, then, we ourselves, as we are at that moment, appear as a sign. Now a sign has, as such, three references: 1st, it is a sign *to* some thought which interprets it; 2d, it is a sign *for* some object to which in that thought it is equivalent; 3d, it is a sign, *in* some respect or quality, which brings it into connection with its object. Let us ask what the three correlates are to which a thought-sign refers.

1. When we think, to what thought does that thought-sign which is ourself address itself? It may, through the medium of outward expression, which it reaches perhaps only after considerable internal development, come to address itself to thought of another person. But whether this happens or not, it is always interpreted by a subsequent thought of our own. If, after any thought, the current of ideas flows on freely, it follows the law of mental association. In that case, each former thought suggests something to the thought which follows it, i.e. is the sign of something to this latter. Our train of thought may, it is true, be interrupted. But we must remember that, in addition to the principal element of thought at any moment, there are a hundred things in our mind to which but a small fraction of attention or consciousness is conceded. It does not, therefore, follow, because a new constituent of thought gets the uppermost, that the train of thought which it displaces is

broken off altogether. On the contrary, from our second principle, that there is no intuition or cognition not determined by previous cognitions, it follows that the striking in of a new experience is never an instantaneous affair, but is an *event* occupying time, and coming to pass by a continuous process. Its prominence in consciousness, therefore, must probably be the consummation of a growing process; and if so, there is no sufficient cause for the thought which had been the leading one just before, to cease abruptly and instantaneously. But if a train of thought ceases by gradually dying out, it freely follows its own law of association as long as it lasts, and there is no moment at which there is a thought belonging to this series, subsequently to which there is not a thought which interprets or repeats it. There is no exception, therefore, to the law that every thought-sign is translated or interpreted in a subsequent one, unless it be that all thought comes to an abrupt and final end in death.

2. The next question is: For what does the thought-sign stand—what does it name—what is its *suppositum*? The outward thing, undoubtedly, when a real outward thing is thought of. But still, as the thought is determined by a previous thought of the same object, it only refers to the thing through denoting this previous thought. Let us suppose, for example, that Toussaint is thought of, and first thought of as a *Negro*, but not distinctly as a man. If this distinctness is afterwards added, it is through the thought that a *Negro* is a *man*; that is to say, the subsequent thought, *man*, refers to the outward thing by being predicated of that previous thought, *Negro*, which has been had of that thing. If we afterwards think of Toussaint as a general, then we think that this Negro, this man, was a general. And so in every case the subsequent thought denotes what was thought in the previous thought.

3. The thought-sign stands for its object in the respect which is thought; that is to say, this respect is the immediate object of consciousness in the thought, or, in other words, it is the thought itself, or at least what the thought is thought to be in the subsequent thought to which it is a sign.

We must now consider two other properties of signs which are of great importance in the theory of cognition. Since a sign is not identical with the thing signified, but differs from the latter in some respects, it must plainly have some characters which belong to it in itself, and have nothing to do with its representative function. These I call the *material* qualities of the sign. As examples of such qualities, take in the word "man" its consisting of three letters—in a picture, its being flat and without relief. In the second place, a sign must be capable of being connected (not in the reason but really) with another sign of the same object, or with the object itself. Thus, words would be of no value at all unless they could be connected into sentences by means of a real copula which joins signs of the same thing. The usefulness of some signs—as a weathercock, a tally, &c.—consists wholly in their being really connected with the very things they signify. In the case of a picture such a connection is not evident, but it exists in the power of association which connects the picture with the brain-sign which labels it. This real, physical connection of a sign with its object, either immediately or by its connection with another sign, I call the *pure demonstrative application* of the sign. Now the representative function of a sign lies neither in its material quality nor in its pure demonstrative application; because it is something which the sign is, not in itself or in a real relation to its object, but which it is *to a thought*, while both of the characters just defined belong to the sign independently of its addressing any thought. And yet if I take all the things which have certain qualities and physically connect them with another series of things, each to each, they become fit to be signs. If they are not regarded as such they are not actually signs, but they are so in the same sense, for example, in which an unseen flower can be said to be *red*, this being also a term relative to a mental affection.

Consider a state of mind which is a conception. It is a conception by virtue of having a *meaning*, a logical comprehension; and if it is applicable to any object, it is because that object has the characters contained in the comprehension of this conception. Now the logical comprehension of a thought is usually said to consist of the thoughts contained in it; but thoughts are events, acts of the mind. Two thoughts are two events separated in time, and one cannot literally be contained in the other. It may be said that all thoughts exactly similar are regarded as one; and that to say that one thought contains another, means that it contains one exactly similar to that other. But how can two thoughts be similar? Two objects can only be *regarded* as similar if they are compared and brought together in the mind. Thoughts have no existence except in the mind; only as they are regarded do they exist. Hence, two thoughts cannot *be* similar unless they are brought together in the mind. But, as to their existence, two thoughts are separated by an interval of time. We are too apt to imagine that we can frame a thought similar to a past thought, by matching it with the latter, as though this past thought were still present to us. But it is plain that the knowledge that one thought is similar to or in any way truly representative of another, cannot be derived from immediate perception, but must be an hypothesis (unquestionably fully justifiable by facts), and that therefore the formation of such a representing thought must be dependent upon a real effective force behind consciousness, and not merely upon a mental comparison. What we must mean, therefore, by saying that one concept is contained in another, is that we normally represent one to be in the other; that is, that we form a particular kind of judgment,[2] of which the subject signifies one concept and the predicate the other.

No thought in itself, then, no feeling in itself, contains any others, but is absolutely simple and unanalyzable; and to say that it is composed of other thoughts and feelings, is like saying that a movement upon a straight line is composed of the two movements of which it is the resultant; that is to say, it is a metaphor, or fiction, parallel to the truth. Every thought, however artificial and complex, is, so far as it is immediately present, a mere sensation without parts, and therefore, in itself, without similarity to any other, but incomparable with any other and absolutely *sui generis*.[3] Whatever is wholly incomparable with anything else is wholly inexplicable, because explanation consists in bringing things under general laws or under natural classes. Hence every thought, in so far as it is a feeling of a peculiar sort, is simply an ultimate, inexplicable fact. Yet this does not conflict with my postulate that no fact should be allowed to stand as inexplicable; for, on the one hand, we never can think, "This is present to me," since, before we have time to make the reflection, the sensation is past, and, on the other hand, when once past, we can never bring back the quality of the feeling as it was *in and for itself*, or know what it was like *in itself*, or even discover the existence of this quality except by a corollary from our general theory of ourselves, and then not in its idiosyncrasy, but only as something present. But, as something present, feelings are all alike and require no explanation, since they contain only what is universal. So that nothing which we can truly predicate of feelings is left inexplicable, but only something which we cannot reflectively know. So that we do not fall into the contradiction of making the Mediate immediate. Finally, no present actual thought (which is a mere feeling) has any meaning, any intellectual value; for this lies not in what is actually thought, but in what

2. A judgment concerning a minimum of information, for the theory of which see my paper on Comprehension and Extension, in the *Proceedings of the American Academy of Arts and Sciences*, vol. 7, p. 426.

3. Observe that I say *in itself*. I am not so wild as to deny that my sensation of red to-day is like my sensation of red yesterday. I only say that the similarity can *consist* only in the physiological force behind consciousness,—which leads me to say, I recognize this feeling the same as the former one, and so does not consist in a community of sensation.

this thought may be connected with in representation by subsequent thoughts; so that the meaning of a thought is altogether something virtual. It may be objected, that if no thought has any meaning, all thought is without meaning. But this is a fallacy similar to saying, that, if in no one of the successive spaces which a body fills there is room for motion, there is no room for motion throughout the whole. At no one instant in my state of mind is there cognition or representation, but in the relation of my states of mind at different instants there is.[4] In short, the Immediate (and therefore in itself unsusceptible of mediation—the Unanalyzable, the Inexplicable, the Unintellectual) runs in a continuous stream through our lives; it is the sum total of consciousness, whose mediation, which is the continuity of it, is brought about by a real effective force behind consciousness.

Thus, we have in thought three elements: 1st, the representative function which makes it a *representation*; 2d, the pure denotative application, or real connection, which brings one thought into *relation* with another; and 3d, the material quality, or how it feels, which gives thought its *quality*.[5]

That a sensation is not necessarily an intuition, or first impression of sense, is very evident in the case of the sense of beauty; and has been shown, upon page 39, in the case of sound. When the sensation beautiful is determined by previous cognitions, it always arises as a predicate; that is, we think that something is beautiful. Whenever a sensation thus arises in consequence of others, induction shows that those others are more or less complicated. Thus, the sensation of a particular kind of sound arises in consequence of impressions upon the various nerves of the ear being combined in a particular way, and following one another with a certain rapidity. A sensation of color depends upon impressions upon the eye following one another in a regular manner, and with a certain rapidity. The sensation of beauty arises upon a manifold of other impressions. And this will be found to hold good in all cases. Secondly, all these sensations are in themselves simple, or more so than the sensations which give rise to them. Accordingly, a sensation is a simple predicate taken in place of a complex predicate; in other words, it fulfills the function of an hypothesis. But the general principle that every thing to which such and such a sensation belongs, has such and such a complicated series of predi-

---

4. Accordingly, just as we say that a body is in motion, and not that motion is in a body we ought to say that we are in thought, and not that thoughts are in us.

5. On quality, relation, and representation, see *Proceedings of the American Academy of Arts and Sciences*, vol. 7, p. 293.

cates, is not one determined by reason (as we have seen), but is of an arbitrary nature. Hence, the class of hypothetic inferences which the arising of a sensation resembles, is that of reasoning from definition to definitum, in which the major premise is of an arbitrary nature. Only in this mode of reasoning, this premise is determined by the conventions of language, and expresses the occasion upon which a word is to be used; and in the formation of a sensation, it is determined by the constitution of our nature, and expresses the occasions upon which sensation, or a natural mental sign, arises. Thus, the sensation, so far as it represents something, is determined, according to a logical law, by previous cognitions; that is to say, these cognitions determine that there shall be a sensation. But so far as the sensation is a mere feeling of a particular sort, it is determined only by an inexplicable, occult power; and so far, it is not a representation, but only the material quality of a representation. For just as in reasoning from definition to definitum, it is indifferent to the logician how the defined word shall sound, or how many letters it shall contain, so in the case of this constitutional word, it is not determined by an inward law how it shall feel in itself. A feeling, therefore, as a feeling, is merely the *material quality* of a mental sign.

But there is no feeling which is not also a representation, a predicate of something determined logically by the feelings which precede it. For if there are any such feelings not predicates, they are the emotions. Now every emotion has a subject. If a man is angry, he is saying to himself that this or that is vile and outrageous. If he is in joy, he is saying "this is delicious." If he is wondering, he is saying "this is strange." In short, whenever a man feels, he is thinking of *something*. Even those passions which have no definite object—as melancholy—only come to consciousness through tinging the *objects of thought*. That which makes us look upon the emotions more as affections of self than other cognitions, is that we have found them more dependent upon our accidental situation at the moment than other cognitions; but that is only to say that they are cognitions too narrow to be useful. The emotions, as a little observation will show, arise when our attention is strongly drawn to complex and inconceivable circumstances. Fear arises when we cannot predict our fate; joy, in the case of certain indescribable and peculiarly complex sensations. If there are some indications that something greatly for my interest, and which I have anticipated would happen, may not happen; and if, after weighing probabilities, and inventing safeguards, and straining for further information, I find myself unable to come to any fixed conclusion in reference to the future, in the place of that intellectual hypothetic inference which I seek, the feeling of *anxiety* arises. When something happens for which I cannot account, I *wonder*. When I endeavor to realize to myself what I never can do, a pleasure in the future, I *hope*. "I do not understand you," is the phrase of an angry man. The indescribable, the ineffable, the incomprehensible, commonly excite emotion; but nothing is so chilling as a scientific explanation. Thus an emotion is always a simple predicate substituted by an operation of the mind for a highly complicated predicate. Now if we consider that a very complex predicate demands explanation by means of an hypothesis, that that hypothesis must be a simpler predicate substituted for that complex one; and that when we have an emotion, an hypothesis, strictly speaking, is hardly possible—the analogy of the parts played by emotion and hypothesis is very striking. There is, it is true, this difference between an emotion and an intellectual hypothesis, that we have reason to say in the case of the latter, that to whatever the simple hypothetic predicate can be applied, of that the complex predicate is true; whereas, in the case of an emotion this is a proposition for which no reason can be given, but which is determined merely by our emotional constitution. But this corresponds precisely to the difference between hypothesis and reasoning from definition to definitum, and thus it would appear that emotion is nothing but sensation. There appears to be a difference, however, between emotion and sensation, and I would state it as follows:

There is some reason to think that, corresponding to every feeling within us, some motion takes place in our bodies. This property of the thought-sign, since it has no rational dependence upon the meaning of the sign, may be compared with what I have called the material quality of the sign; but it differs from the latter inasmuch as it is not essentially necessary that it should be felt in order that there should be any thought-sign. In the case of a sensation, the manifold of impressions which precede and determine it are not of a kind, the bodily motion corresponding to which comes from any large ganglion or from the brain, and probably for this reason the sensation produces no great commotion in the bodily organism; and the sensation itself is not a thought which has a very strong influence upon the current of thought except by virtue of the information it may serve to afford. An emotion, on the other hand, comes much later in the development of thought—I mean, further from the first beginning of the cognition of its object—and the thoughts which determine it already have motions corresponding to them in the brain, or the chief ganglion; consequently, it produces large movements in the body, and independently of its representative value, strongly affects the current of thought. The animal motions to which I allude, are, in the first place and obviously, blush-

ing, blenching, staring, smiling, scowling, pouting, laughing, weeping, sob-
bing, wriggling, flinching, trembling, being petrified, sighing, sniffing,
shrugging, groaning, heartsinking, trepidation, swelling of the heart, etc.,
etc. To these may, perhaps, be added, in the second place, other more complicated actions, which nevertheless spring from a direct impulse and not from
deliberation.

That which distinguishes both sensations proper and emotions from the
feeling of a thought, is that in the case of the two former the material quality
is made prominent, because the thought has no relation of reason to the
thoughts which determine it, which exists in the last case and detracts from
the attention given to the mere feeling. By there being no relation of reason
to the determining thoughts, I mean that there is nothing in the content of the
thought which explains why it should arise only on occasion of these determining thoughts. If there is such a relation of reason, if the thought is essentially limited in its application to these objects, then the thought comprehends
a thought other than itself; in other words, it is then a complex thought. An
incomplex thought can, therefore, be nothing but a sensation or emotion,
having no rational character. This is very different from the ordinary doctrine,
according to which the very highest and most metaphysical conceptions are
absolutely simple. I shall be asked how such a conception of a *being* is to be
analyzed, or whether I can ever define *one, two,* and *three,* without a diallele.
Now I shall admit at once that neither of these conceptions can be separated
into two others higher than itself; and in that sense, therefore, I fully admit
that certain very metaphysical and eminently intellectual notions are absolutely simple. But though these concepts cannot be defined by genus and
difference, there is another way in which they can be defined. All determination is by negation; we can first recognize any character only by putting an
object which possesses it into comparison with an object which possesses it
not. A conception, therefore, which was quite universal in every respect
would be unrecognizable and impossible. We do not obtain the conception of
Being, in the sense implied in the copula, by observing that all the things
which we can think of have something in common, for there is no such thing
to be observed. We get it by reflecting upon signs—words or thoughts;—we
observe that different predicates may be attached to the same subject, and that
each makes some conception applicable to the subject; then we imagine that
a subject has something true of it merely because a predicate (no matter what)
is attached to it,—and that we call Being. The conception of being is, therefore, a conception about a sign—a thought, or word;—and since it is not

applicable to every sign, it is not primarily universal, although it is so in its mediate application to things. Being, therefore, may be defined; it may be defined, for example, as that which is common to the objects included in any class, and to the objects not included in the same class. But it is nothing new to say that metaphysical conceptions are primarily and at bottom thoughts about words, or thoughts about thoughts; it is the doctrine both of Aristotle (whose categories are parts of speech) and of Kant (whose categories are the characters of different kinds of propositions).

Sensation and the power of abstraction or attention may be regarded as, in one sense, the sole constituents of all thought. Having considered the former, let us now attempt some analysis of the latter. By the force of attention, an emphasis is put upon one of the objective elements of consciousness. This emphasis is, therefore, not itself an object of immediate consciousness; and in this respect it differs entirely from a feeling. Therefore, since the emphasis, nevertheless, consists in some effect upon consciousness, and so can exist only so far as it affects our knowledge; and since an act cannot be supposed to determine that which precedes it in time, this act can consist only in the capacity which the cognition emphasized has for producing an effect upon memory, or otherwise influencing subsequent thought. This is confirmed by the fact that attention is a matter of continuous quantity; for continuous quantity, so far as we know it, reduces itself in the last analysis to time. Accordingly, we find that attention does, in fact, produce a very great effect upon subsequent thought. In the first place, it strongly affects memory, a thought being remembered for a longer time the greater the attention originally paid to it. In the second place, the greater the attention, the closer the connection and the more accurate the logical sequence of thought. In the third place, by attention a thought may be recovered which has been forgotten. From these facts, we gather that attention is the power by which thought at one time is connected with and made to relate to thought at another time; or, to apply the conception of thought as a sign, that it is the *pure demonstrative application* of a thought-sign.

Attention is roused when the same phenomenon presents itself repeatedly on different occasions, or the same predicate in different subjects. We see that A has a certain character, that B has the same, C has the same; and this excites our attention, so that we say, "*These* have this character." Thus attention is an act of induction; but it is an induction which does not increase our knowledge, because our "these" covers nothing but the instances experienced. It is, in short, an argument from enumeration.

Attention produces effects upon the nervous system. These effects are habits, or nervous associations. A habit arises, when, having had the sensation of performing a certain act, *m*, on several occasions *a, b, c*, we come to do it upon every occurrence of the general event, *l*, of which *a, b*, and *c* are special cases. That is to say, by the cognition that

Every case of *a, b*, or *c*, is a case of *m*,

is determined the cognition that

Every case of *l* is a case of *m*.

Thus the formation of a habit is an induction, and is therefore necessarily connected with attention or abstraction. Voluntary actions result from the sensations produced by habits, as instinctive actions result from our original nature.

We have thus seen that every sort of modification of consciousness— Attention, Sensation, and Understanding—is an inference. But the objection may be made that inference deals only with general terms, and that an image, or absolutely singular representation, cannot therefore be inferred.

"Singular" and "individual" are equivocal terms. A singular may mean that which can be but in one place at one time. In this sense it is not opposed to general. *The sun* is a singular in this sense, but, as is explained in every good treatise on logic, it is a general term. I may have a very general conception of Hermolaus Barbarus, but still I conceive him only as able to be in one place at one time. When an image is said to be singular, it is meant that it is absolutely determinate in all respects. Every possible character, or the negative thereof, must be true of such an image. In the words of the most eminent expounder of the doctrine, the image of a man "must be either of a white, or a black, or a tawny; a straight, or a crooked; a tall, or a low, or a middle-sized man." It must be of a man with his mouth open or his mouth shut, whose hair is precisely of such and such a shade, and whose figure has precisely such and such proportions. No statement of Locke has been so scouted by all friends of images as his denial that the "idea" of a triangle must be either of an obtuse-angled, right-angled, or acute-angled triangle. In fact, the image of a triangle must be of one, each of whose angles is of a certain number of degrees, minutes, and seconds.

This being so, it is apparent that no man has a true image of the road to his office, or of any other real thing. Indeed he has no image of it at all unless he can not only recognize it, but imagines it (truly or falsely) in all its infinite details. This being the case, it becomes very doubtful whether we ever have any such thing as an image in our imagination. Please, reader, to look at a bright red book, or other brightly colored object, and then to shut your eyes and say whether you *see* that color, whether brightly or faintly—whether, indeed, there is anything like sight there. Hume and the other followers of Berkeley maintain that there is no difference between the sight and the memory of the red book except in "their different degrees of force and vivacity." "The colors which the memory employs," says Hume, "are faint and dull compared with those in which our original perceptions are clothed." If this were a correct statement of the difference, we should remember the book as being less red than it is; whereas, in fact, we remember the color with very great precision for a few moments [please to test this point, reader], although we do not see anything like it. We carry away absolutely nothing of the color except the *consciousness that we could recognize it.* As a further proof of this, I will request the reader to try a little experiment. Let him call up, if he can, the image of a horse—not of one which he has ever seen, but of an imaginary one,—and before reading further let him by contemplation[6]

6. No person whose native tongue is English will need to be informed that contemplation is essentially (1) protracted, (2) voluntary, and (3) an action, and that it is never used for that which is set forth to the mind in this act. A foreigner can convince himself of this by the proper study of English writers. Thus, Locke (*Essay concerning Human Understanding*, Book II, chap. 19, §1) says, "If it [an idea] be held there [in view] long under attentive consideration, 'tis *Contemplation*"; and again (*Ibid.*, Book II, chap. 10, §1), "Keeping the *Idea*, which is brought into it [the mind] for some time actually in view, which is called *Contemplation*." This term is therefore unfitted to translate *Anschauung*; for this latter does not imply an act which is necessarily protracted or voluntary, and denotes most usually a mental presentation, sometimes a faculty, less often the reception of an impression in the mind, and seldom, if ever, an action. To the translation of *Anschauung* by intuition, there is, at least, no such insuperable objection. Etymologically, the two words precisely correspond. The original philosophical meaning of intuition was a cognition of the present manifold in that character; and it is now commonly used, as a modern writer says, "to include all the products of the perceptive (external or internal) and imaginative faculties; every act of consciousness, in short, of which the immediate object is an *individual*, thing, act, or state of mind, presented under the condition of distinct existence in space and time." Finally, we have the authority of Kant's own example for translating his *Anschauung* by *Intuitus*; and, indeed, this is the common usage of Germans writing Latin. Moreover, *intuitiv* frequently replaces *anschauend* or *anschaulich*. If this constitutes a misunderstanding of Kant, it is one which is shared by himself and nearly all his countrymen.

fix the image in his memory. . . . Has the reader done as requested? for I protest that it is not fair play to read further without doing so.—Now, the reader can say in general of what color that horse was, whether grey, bay, or black. But he probably cannot say *precisely* of what shade it was. He cannot state this as exactly as he could just after having *seen* such a horse. But why, if he had an image in his mind which no more had the general color than it had the particular shade, has the latter vanished so instantaneously from his memory while the former still remains? It may be replied, that we always forget the details before we do the more general characters; but that this answer is insufficient is, I think, shown by the extreme disproportion between the length of time that the exact shade of something looked at is remembered as compared with that instantaneous oblivion to the exact shade of the thing imagined, and the but slightly superior vividness of the memory of the thing seen as compared with the memory of the thing imagined.

The nominalists, I suspect, confound together thinking a triangle without thinking that it is either equilateral, isosceles, or scalene, and thinking a triangle without thinking whether it is equilateral, isosceles, or scalene.

It is important to remember that we have no intuitive power of distinguishing between one subjective mode of cognition and another; and hence often think that something is presented to us as a picture, while it is really constructed from slight data by the understanding. This is the case with dreams, as is shown by the frequent impossibility of giving an intelligible account of one without adding something which we feel was not in the dream itself. Many dreams, of which the waking memory makes elaborate and consistent stories, must probably have been in fact mere jumbles of these feelings of the ability to recognize this and that which I have just alluded to.

I will now go so far as to say that we have no images even in actual perception. It will be sufficient to prove this in the case of vision; for if no picture is seen when we look at an object, it will not be claimed that hearing, touch, and the other senses, are superior to sight in this respect. That the picture is not painted on the nerves of the retina is absolutely certain, if, as physiologists inform us, these nerves are needle-points pointing to the light and at distances considerably greater than the *minimum visibile*. The same thing is shown by our not being able to perceive that there is a large blind spot near the middle of the retina. If, then, we have a picture before us when we see, it is one constructed by the mind at the suggestion of previous sensations. Supposing these sensations to be signs, the understanding by reasoning from them could attain all the knowledge of outward things which we derive from sight, while the sensations are quite inadequate to forming an image or representation absolutely determinate. If we have such an image or picture, we must have in our minds a representation of a surface which is only a part of every surface we see, and we must see that each part, however small, has such and such a color. If we look from some distance at a speckled surface, it seems as if we did not see whether it were speckled or not; but if we have an image before us, it must appear to us either as speckled, or as not speckled. Again, the eye by education comes to distinguish minute differences of color; but if we see only absolutely determinate images, we must, no less before our eyes are trained than afterwards, see each color as particularly such and such a shade. Thus to suppose that we have an image before us when we see, is not only a hypothesis which explains nothing whatever, but is one which actually creates difficulties which require new hypotheses in order to explain them away.

One of these difficulties arises from the fact that the details are less easily distinguished than, and forgotten before, the general circumstances. Upon this theory, the general features exist in the details: the details are, in fact, the whole picture. It seems, then, very strange that that which exists only secondarily in the picture should make more impression than the picture itself. It is true that in an old painting the details are not easily made out; but this is because we know that the blackness is the result of time, and is no part of the picture itself. There is no difficulty in making out the details of the picture as it looks at present; the only difficulty is in guessing what it used to be. But if we have a picture on the retina, the minutest details are there as much as, nay, more than, the general outline and significancy of it. Yet that which must actually be seen, it is extremely difficult to recognize; while that which is only abstracted from what is seen is very obvious.

But the conclusive argument against our having any images, or absolutely determinate representations in perception, is that in that case we have the materials in each such representation for an infinite amount of conscious cognition, which we yet never become aware of. Now there is no meaning in saying that we have something in our minds which never has the least effect on what we are conscious of knowing. The most that can be said is, that when we see we are put in a condition in which we are able to get a very large and perhaps indefinitely great amount of knowledge of the visible qualities of objects.

Moreover, that perceptions are not absolutely determinate and singular is obvious from the fact that each sense is an abstracting mechanism. Sight by itself informs us only of colors and forms. No one can pretend that the images of sight are determinate in reference to taste. They are, therefore, so far general that they are neither sweet nor non-sweet, bitter nor non-bitter, having savor or insipid.

The next question is whether we have any general conceptions except in judgments. In perception, where we know a thing as existing, it is plain that there is a judgment that the thing exists, since a mere general concept of a thing is in no case a cognition of it as existing. It has usually been said, however, that we can call up any concept without making any judgment; but it seems that in this case we only arbitrarily suppose ourselves to have an experience. In order to conceive the number 7, I suppose, that is, I arbitrarily make the hypothesis or judgment, that there are certain points before my eyes, and I judge that these are seven. This seems to be the most simple and rational view of the matter, and I may add that it is the one which has been adopted by the best logicians. If this be the case, what goes by the name of the association of images is in reality an association of judgments. The association of ideas is said to proceed according to three principles—those of resemblance, of contiguity, and of causality. But it would be equally true to say that signs denote what they do on the three principles of resemblance, contiguity, and causality. There can be no question that anything *is* a sign of whatever is associated with it by resemblance, by contiguity, or by causality: nor can there be any doubt that any sign recalls the thing signified. So, then, the association of ideas consists in this, that a judgment occasions another judgment, of which it is the sign. Now this is nothing less nor more than inference.

Everything in which we take the least interest creates in us its own particular emotion, however slight this may be. This emotion is a sign and a predicate of the thing. Now, when a thing resembling this thing is presented to us, a similar emotion arises; hence, we immediately infer that the latter is like the former. A formal logician of the old school may say, that in logic no term can enter into the conclusion which had not been contained in the premises, and that therefore the suggestion of something new must be essentially different from inference. But I reply that that rule of logic applies only to those arguments which are technically called completed. We can and do reason—

> Elias was a man;
> ∴ He was mortal.

And this argument is just as valid as the full syllogism, although it is so only because the major premise of the latter happens to be true. If to pass from the judgment "Elias was a man" to the judgment "Elias was mortal,"

without actually saying to one's self that "All men are mortal," is not inference, then the term "inference" is used in so restricted a sense that inferences
hardly occur outside of a logic-book.

What is here said of association by resemblance is true of all association.
All association is by signs. Everything has its subjective or emotional qualities, which are attributed either absolutely or relatively, or by conventional
imputation to anything which is a sign of it. And so we reason,

The sign is such and such;
∴ The sign is that thing.

This conclusion receiving, however, a modification, owing to other considerations, so as to become—

The sign is almost (is representative of) that thing.

We come now to the consideration of the last of the four principles whose
consequences we were to trace; namely, that the absolutely incognizable is
absolutely inconceivable. That upon Cartesian principles the very realities of
things can never be known in the least, most competent persons must long
ago have been convinced. Hence the breaking forth of idealism, which is
essentially anti-Cartesian, in every direction, whether among empiricists
(Berkeley, Hume), or among noologists (Hegel, Fichte). The principle now
brought under discussion is directly idealistic; for, since the meaning of a
word is the conception it conveys, the absolutely incognizable has no meaning
because no conception attaches to it. It is, therefore, a meaningless word;
and, consequently, whatever is meant by any term as "the real" is cognizable
in some degree, and so is of the nature of a cognition, in the objective sense
of that term.

At any moment we are in possession of certain information, that is, of
cognitions which have been logically derived by induction and hypothesis
from previous cognitions which are less general, less distinct, and of which
we have a less lively consciousness. These in their turn have been derived
from others still less general, less distinct, and less vivid; and so on back to
the ideal[7] first, which is quite singular, and quite out of consciousness. This
ideal first is the particular thing-in-itself. It does not exist *as such*. That is,
there is no thing which is in-itself in the sense of not being relative to the
mind, though things which are relative to the mind doubtless are, apart from

7. By an ideal, I mean the limit which the possible cannot attain.

that relation. The cognitions which thus reach us by this infinite series of inductions and hypotheses (which though infinite *a parte ante logice*, is yet as one continuous process not without a beginning *in time*) are of two kinds, the true and the untrue, or cognitions whose objects are *real* and those whose objects are *unreal*. And what do we mean by the real? It is a conception which we must first have had when we discovered that there was an unreal, an illusion; that is, when we first corrected ourselves. Now the distinction for which alone this fact logically called, was between an *ens* relative to private inward determinations, to the negations belonging to idiosyncrasy, and an *ens* such as would stand in the long run. The real, then, is that which, sooner or later, information and reasoning would finally result in, and which is therefore independent of the vagaries of me and you. Thus, the very origin of the conception of reality shows that this conception essentially involves the notion of a COMMUNITY, without definite limits, and capable of an indefinite increase of knowledge. And so those two series of cognitions—the real and the unreal—consist of those which, at a time sufficiently future, the community will always continue to reaffirm; and of those which, under the same conditions, will ever after be denied. Now, a proposition whose falsity can never be discovered, and the error of which therefore is absolutely incognizable, contains, upon our principle, absolutely no error. Consequently, that which is thought in these cognitions is the real, as it really is. There is nothing, then, to prevent our knowing outward things as they really are, and it is most likely that we do thus know them in numberless cases, although we can never be absolutely certain of doing so in any special case.

But it follows that since no cognition of ours is absolutely determinate, generals must have a real existence. Now this scholastic realism is usually set down as a belief in metaphysical fictions. But, in fact, a realist is simply one who knows no more recondite reality than that which is represented in a true representation. Since, therefore, the word "man" is true of something, that which "man" means is real. The nominalist must admit that man is truly applicable to something; but he believes that there is beneath this a thing in itself, an incognizable reality. His is the metaphysical figment. Modern nominalists are mostly superficial men, who do not know, as the more thorough Roscellinus and Occam did, that a reality which has no representation is one which has no relation and no quality. The great argument for nominalism is that there is no man unless there is some particular man. That, however, does not affect the realism of Scotus; for although there is no man of whom all further determination can be denied, yet there is a man, abstraction being made of all further determination. There is a real difference between man irrespective of what the other determinations may be, and man with this or that particular series of determinations, although undoubtedly this difference is only relative to the mind and not *in re*. Such is the position of Scotus.[8] Occam's great objection is, there can be no real distinction which is not *in re*, in the thing-in-itself; but this begs the question, for it is itself based only on the notion that reality is something independent of representative relation.[9]

Such being the nature of reality in general, in what does the reality of the mind consist? We have seen that the content of consciousness, the entire phenomenal manifestation of mind, is a sign resulting from inference. Upon our principle, therefore, that the absolutely incognizable does not exist, so that the phenomenal manifestation of a substance is the substance, we must conclude that the mind is a sign developing according to the laws of inference. What distinguishes a man from a word? There is a distinction doubtless. The material qualities, the forces which constitute the pure denotative application, and the meaning of the human sign, are all exceedingly complicated in comparison with those of the word. But these differences are only relative. What other is there? It may be said that man is conscious, while a word is not. But consciousness is a very vague term. It may mean that emotion which accompanies the reflection that we have animal life. This is a consciousness which is dimmed when animal life is at its ebb in old age, or sleep, but which is not dimmed when the spiritual life is at its ebb; which is the more lively the better *animal* a man is, but which is not so, the better *man* he is. We do not attribute this sensation to words, because we have reason to believe that it is dependent upon the possession of an animal body. But this consciousness, being a mere sensation, is only a part of the *material quality* of the man-sign. Again, consciousness is sometimes used to signify the *I think*, or unity in thought; but this unity is nothing but consistency, or the recognition of it. Consistency belongs to every sign, so far as it is a sign; and therefore every sign, since it signifies primarily that it is a sign, signifies its own consistency. The man-sign acquires information, and comes to mean more than he did before. But

8. "Eadem natura est, quæ in existentia per gradum singularitatis est determinata, et in intellectu, hoc est ut habet relationem ad intellectum ut cognitum ad cognoscens, est indeterminata." ["It is the same nature that in existence is determinate through the grade of singularity and that in the intellect, that is as having to the intellect the relation of known to knower, is indeterminate."]—*Quæstiones Subtillissimæ*, lib. 7, qu. 18.

9. See his argument *Summa logices* [*Summa logicae* (Paris: Johannes Higman, 1488)], part 1, cap. 16.

so do words. Does not electricity mean more now than it did in the days of Franklin? Man makes the word, and the word means nothing which the man has not made it mean, and that only to some man. But since man can think only by means of words or other external symbols, these might turn round and say: "You mean nothing which we have not taught you, and then only so far as you address some word as the interpretant of your thought." In fact, therefore, men and words reciprocally educate each other; each increase of a man's information involves and is involved by, a corresponding increase of a word's information.

Without fatiguing the reader by stretching this parallelism too far, it is sufficient to say that there is no element whatever of man's consciousness which has not something corresponding to it in the word; and the reason is obvious. It is that the word or sign which man uses *is* the man himself. For, as the fact that every thought is a sign, taken in conjunction with the fact that life is a train of thought, proves that man is a sign; so, that every thought is an *external* sign, proves that man is an external sign. That is to say, the man and the external sign are identical, in the same sense in which the words *homo* and *man* are identical. Thus my language is the sum total of myself; for the man is the thought.

It is hard for man to understand this, because he persists in identifying himself with his will, his power over the animal organism, with brute force. Now the organism is only an instrument of thought. But the identity of a man consists in the *consistency* of what he does and thinks, and consistency is the intellectual character of a thing; that is, is its expressing something.

Finally, as what anything really is, is what it may finally come to be known to be in the ideal state of complete information, so that reality depends on the ultimate decision of the community; so thought is what it is, only by virtue of its addressing a future thought which is in its value as thought identical with it, though more developed. In this way, the existence of thought now, depends on what is to be hereafter; so that it has only a potential existence, dependent on the future thought of the community.

The individual man, since his separate existence is manifested only by ignorance and error, so far as he is anything apart from his fellows, and from what he and they are to be, is only a negation. This is man,

proud man,
Most ignorant of what he's most assured,
His glassy essence.

6

■   ■   ■

Grounds of Validity
of the Laws of Logic:
Further Consequences
of Four Incapacities

In this third and final essay in the Cognition Series, Peirce attempts to reconcile what seemed to be both a logical contradiction and a contradiction of the possibility of logic in the first two essays. In them he had maintained that everything real can be known. Yet he also held that human beings have no intuitive consciousness or direct knowledge of their thoughts but only inference from signs. How then can they know that there is anything real on which to ground the validity of the science of thinking—that is, logic—whether deductive, inductive, or hypothetic (abductive) logic?

Deductive inference, Peirce argues, is syllogistic. Its validity as a way of reasoning toward truth is undeniable to anyone sufficiently honest to admit that he or she does not doubt that if two signs ("terms," in the language of formal logic) represent the same object, they are interchangeable. So if "S is M" and "M is P," then "S is P."

Induction and hypothesis, according to Peirce, are types of statistical inference. The basis of his argument for their validity as modes of reasoning is the theory of semiotic realism for which he argued in the second essay; the real is essentially of the nature of a representation, so the most basic metaphysical conceptions are semiotic relations rather than simple unities. We may therefore reason from particulars to generals because "parts make up and constitute the whole." No single induction or hypothesis can be absolutely certain, but generally or in the long run, Peirce argues, such reasoning must ever more closely approximate the truth.

In the previous essay Peirce first stated his view that the conception of reality is inseparable from the notion of a community of inquirers. Some commentators have argued on this basis that Peirce therefore believed logic to be an essentially social process. They may wish to examine carefully the argument near the end of this essay that it is the other way around, that "the social principle is rooted intrinsically in logic."

Source: *Writings of Charles S. Peirce*, 2:242–72.
Originally published in *Journal of Speculative Philosophy* 2
(1869): 193–208.

If, as I maintained in an article in the last number of this Journal, every judgment results from inference, to doubt every inference is to doubt everything. It has often been argued that absolute scepticism is self-contradictory; but this is a mistake: and even if it were not so, it would be no argument against the absolute sceptic, inasmuch as he does not admit that no contradictory propositions are true. Indeed, it would be impossible to move such a man, for his scepticism consists in considering every argument and never deciding upon its validity; he would, therefore, act in this way in reference to the arguments brought against him.

But then there are no such beings as absolute sceptics. Every exercise of the mind consists in inference, and so, though there are inanimate objects without beliefs, there are no intelligent beings in that condition.

Yet it is quite possible that a person should doubt every principle of inference. He may not have studied logic, and though a logical formula may sound very obviously true to him, he may feel a little uncertain whether some subtle deception may not lurk in it. Indeed, I certainly shall have, among the most cultivated and respected of my readers, those who deny that those laws of logic which men generally admit have universal validity. But I address myself, also, to those who have no such doubts, for even to them it may be interesting to consider how it is that these principles come to be true. Finally, having put forth in former numbers of this Journal some rather heretical principles of philosophical research, one of which is nothing can be admitted to be absolutely inexplicable, it behooves me to take up a challenge which has been given me to show how upon my principles the validity of the laws of logic can be other than inexplicable.

I shall be arrested, at the outset, by a sweeping objection to my whole undertaking. It will be said that my deduction of logical principles, being itself an argument, depends for its whole virtue upon the truth of the very principles in question; so that whatever my proof may be, it must take for granted the very things to be proved. But to this I reply, that I am neither addressing absolute sceptics, nor men in any state of fictitious doubt whatever. I require the reader to be candid; and if he becomes convinced of a conclusion, to admit it. There is nothing to prevent a man's perceiving the force of certain special arguments, although he does not yet know that a certain general law of arguments holds good; for the general rule may hold good in some cases and not in others. A man may reason well without understanding the principles of reasoning, just as he may play billiards well without understanding analytical mechanics. If you, the reader, actually find that my arguments have a convincing force with you, it is a mere pretence to call them illogical.

That if one sign denotes generally everything denoted by a second, and this second denotes generally everything denoted by a third, then the first denotes generally everything denoted by the third, is not doubted by anybody who distinctly apprehends the meaning of these words. The deduction of the general form of syllogism, therefore, will consist only of an explanation of the *suppositio communis*.[1] Now, what the formal logician means by an expression

---

1. The word *suppositio* is one of the useful technical terms of the middle ages which was condemned by the purists of the *renaissance* as incorrect. The early logicians made a distinction between *significatio* and *suppositio*. *Significatio* is defined as "rei per vocem secundum placitum representatio." It is a mere affair of lexicography, and depends on a special convention (*secundum placitum*), and not on a general principle. *Suppositio* belongs, not directly to the *vox*, but to the *vox* as having this or that *significatio*. "Unde significatio prior est suppositione et differunt in hoc, quia significatio est vocis, suppositio vero est termini jam compositi ex voce et significatione." ["Signification is thus prior to supposition, and they differ in that signification belongs to the word, whereas supposition belongs to the term already composed of the word and its signification." Petrus Hispanus, *Compendiarius Parvorum logicalium continens perutiles Petri Hispani tractatus priores sex & clarissimi philosophi Marsilij dialectices documenta*, edited by Konrad Pschlacher (Vienna, 1512), Tract 6.] The various *suppositiones* which may belong to one word with one *significatio* are the different senses in which the word may be taken, according to the general principles of the language or of logic. Thus, the word *table* has different *significationes* in the expressions "table of logarithms" and "writing-table"; but the word *man* has one and the same *significatio*, and only different *suppositiones*, in the following sentences: "A

of the form, "Every M is P," is that anything of which M is predicable is P; thus, if S is M, that S is P. The premise that "Every M is P" may, therefore, be denied; but to admit it, unambiguously, in the sense intended, is to admit that the inference is good that S is P if S is M. He, therefore, who does not deny that S is P—M, S, P, being any terms such that S is M and every M is P—denies nothing that the formal logician maintains in reference to this matter; and he who does deny this, simply is deceived by an ambiguity of language. How we come to make any judgments in the sense of the above "Every M is P," may be understood from the theory of reality put forth in the article in the last number. It was there shown that real things are of a cognitive and therefore significative nature, so that the real is that which signifies something real. Consequently, to predicate anything of anything real is to predicate it of that of which that subject [the real] is itself predicated; for to predicate one thing of another is to state that the former is a sign of the latter.

These considerations show the reason of the validity of the formula,

$$S \text{ is } M; M \text{ is } P:$$
$$\therefore S \text{ is } P.$$

They hold good whatever S and P may be, provided that they be such that any middle term between them can be found. That P should be a negative term, therefore, or that S should be a particular term, would not interfere at all with the validity of this formula. Hence, the following formulæ are also valid:

$$S \text{ is } M; M \text{ is not } P:$$
$$\therefore S \text{ is not } P.$$

$$\text{Some } S \text{ is } M; M \text{ is } P:$$
$$\therefore \text{Some } S \text{ is } P.$$

$$\text{Some } S \text{ is } M; M \text{ is not } P:$$
$$\therefore \text{Some } S \text{ is not } P.$$

---

man is an animal," "a butcher is a man," "man cooks his food," "man appeared upon the earth at such a date," &c. Some later writers have endeavored to make "*acceptio*" do service for "*suppositio*"; but it seems to me better, now that scientific terminology is no longer forbidden, to revive *supposition*. I should add that as the principles of logic and language for the different uses of the different parts of speech are different, *supposition* must be restricted to the acceptation of a *substantive*. The term *copulatio* was used for the acceptation of an adjective or verb.

Moreover, as all that class of inferences which depend upon the introduction of relative terms can be reduced to the general form, they also are shown to be valid. Thus, it is proved to be correct to reason thus:

Every relation of a subject to its predicate is a relation of the relative "not X'd, except by the X of some," to its correlate, where X is any relative I please.

Every relation of "man" to "animal" is a relation of a subject to its predicate.

∴ Every relation of "man" to "animal" is a relation of the relative "not X'd, except by the X of some," to its correlate, where X is any relative I please.

Every relation of the relative "not X'd, except by the X of some," to its correlate, where X is any relative I please, is a relation of the relative "not *headed*, except by the *head* of some," to its correlate.

∴ Every relation of "man" to "animal" is a relation of the relative "not headed, except by the head of some," to its correlate.[2]

At the same time, as will be seen from this example, the proof of the validity of these inferences depends upon the assumption of the truth of certain general statements concerning relatives. These formulæ can all be deduced from the principle, that in a system of signs in which no sign is taken in two different senses, two signs which differ only in their manner of representing their object, but which are equivalent in meaning, can always be substituted for one another. Any case of the falsification of this principle would be a case of the dependence of the mode of existence of the thing represented upon the mode of this or that representation of it, which, as has been shown in the article in the last number, is contrary to the nature of reality.

The next formula of syllogism to be considered is the following:

$$S \text{ is other than } P; \ M \text{ is } P:$$
$$\therefore S \text{ is other than } M.$$

The meaning of "not" or "other than" seems to have greatly perplexed the German logicians, and it may be, therefore, that it is used in different senses.

2. "If any one will by ordinary syllogism prove that because every man is an animal, therefore every head of a man is a head of an animal, I shall be ready to—set him another question."—*De Morgan*: "On the Syllogism No. IV, and on the Logic of Relations" [*Transactions of the Cambridge Philosophical Society* 10 (1864): 337].

If so, I propose to defend the validity of the above formula only when *other than* is used in a particular sense. By saying that one thing or class is other than a second, I mean that any third whatever is identical with the class which is composed of that third and of whatever is, at once, the first and second. For example, if I say that rats are not mice, I mean that any third class as dogs is identical with dogs and rats-which-are-mice; that is to say, the addition of rats-which-are-mice, to anything, leaves the latter just what it was before. This being all that I mean by S is other than P, I mean absolutely the same thing when I say that S is other than P, that I do when I say that P is other than S; and the same when I say that S is other than M, that I do when I say that M is other than S. Hence the above formula is only another way of writing the following:

$$M \text{ is } P; P \text{ is not } S:$$
$$\therefore M \text{ is not } S.$$

But we have already seen that this is valid.

A very similar formula to the above is the following:

$$S \text{ is } M; \text{ some } S \text{ is } P:$$
$$\therefore \text{ Some } M \text{ is } P.$$

By saying that some of a class is of any character, I mean simply that no statement which implies that none of that class is of that character is true. But to say that none of that class is of that character, is, as I take the word "not," to say that nothing of that character is of that class. Consequently, to say that some of A is B, is, as I understand words and in the only sense in which I defend this formula, to say that some B is A. In this way the formula is reduced to the following, which has already been shown to be valid:

$$\text{Some } P \text{ is } S; S \text{ is } M:$$
$$\therefore \text{ Some } P \text{ is } M.$$

The only demonstrative syllogisms which are not included among the above forms are the Theophrastean moods, which are all easily reduced by means of simple conversions.

Let us now consider what can be said against all this, and let us take up the objections which have actually been made to the syllogistic formulæ, beginning with those which are of a general nature and then examining those sophisms which have been pronounced irresolvable by the rules of ordinary logic.

It is a very ancient notion that no proof can be of any value, because it rests on premises which themselves equally require proof, which again must rest on other premises, and so back to infinity. This really does show that nothing can be proved beyond the *possibility* of a doubt; that no argument could be legitimately used against an absolute sceptic; and that inference is only a transition from one cognition to another, and not the creation of a cognition. But the objection is intended to go much further than this, and to show (as it certainly seems to do) that inference not only cannot produce *infallible* cognition, but that it cannot *produce* cognition at all. It is true, that since some judgment precedes every judgment inferred, either the first premises were not inferred, or there have been no first premises. But it does not follow that because there has been no first in a series, therefore that series has had no beginning in time; for the series may be *continuous*, and may have begun gradually, as was shown in an article in No. 3 of this volume [pages 51–53 of this book], where this difficulty has already been resolved.

A somewhat similar objection has been made by Locke and others, to the effect that the ordinary demonstrative syllogism is a *petitio principii*, inasmuch as the conclusion is already implicitly stated in the major premise. Take, for example, the syllogism,

All men are mortal;
Socrates is a man:
∴ Socrates is mortal.

This attempt to prove that Socrates is mortal begs the question, it is said, since if the conclusion is denied by anyone, he thereby denies that all men are mortal. But what such considerations really prove is that the syllogism is demonstrative. To call it a *petitio principii* is a mere confusion of language. It is strange that philosophers, who are so suspicious of the words *virtual* and *potential*, should have allowed this "implicit" to pass unchallenged. A *petitio principii* consists in reasoning from the unknown to the unknown. Hence, a logician who is simply engaged in stating what general forms of argument are valid, can, at most, have nothing more to do with the consideration of this fallacy than to note those cases in which from logical principles a premise of a certain form cannot be better known than a conclusion of the corresponding form. But it is plainly beyond the province of the logician, who has only proposed to state what forms of facts involve what others, to inquire whether man can have a knowledge of universal propositions without a knowledge of every particular contained under them, by means of natural insight, divine revelation, induction, or testimony. The only *petitio principii*, therefore, which he can notice is the assumption of the conclusion itself in the premise; and this, no doubt, those who call the syllogism a *petitio principii* believe is done in that formula. But the proposition "All men are mortal" does not in itself involve the statement that Socrates is mortal, but only that "whatever has man truly predicated of it is mortal." In other words, the *conclusion* is not involved in the meaning of the premise, but only the *validity of the syllogism*. So that this objection merely amounts to arguing that the syllogism is not valid, because it is demonstrative.[3]

A much more interesting objection is that a syllogism is a purely mechanical process. It proceeds according to a bare rule or formula; and a machine might be constructed which would so transpose the terms of premises. This being so (and it is so), it is argued that this cannot be *thought*; that there is no life in it. Swift has ridiculed the syllogism in the "Voyage to Laputa," by describing a machine for making science:

> By this contrivance, the most ignorant person, at a reasonable charge, and with little bodily labor, might write books in philosophy, poetry, politics, laws, mathematics, and theology, without the least assistance from genius or study.

The idea involved in this objection seems to be that it requires mind to apply any formula or use any machine. If, then, this mind is itself only another formula, it requires another mind behind it to set it into operation, and so on *ad infinitum*. This objection fails in much the same way that the first one which we considered failed. It is as though a man should address a land surveyor as follows:—"You do not make a true representation of the land; you only measure lengths from point to point—that is to say, lines. If you observe angles, it is only to solve triangles and obtain the lengths of their sides. And when you come to make your map, you use a pencil which can

---

3. Mr. Mill thinks the syllogism is merely a formula for recalling forgotten facts. Whether he means to deny, what all logicians since Kant have held, that the syllogism serves to render confused thoughts distinct, or whether he does not know that this is the usual doctrine, does not appear [John Stuart Mill, *A System of Logic, Ratiocinative and Inductive: Being a Connected View of the Principles of Evidence, and the Methods of Scientific Investigation*, 2 vols., 6th ed. (London: Longmans, Green, 1865), 1:204].

only make lines, again. So, you have to do solely with lines. But the land is a surface; and no number of lines, however great, will make any surface, however small. You, therefore, fail entirely to represent the land." The surveyor, I think, would reply, "Sir, you have proved that my lines cannot make up the land, and that, therefore, my map *is not* the land. I never pretended that it was. But that does not prevent it from truly representing the land, as far as it goes. It cannot, indeed, represent every blade of grass; but it does not represent that there is not a blade of grass where there is. To abstract from a circumstance is not to deny it." Suppose the objector were, at this point, to say, "To abstract from a circumstance *is* to deny it. Wherever your map does not represent a blade of grass, it represents there is no blade of grass. Let us take things on their own valuation." Would not the surveyor reply: "This map is my description of the country. Its own valuation can be nothing but what I say, and all the world understands, that I mean by it. Is it very unreasonable that I should demand to be taken as I mean, especially when I succeed in making myself understood?" What the objector's reply to this question would be, I leave it to anyone to say who thinks his position well taken. Now this line of objection is parallel to that which is made against the syllogism. It is shown that no number of syllogisms can constitute the sum total of any mental action, however restricted. This may be freely granted, and yet it will not follow that the syllogism does not truly represent the mental action, as far as it purports to represent it at all. There is reason to believe that the action of the mind is, as it were, a continuous movement. Now the doctrine embodied in syllogistic formulæ (so far as it applies to the mind at all) is, that if two successive positions, occupied by the mind in this movement, be taken, they will be found to have certain relations. It is true that no number of successions of positions can make up a continuous movement; and this, I suppose, is what is meant by saying that a syllogism is a dead formula, while thinking is a living process. But the reply is that the syllogism is not intended to represent the mind, as to its life or deadness, but only as to the relation of its different judgments concerning the same thing. And it should be added that the relation between syllogism and thought does not spring from considerations of formal logic, but from those of psychology. All that the formal logician has to say is, that if facts capable of expression in such and such forms of words are true, another fact whose expression is related in a certain way to the expression of these others is also true.

Hegel taught that ordinary reasoning is "one-sided." A part of what he meant was that by such inference a part only of all that is true of an object can be learned, owing to the generality or abstractedness of the predicates inferred. This objection is, therefore, somewhat similar to the last; for the point of it is that no number of syllogisms would give a complete knowledge of the object. This, however, presents a difficulty which the other did not; namely, that if nothing incognizable exists, and all knowledge is by mental action, by mental action everything is cognizable. So that if by syllogism everything is not cognizable, syllogism does not exhaust the modes of mental action. But grant the validity of this argument and it proves too much; for it makes, not the syllogism particularly, but all finite knowledge to be worthless. However much we know, more may come to be found out. Hence, all can never be known. This seems to contradict the fact that nothing is absolutely incognizable; and it would really do so *if our knowledge* were something absolutely limited. For, to say that all can never be known, means that information may increase beyond any assignable point; that is, that an absolute termination of all increase of knowledge is absolutely incognizable, and therefore does not exist. In other words, the proposition merely means that the sum of all that will be known up to any time, however advanced, into the future, has a ratio less than any assignable ratio to all that may be known at a time still more advanced. This does not contradict the fact that everything is cognizable; it only contradicts a proposition, which no one can maintain, that everything will be known at some time some number of years into the future. It may, however, very justly be said that the difficulty still remains, how at every future time, however late, there can be something yet to happen. It is no longer a contradiction, but it is a difficulty; that is to say, *lengths of time* are shown not to afford an adequate conception of futurity in general; and the question arises, in what other way we are to conceive of it. I might indeed, perhaps, fairly drop the question here, and say that the difficulty had become so entirely removed from the syllogism in particular, that the formal logician need not feel himself specially called on to consider it. The solution, however, is very simple. It is that we conceive of the future, as a whole, by considering that this *word*, like any other general term, as "inhabitant of St. Louis," may be taken distributively or collectively. We conceive of the infinite, therefore, not directly or on the side of its infinity, but by means of a consideration concerning words or a second intention.

Another objection to the syllogism is that its "therefore" is merely subjective; that, because a certain conclusion syllogistically follows from a premise, it does not follow that the fact denoted by the conclusion really depends upon the fact denoted by the premise, so that the syllogism does not represent things as they really are. But it has been fully shown that if the facts are as the premises represent, they are also as the conclusion represents. Now this is a purely objective statement: therefore, there is a real connection between the facts stated as premises and those stated as conclusion. It is true that there is often an appearance of reasoning deductively from effects to causes. Thus we may reason as follows:—"There is smoke; there is never smoke without fire: hence, there has been fire." Yet smoke is not the cause of fire, but the effect of it. Indeed, it is evident, that in many cases an event is a demonstrative sign of a certain previous event having occurred. Hence, we can reason deductively from relatively future to relatively past, whereas causation really determines events in the direct order of time. Nevertheless, if we can thus reason against the stream of time, it is because there really are such facts as that "If there is smoke, there has been fire," in which the following event is the antecedent. Indeed, if we consider the manner in which such a proposition became known to us, we shall find that what it really means is that "If we find smoke, we *shall* find evidence on the whole that there has been fire"; and this, if reality consists in the agreement that the whole community would eventually come to, is the very same thing as to say that there really has been fire. In short, the whole present difficulty is resolved instantly by this theory of reality, because it makes all reality something which is constituted by an event indefinitely future.

Another objection, for which I am quite willing to allow a great German philosopher the whole credit, is that sometimes the conclusion is false, although both the premises and the syllogistic form are correct.[4] Of this he gives the following examples. From the middle term that a wall has been painted blue, it may correctly be concluded that it is blue; but notwithstanding this syllogism it may be green if it has also received a coat of yellow, from which last circumstance by itself it would follow that it is yellow. If from the middle term of the sensuous faculty it be concluded that man is neither good nor bad, since neither can be predicated of the sensuous, the syllogism is correct; but the conclusion is false, since of man in the concrete, spirituality is equally

4. "So zeigt sich jener Schlussatz dadurch als falsch, obleich für sich dessen Prämissen und ebenso dessen Consequenz ganz richtig sind."—Hegel's *Werke* [*Werke: Vollständige Ausgabe durch einen Verein des Verewigten*, 18 vols., edited by Philipp Marheineke et al. (Berlin: Duncker and Humblot, 1832–40)], vol. v, p. 124.

true, and may serve as middle term in an opposite syllogism. From the middle term of the gravitation of the planets, satellites, and comets, towards the sun, it follows correctly that these bodies fall into the sun; but they do not fall into it, because (!) they equally gravitate to their own centres, or, in other words (!!), they are supported by centrifugal force. Now, does Hegel mean to say that these syllogisms satisfy the rules for syllogism given by those who defend syllogism? or does he mean to grant that they do not satisfy *those* rules, but to set up some rules of his own for syllogism which shall insure its yielding false conclusions from true premises? If the latter, he ignores the real issue, which is whether the syllogism as defined by the rules of formal logic is correct, and not whether the syllogism as represented by Hegel is correct. But if he means that the above examples satisfy the usual definition of a true syllogism, he is mistaken. The first, stated in form, is as follows:

> Whatever has been painted blue is blue;
> This wall has been painted blue:
> ∴ This wall is blue.

Now "painted blue" may mean painted with blue paint, or painted so as to be blue. If, in the example, the former were meant, the major premise would be false. As he has stated that it is true, the latter meaning of "painted blue" must be the one intended. Again, "blue" may mean blue at some time, or blue at this time. If the latter be meant, the major premise is plainly false; therefore, the former is meant. But the conclusion is said to contradict the statement that the wall is yellow. If blue were here taken in the more general sense, there would be no such contradiction. Hence, he means in the conclusion that this wall is now blue; that is to say, he reasons thus:

> Whatever had been made blue has been blue;
> This has been made blue:
> ∴ This is blue now.

Now substituting letters for the subjects and predicates, we get the form,

> M is P;
> S is M:
> ∴ S is Q.

This is not a syllogism in the ordinary sense of that term, or in any sense in which anybody maintains that the syllogism is valid.

The second example given by Hegel, when written out in full, is as follows:

> Sensuality is neither good nor bad;
> Man *has* (not *is*) sensuality:
> ∴ Man is neither good nor bad.

Or, the same argument may be stated as follows:

> The sensuous, *as such*, is neither good nor bad;
> Man is sensuous:
> ∴ Man is neither good nor bad.

When letters are substituted for subject and predicate in either of these arguments, it takes the form,

> M is P;
> S is N:
> ∴ S is P.

This, again, bears but a very slight resemblance to a syllogism.

The third example, when stated at full length, is as follows:

> Whatever tends towards the sun, *on the whole*, falls into the sun;
> The planets tend toward the sun:
> ∴ The planets fall into the sun.

This is a fallacy similar to the last.

I wonder that this eminent logician did not add to his list of examples of correct syllogism the following:

> It either rains, or it does not rain;
> It does not rain:
> ∴ It rains.

This is fully as deserving of serious consideration as any of those which he has brought forward. The rainy day and the pleasant day are both, in the first place, day. Secondly, each is the negation of a day. It is indifferent which be regarded as the positive. The pleasant is Other to the rainy, and the rainy is in like manner Other to the pleasant. Thus, both are equally Others. Both are Others of each other, or each is Other for itself. So this day being other than rainy, that to which it is Other is itself. But it is Other than itself. Hence, it is itself Rainy.

Some sophisms have, however, been adduced, mostly by the Eleatics and Sophists, which really are extremely difficult to resolve by syllogistic rules; and according to some modern authors this is actually impossible. These sophisms fall into three classes: *1st*, those which relate to continuity; *2d*, those which relate to consequences of supposing things to be other than they are; *3d*, those which relate to propositions which imply their own falsity. Of the first class, the most celebrated are Zeno's arguments concerning motion. One of these is, that if Achilles overtakes a tortoise in any finite time, and the tortoise has the start of him by a distance which may be called *a*, then Achilles has to pass over the sum of distances represented by the polynomial

$$\frac{1}{2}a + \frac{1}{4}a + \frac{1}{8}a + \frac{1}{16}a + \frac{1}{32}a \ \&c.$$

up to infinity. Every term of this polynomial is finite, and it has an infinite number of terms; consequently, Achilles must in a finite time pass over a distance equal to the sum of an infinite number of finite distances. Now this distance must be infinite, because no finite distance, however small, can be multiplied by an infinite number without giving an infinite distance. So that even if none of these finite distances were larger than the smallest (which is finite since all are finite), the sum of the whole would be infinite. But Achilles cannot pass over an infinite distance in a finite time; therefore, he cannot overtake the tortoise in any time, however great.

The solution of this fallacy is as follows: The conclusion is dependent on the fact that Achilles cannot overtake the tortoise without passing over an infinite number of terms of that series of finite distances. That is, no case of his overtaking the tortoise would be a case of his not passing over a non-finite number of terms; that is (by simple conversion), no case of his not passing over a non-finite number of terms would be a case of his overtaking the tortoise. But if he does not pass over a non-finite number of terms, he either passes over a finite number, or he passes over none; and conversely. Consequently, nothing more has been said than that every case of his passing over only a finite number of terms, or of his not passing over any, is a case of his not overtaking the tortoise. Consequently, nothing more can be concluded than that he passes over a distance greater than the sum of any finite number of the above series of terms. But because a quantity is greater than any quantity of a certain series, it does not follow that it is greater than any quantity.

In fact, the reasoning in this sophism may be exhibited as follows:—We start with the series of numbers,

$$\frac{1}{2}a$$
$$\frac{1}{2}a + \frac{1}{4}a$$
$$\frac{1}{2}a + \frac{1}{4}a + \frac{1}{8}a$$
$$\frac{1}{2}a + \frac{1}{4}a + \frac{1}{8}a + \frac{1}{16}a$$
&c. &c. &c.

Then, the implied argument is

Any number of this series is less than a;
But any number you please is less than the number of terms of this
series:
Hence, any number you please is less than a.

This involves an obvious confusion between the number of terms and the value of the greatest term.

Another argument by Zeno against motion, is that a body fills a space no larger than itself. In that place there is no room for motion. Hence, while in the place where it is, it does not move. But it never is other than in the place where it is. Hence, it never moves. Putting this into form, it will read:

No body in a place no larger than itself is moving;
But every body is a body in a place no larger than itself:
∴ No body is moving.

The error of this consists in the fact that the minor premise is only true in the sense that during a time sufficiently short the space occupied by a body is as little larger than itself as you please. All that can be inferred from this is, that during no time a body will move no distance.

All the arguments of Zeno depend on supposing that a *continuum* has ultimate parts. But a *continuum* is precisely that, every part of which has parts, in the same sense. Hence, he makes out his contradictions only by making a self-contradictory supposition. In ordinary and mathematical language, we allow ourselves to speak of such parts—*points*—and whenever we are led into contradiction thereby, we have simply to express ourselves more accurately to resolve the difficulty.

Suppose a piece of glass to be laid on a sheet of paper so as to cover half of it. Then, every part of the paper is *covered*, or *not covered*; for "not" means merely outside of, or other than. But is the line under the edge of the glass covered or not? It is no more on one side of the edge than it is on the other. Therefore, it is either on both sides, or neither side. It is not on neither side; for if it were it would be *not* on either side, therefore not on the covered side, therefore not covered, therefore on the uncovered side. It is not partly on one side and partly on the other, because it has no width. Hence, it is wholly on both sides, or both covered and not covered.

The solution of this is, that we have supposed a part too narrow to be partly uncovered and partly covered; that is to say, a part which has no parts in a continuous surface, which by definition has no such parts. The reasoning, therefore, simply serves to reduce this supposition to an absurdity.

It may be said that there really is such a thing as a line. If a shadow falls on a surface, there really is a division between the light and the darkness. That is true. But it does not follow that because we attach a definite meaning to the part of a surface being covered, therefore we know what we mean when we say that a line is covered. We may define a covered line as one which separates two surfaces both of which are covered, or as one which separates two surfaces *either* of which is covered. In the former case, the line under the edge is uncovered; in the latter case, it is covered.

In the sophisms thus far considered, the appearance of contradiction depends mostly upon an ambiguity; in those which we are now to consider, two true propositions really do in form conflict with one another. We are apt to think that formal logic forbids this, whereas a familiar argument, the *reductio ad absurdum*, depends on showing that contrary predicates are true of a subject, and *that therefore that subject does not exist*. Many logicians, it is true, make affirmative propositions assert the existence of their subjects.[5] The objection to this is that it cannot be extended to hypotheticals. The proposition

If *A* then *B*

may conveniently be regarded as equivalent to

Every case of the truth of *A* is a case of the truth of *B*.

But this cannot be done if the latter proposition asserts the existence of its subject; that is, asserts that *A* really happens. If, however, a categorical affir-

---

5. The usage of ordinary language has no relevancy in the matter.

mative be regarded as asserting the existence of its subject, the principle of the *reductio ad absurdum* is that two propositions of the forms,

If *A* were true, *B* would not be true,

and

If *A* were true, *B* would be true,

may both be true at once; and that if they are so, *A* is not true. It will be well, perhaps, to illustrate this point. No man of common sense would deliberately upset his inkstand if there were ink in it; that is, if any ink would run out. Hence, by simple conversion,

If he were deliberately to upset his inkstand,
no ink would be spilt.

But suppose there is ink in it. Then, it is also true, that

If he were deliberately to upset his inkstand,
the ink would be spilt.

These propositions are both true, and the law of contradiction is not violated which asserts only that nothing has contradictory predicates: only, it follows from these propositions that the man will not deliberately overturn his inkstand.

There are two ways in which deceptive sophisms may result from this circumstance. In the first place, contradictory propositions are never both true. Now, as a universal proposition may be true when the subject does not exist, it follows that the contradictory of a universal—that is, a particular—cannot be taken in such a sense as to be true when the subject does not exist. But a particular simply asserts a part of what is asserted in the universal over it; therefore, the universal over it asserts the subject to exist. Consequently, there are two kinds of universals, those which do not assert the subject to exist, and these have no particular propositions under them, and those which do assert that the subject exists, and these strictly speaking have no contradictories. For example, there is no use of such a form of proposition as "Some griffins would be dreadful animals," as particular under the useful form "The griffin would be a dreadful animal"; and the apparent contradictories "All of John Smith's family are ill," and "Some of John Smith's family are not ill," are both false at once if John Smith has no family. Here, though an inference from a universal to the particular under it is always valid, yet a procedure which greatly resembles this would be sophistical if the universal were one of those propositions which does not assert the existence of its subject. The following sophism depends upon this; I call it the True Gorgias:

Gorgias. What say you, Socrates, of black? Is any black, white?

Socrates. No, by Zeus!

Gor. Do you say, then, that no black is white? *Soc.* None at all.

Gor. But is everything either black or non-black? *Soc.* Of course.

Gor. And everything either white or non-white? *Soc.* Yes.

Gor. And everything either rough or smooth? *Soc.* Yes.

Gor. And everything either real or unreal? *Soc.* Oh, bother! yes.

Gor. Do you say, then, that all black is either rough black or smooth black? *Soc.* Yes.

Gor. And that all white is either real white or unreal white? *Soc.* Yes.

Gor. And yet is no black, white? *Soc.* None at all.

Gor. Nor no white, black? *Soc.* By no means.

Gor. What? Is no smooth black, white? *Soc.* No; you cannot prove that, Gorgias.

Gor. Nor no rough black, white? *Soc.* Neither.

Gor. Nor no real white, black? *Soc.* No.

Gor. Nor no unreal white, black? *Soc.* No, I say. No white at all is black.

Gor. What if black is smooth, is it not white? *Soc.* Not in the least.

Gor. And if the last is false, is the first false? *Soc.* It follows.

Gor. If, then, black is white, does it follow, that black is not smooth? *Soc.* It does.

Gor. Black-white is not smooth? *Soc.* What do you mean?

Gor. Can any dead man speak? *Soc.* No, indeed.

Gor. And is any speaking man dead? *Soc.* I say, no.

Gor. And is any good king tyrannical? *Soc.* No.

Gor. And is any tyrannical king good? *Soc.* I just said no.

Gor. And you said, too, that no rough black is white, did you not? *Soc.* Yes.

Gor. Then, is any black-white, rough? *Soc.* No.

Gor. And is any unreal black, white? *Soc.* No.

Gor. Then, is any black-white unreal? *Soc.* No.

Gor. No black-white is rough? *Soc.* None.

Gor. All black-white, then, is non-rough? *Soc.* Yes.

Gor. And all black-white, non-unreal? *Soc.* Yes.

Gor. All black-white is then smooth? *Soc.* Yes.

Gor. And all real? *Soc.* Yes.

Gor. Some smooth, then, is black-white? *Soc.* Of course.

Gor. And some real is black-white? *Soc.* So it seems.

Gor. Some black-white smooth is black-white? *Soc.* Yes.

Gor. Some black smooth is black-white? *Soc.* Yes.

Gor. Some black smooth is white? *Soc.* Yes.

Gor. Some black real is black-white? *Soc.* Yes.

Gor. Some black real is white? *Soc.* Yes.

Gor. Some real black is white? *Soc.* Yes.

Gor. And some smooth black is white? *Soc.* Yes.

Gor. Then, some black is white? *Soc.* I think so myself.

The principle of the *reductio ad absurdum* also occasions deceptions in another way, owing to the fact that we have many words, such as *can, may, must*, &c., which imply more or less vaguely an otherwise unexpressed condition, so that these propositions are in fact hypotheticals. Accordingly, if the unexpressed condition is some state of things which does not actually come to pass, the two propositions may appear to be contrary to one another. Thus, the moralist says, "You ought to do this, and you can do it." This "You can do it" is principally hortatory in its force: so far as it is a statement of fact, it means merely, "If you try, you will do it." Now, if the act is an outward one and the act is not performed, the scientific man, in view of the fact that every event in the physical world depends exclusively on physical antecedents, says that in this case the laws of nature prevented the thing from being done, and that therefore, "Even if you had tried, you would not have done it." Yet the reproachful conscience still says you might have done it; that is, that "If you had tried, you would have done it." This is called the paradox of freedom and fate; and it is usually supposed that one of these propositions must be true and the other false. But since, in fact, you have not tried, there is no reason why the supposition that you have tried should not be reduced to an absurdity. In the same way, if you had tried and had performed the action, the conscience might say, "If you had not tried, you would not have done it"; while the understanding would say, "Even if you had not tried, you would have done it." These propositions are perfectly consistent, and only serve to reduce the supposition that you did not try to an absurdity.[6]

6. This seems to me to be the main difficulty of freedom and fate. But the question is overlaid with many others. The Necessitarians seem now to maintain less that every

The third class of sophisms consists of the so-called *Insolubilia*. Here is an example of one of them with its resolution:

THIS PROPOSITION IS NOT TRUE.
IS IT TRUE OR NOT?

Suppose it true.	Suppose it not true.
Then,	Then,
The proposition is true;	It is not true.
But, that it is not true is the	∴ It is true that it is not true.
proposition:	But, the proposition is that it is
∴ That it is not true is true;	not true.
∴ It is not true.	∴ The proposition is true.
Besides,	Besides,
It is true.	The proposition is not true.
∴ It is true that it is true,	But that it is not true is the
∴ It is not true that it is not true;	proposition.
But, the proposition is that it is	∴ That it is not true, is not true.
not true,	∴ That it is true, is true.
∴ The proposition is not true.	∴ It is true.

∴ Whether it is true or not, it is both true and not.
∴ It is both true and not,
which is absurd.

---

physical event is completely determined by physical causes (which seems to me irrefragable), than that every act of will is determined by the strongest motive. This has never been proved. Its advocates seem to think that it follows from universal causation, but why need the cause of an act lie within the consciousness at all? If I act from a reason at all, I act voluntarily; but which of two reasons shall appear strongest to me on a particular occasion may be owing to what I have eaten for dinner. Unless there is a perfect regularity as to what is the strongest motive with me, to say that I act from the strongest motive is mere tautology. If there is no calculating how a man will act except by taking into account external facts, the character of his motives does not determine how he acts. Mill and others have, therefore, not shown that a man always acts from the strongest motive. Hobbes maintained that a man always acts from a reflection upon what will please him most. This is a very crude opinion. Men are not always thinking of themselves.

Self-control seems to be the capacity for rising to an extended view of a practical subject instead of seeing only temporary urgency. This is the only freedom of which

Since the conclusion is false, the reasoning is bad, or the premises are not all true. But the reasoning is a dilemma; either, then, the disjunctive principle that it is either true or not is false, or the reasoning under one or the other branch is bad, or the reasoning is altogether valid. If the principle that it is either true or not is false, it is other than true and other than not true; that is, not true and not not true; that is, not true and true. But this is absurd. Hence, the disjunctive principle is valid. There are two arguments under each horn of the dilemma; both the arguments under one or the other branch must be false. But, in each case, the second argument involves all the premises and forms of inference involved in the first; hence, if the first is false, the second necessarily is so. We may, therefore, confine our attention to the first arguments in the two branches. The forms of argument contained in these are two: first, the simple syllogism in Barbara, and, second, the consequence from the truth of a proposition to the proposition itself. These are both correct. Hence, the whole form of reasoning is correct, and nothing remains to be false but a premise. But since the repetition of an alternative supposition is not a premise, there is, properly speaking, but one premise in the whole. This is that the proposition is the same as that that proposition is not true. This, then, must be false. Hence the proposition signifies either less or more than this. If it does not signify as much as this, it signifies nothing, and hence it is not true, and hence another proposition which says of it what it says of itself is true. But if the proposition in question signifies something more than that it is itself not true, then the premise that

> Whatever is said in the proposition is
> that it is not true,

is not true. And as a proposition is true only if whatever is said in it is true, but is false if anything said in it is false, the first argument on the second side of the dilemma contains a false premise, and the second an undistributed middle. But the first argument on the first side remains good. Hence, if the proposition means more than that it is not true, it is not true, and another proposition which repeats this of it is true. Hence, whether the proposition does or does not mean that it is not true, it is not true, and a proposition which repeats this of it is true.

---

man has any reason to be proud; and it is because love of what is good for all on the whole, which is the widest possible consideration, is the essence of Christianity, that it is said that the service of Christ is perfect freedom.

Since this repeating proposition is true, it has a meaning. Now, a proposition has a meaning if any part of it has a meaning. Hence the original proposition (a part of which repeated has a meaning) has itself a meaning. Hence, it must imply something besides that which it explicitly states. But it has no particular determination to any further implication. Hence, what more it signifies it must signify by virtue of being a proposition at all. That is to say, every proposition must imply something analogous to what this implies. Now, the repetition of this proposition does not contain this implication, for otherwise it could not be true; hence, what every proposition implies must be something concerning itself. What every proposition implies concerning itself must be something which is false of the proposition now under discussion, for the whole falsity of this proposition lies therein, since all that it explicitly lays down is true. It must be something which would not be false if the proposition were true, for in that case some true proposition would be false. Hence, it must be that it is itself true. That is, *every proposition asserts its own truth.*

The proposition in question, therefore, is true in all other respects but its implication of its own truth.[7]

The difficulty of showing how the law of deductive reasoning is true depends upon our inability to conceive of its not being true. In the case of probable reasoning the difficulty is of quite another kind; here, where we see precisely what the procedure is, we wonder how such a process can have any validity at all. How magical it is that by examining a part of a class, we can know what is true of the whole of the class, and by study of the past can know the future; in short, that we can know what we have not experienced!

7. This is the principle which was most usually made the basis of the resolution of the *Insolubilia*. See, for example, *Pauli Veneti Sophismata Aurea* [Paulus Venetus, *Sophismata aurea et perutilia* (Pavia, 1483)], Sophisma 50. The authority of Aristotle is claimed for this mode of solution. *Sophistici Elenchi*, cap. 25. The principal objection which was made to this mode of solution, viz., that the principle that every proposition implies its own truth, cannot be proved, I believe that I have removed. The only arguments against the truth of this principle were based on the imperfect doctrines of *modales* and *obligationes*. Other methods of solution suppose that a part of a proposition cannot denote the whole proposition, or that no intellection is a formal cognition of itself. A solution of this sort will be found in Occam's *Summa Totius Logices* [*Summa logicae* (Paris: Johannes Higman, 1488)], 3d part of 3d part, cap. 38. Such modern authors as think the solution "very easy" do not understand its difficulties. See Mansel's Aldrich [Henry Aldrich, *Artis logicæ rudimenta*, 4th ed., edited by H. L. Mansel (London: Rivingtons, 1862)], p. 145.

Is not this an intellectual intuition! Is it not that besides ordinary experience which is dependent on there being a certain physical connection between our organs and the thing experienced, there is a second avenue of truth dependent only on there being a certain intellectual connection between our previous knowledge and what we learn in that way? Yes, this is true. Man has this faculty, just as opium has a somnific virtue; but some further questions may be asked, nevertheless. How is the existence of this faculty accounted for? In one sense, no doubt, by natural selection. Since it is absolutely essential to the preservation of so delicate an organism as man's, no race which had it not has been able to sustain itself. This accounts for the prevalence of this faculty, provided it was only a possible one. But how can it be possible? What could enable the mind to know physical things which do not physically influence it and which it does not influence? The question cannot be answered by any statement concerning the human mind, for it is equivalent to asking what makes the facts usually to be, as inductive and hypothetic conclusions from true premises represent them to be? Facts of a certain kind are usually true when facts having certain relations to them are true; what is the cause of this? That is the question.

The usual reply is that nature is everywhere regular; as things have been, so they will be; as one part of nature is, so is every other. But this explanation will not do. Nature is not regular. No disorder would be less orderly than the existing arrangement. It is true that the special laws and regularities are in-numerable; but nobody thinks of the irregularities, which are infinitely more frequent. Every fact true of any one thing in the universe is related to every fact true of every other. But the immense majority of these relations are for-tuitous and irregular. A man in China bought a cow three days and five min-utes after a Greenlander had sneezed. Is that abstract circumstance connected with any regularity whatever? And are not such relations infinitely more fre-quent than those which are regular? But if a very large number of qualities were to be distributed among a very large number of things in almost any way, there would chance to be some few regularities. If, for example, upon a checker-board of an enormous number of squares, painted all sorts of colors, myriads of dice were to be thrown, it could hardly fail to happen, that upon some color, or shade of color, out of so many, some one of the six numbers should not be uppermost on any die. This would be a regularity; for, the universal proposition would be true that upon that color that number is never turned up. But suppose this regularity abolished, then a far more remarkable regularity would be created, namely, that on every color every number is turned up. Either way, therefore, a regularity must occur. Indeed, a little reflection will show that although we have here only variations of color and of the numbers of the dice, many regularities must occur. And the greater the number of objects, the more respects in which they vary, and the greater the number of varieties in each respect, the greater will be the number of regularities. Now, in the universe, all these numbers are infinite. Therefore, however disorderly the chaos, the *number* of regularities must be infinite. The orderliness of the universe, therefore, if it exists, must consist in the large *proportion* of relations which present a regularity to those which are quite irregular. But this proportion in the actual universe is, as we have seen, as small as it can be; and, therefore, the orderliness of the universe is as little as that of any arrangement whatever.

But even if there were such an orderliness in things, it never could be discovered. For it would belong to things either collectively or distributively. If it belonged to things collectively, that is to say, if things formed a system, the difficulty would be that a system can only be known by seeing some considerable proportion of the whole. Now we never can know how great a part of the whole of nature we have discovered. If the order were distributive, that is, belonged to all things only by belonging to each thing, the difficulty would be that a character can only be known by comparing something which has it with something which has it not. *Being, quality, relation*, and other universals are not known except as characters of words or other signs, attributed by a figure of speech to things. Thus, in neither case could the order of things be known. But the order of things would not help the validity of our reasoning—that is, would not help us to reason correctly—unless we knew what the order of things required the relation between the known reasoned *from* to the unknown reasoned *to*, to be.

But even if this order both existed and were known, the knowledge would be of no use except as a general principle, from which things could be deduced. It would not explain how knowledge could be increased (in contradistinction to being rendered more distinct), and so it would not explain how it could itself have been acquired.

Finally, if the validity of induction and hypothesis were dependent on a particular constitution of the universe, we could imagine a universe in which these modes of inference should not be valid, just as we can imagine a universe in which there would be no attraction, but things should merely drift about. Accordingly, J. S. Mill, who explains the validity of induction by the uniformity of nature,[8] maintains that he can imagine a universe without any regularity, so that no probable inference would be valid in it.[9] In the universe as it is, probable arguments sometimes fail, nor can any definite proportion of cases be stated in which they hold good; all that can be said is that in the long run they prove approximately correct. Can a universe be imagined in which this would not be the case? It must be a universe where probable argument can have some application, in order that it may fail half the time. It must, therefore, be a universe experienced. Of the finite number of propositions true of a finite amount of experience of such a universe, no one would be universal in form, unless the subject of it were an individual. For if there were a plural universal proposition, inferences by analogy from one particular to another would hold good invariably in reference to that subject. So that these arguments might be no better than guesses in reference to other parts of the universe, but they would invariably hold good in a finite proportion of it, and so would on the whole be somewhat better than guesses. There could, also, be no individuals in that universe, for there must be some general class—that is, there must be some things more or less alike—or probable argument would find no premises there; therefore, there must be two mutually exclusive classes, since every class has a residue outside of it; hence, if there were any individual, that individual would be wholly excluded from one or other of these classes. Hence, the universal plural proposition would be true, that no one of a certain class was that individual. Hence, no universal proposition would be true. Accordingly, every combination of characters would occur in such a universe. But this would not be disorder, but the simplest order; it would not be unintelligible, but, on the contrary, everything conceivable would be found in it with equal frequency. The notion, therefore, of a universe in which probable arguments should fail as often as hold true, is

8. *Logic*, Book 3, chap. 3, sec. 1.

9. *Ibid.*, Book 3, chap. 21, sec. 1. "I am convinced that any one accustomed to abstraction and analysis, who will fairly exert his faculties for the purpose, will, when his imagination has once learnt to entertain the notion, find no difficulty in conceiving that in some one, for instance, of the many firmaments into which sidereal astronomy divides the universe, events may succeed one another at random, without any fixed law; nor can anything in our experience or mental nature constitute a sufficient, or indeed any, reason for believing that this is nowhere the case.

"Were we to suppose (what it is perfectly possible to imagine) that the present order of the universe were brought to an end, and that a chaos succeeded, in which there was no fixed succession of events, and the past gave no assurance of the future," &c.

absurd. We can suppose it in general terms, but we cannot specify how it should be other than self-contradictory.[10]

Since we cannot conceive of probable inferences as not generally holding good, and since no special supposition will serve to explain their validity, many logicians have sought to base this validity on that of deduction, and that in a variety of ways. The only attempt of this sort, however, which deserves to be noticed is that which seeks to determine the probability of a future event by the theory of probabilities, from the fact that a certain number of similar events have been observed. Whether this can be done or not depends on the meaning assigned to the word *probability*. But if this word is to be taken in such a sense that a form of conclusion which is probable is valid; since the validity of an inference (or its correspondence with facts) consists solely in this, that when such premises are true, such a conclusion is generally true, then probability can mean nothing but the ratio of the frequency of occurrence of a specific event to a general one over it. In this sense of the term, it is plain that the probability of an inductive conclusion cannot be *deduced* from the premises; for from the inductive premises

$$S', S'', S''' \text{ are } M,$$
$$S', S'', S''' \text{ are } P,$$

nothing follows deductively, except that any M, which is S', or S'', or S''' is P; or, less explicitly, that some M is P.

Thus, we seem to be driven to this point. On the one hand, no determination of things, no *fact*, can result in the validity of probable argument; nor, on the other hand, is such argument reducible to that form which holds good, however the facts may be. This seems very much like a reduction to absurdity of the validity of such reasoning; and a paradox of the greatest difficulty is presented for solution.

There can be no doubt of the importance of this problem. According to

---

10. Boole (*Laws of Thought*, p. 370) [George Boole, *An Investigation of the Laws of Thought, on Which Are Founded the Mathematical Theories of Logic and Probabilities* (London: Walton and Maberly, 1854)] has shown, in a very simple and elegant manner, that an *infinite* number of balls may have characters distributed in such a way, that from the characters of the balls already drawn, we could infer nothing in regard to that of the characters of the next one. The same is true of some arrangements of a finite number of balls, provided the inference takes place after a fixed number of drawings. But this does not invalidate the reasoning above, although it is an important fact without doubt.

Kant, the central question of philosophy is "How are synthetical judgments *a priori* possible?" But antecedently to this comes the question how synthetical judgments in general, and still more generally, how synthetical reasoning is possible at all. When the answer to the general problem has been obtained, the particular one will be comparatively simple. This is the lock upon the door of philosophy.

All probable inference, whether induction or hypothesis, is inference from the parts to the whole. It is essentially the same, therefore, as statistical inference. Out of a bag of black and white beans I take a few handfuls, and from this sample I can judge approximately the proportions of black and white in the whole. This is identical with induction. Now we know upon what the validity of this inference depends. It depends upon the fact that in the long run, any one bean would be taken out as often as any other. For were this not so, the mean of a large number of results of such testings of the contents of the bag would not be precisely the ratio of the numbers of the two colors of beans in the bag. Now we may divide the question of the validity of induction into two parts: 1st, why of all inductions, premises for which occur, the generality should hold good, and 2d, why men are not fated always to light upon the small proportion of worthless inductions. Then, the first of these two questions is readily answered. For since all the members of any class are the same as all that are to be known; and since from any part of those which are to be known an induction is competent to the rest, in the long run any one member of a class will occur as the subject of a premise of a possible induction as often as any other, and, therefore, the validity of induction depends simply upon the fact that the parts make up and constitute the whole. This in its turn depends simply upon there being such a state of things that any general terms are possible. But it has been shown, p. 82, that being at all is being in general. And thus this part of the validity of induction depends merely on there being any reality.

From this it appears that we cannot say that the generality of inductions are true, but only that in the long run they approximate to the truth. This is the truth of the statement, that the universality of an inference from induction is only the analogue of true universality. Hence, also, it cannot be said that we know an inductive conclusion to be true, however loosely we state it; we only know that by accepting inductive conclusions, in the long run our errors balance one another. In fact, insurance companies proceed upon induction;— they do not know what will happen to this or that policyholder; they only know that they are secure in the long run.

The other question relative to the validity of induction, is why men are not fated always to light upon those inductions which are highly deceptive. The explanation of the former branch of the problem we have seen to be that there is something real. Now, since if there is anything real, then (on account of this reality consisting in the ultimate agreement of all men, and on account of the fact that reasoning from parts to whole, is the only kind of synthetic reasoning which men possess) it follows necessarily that a sufficiently long succession of inferences from parts to whole will lead men to a knowledge of it, so that in that case they cannot be fated on the whole to be thoroughly unlucky in their inductions. This second branch of the problem is in fact equivalent to asking why there is anything real, and thus its solution will carry the solution of the former branch one step further.

The answer to this question may be put into a general and abstract, or a special detailed form. If men were not to be able to learn from induction, it must be because as a general rule, when they had made an induction, the order of things (as they appear in experience), would then undergo a revolution. Just herein would the unreality of such a universe consist; namely, that the order of the universe should depend on how much men should know of it. But this general rule would be capable of being itself discovered by induction; and so it must be a law of such a universe, that when this was discovered it would cease to operate. But this second law would itself be capable of discovery. And so in such a universe there would be nothing which would not sooner or later be known; and it would have an order capable of discovery by a sufficiently long course of reasoning. But this is contrary to the hypothesis, and therefore that hypothesis is absurd. This is the particular answer. But we may also say, in general, that if nothing real exists, then, since every question supposes that something exists—for it maintains its own urgency—it supposes only illusions to exist. But the existence even of an illusion is a reality; for an illusion affects all men, or it does not. In the former case, it is a reality according to our theory of reality; in the latter case, it is independent of the state of mind of any individuals except those whom it happens to affect. So that the answer to the question, Why is anything real? is this: That question means, "supposing anything to exist, why is something real?" The answer is, that that very existence is reality by definition.

All that has here been said, particularly of induction, applies to all inference from parts to whole, and therefore to hypothesis, and so to all probable inference.

Thus, I claim to have shown, in the first place, that it is possible to hold a consistent theory of the validity of the laws of ordinary logic.

But now let us suppose the idealistic theory of reality, which I have in this paper taken for granted to be false. In that case, inductions would not be true unless the world were so constituted that every object should be presented in experience as often as any other; and further, unless we were so constituted that we had no more tendency to make bad inductions than good ones. These facts might be explained by the benevolence of the Creator; but, as has already been argued, they could not explain, but are absolutely refuted by the fact that no state of things can be conceived in which probable arguments should not lead to the truth. This affords a most important argument in favor of that theory of reality, and thus of those denials of certain faculties from which it was deduced, as well as of the general style of philosophizing by which those denials were reached.

Upon our theory of reality and of logic, it can be shown that no inference of any individual can be thoroughly logical without certain determinations of his mind which do not concern any one inference immediately; for we have seen that that mode of inference which alone can teach us anything, or carry us at all beyond what was implied in our premises—in fact, does not give us to know any more than we knew before; only, we know that, by faithfully adhering to that mode of inference, we shall, on the whole, approximate to the truth. Each of us is an insurance company, in short. But, now, suppose that an insurance company, among its risks, should take one exceeding in amount the sum of all the others. Plainly, it would then have no security whatever. Now, has not every single man such a risk? What shall it profit a man if he shall gain the whole world and lose his own soul? If a man has a transcendent personal interest infinitely outweighing all others, then, upon the theory of validity of inference just developed, he is devoid of all security, and can make no valid inference whatever. What follows? That logic rigidly requires, before all else, that no determinate fact, nothing which can happen to a man's self, should be of more consequence to him than everything else. He who would not sacrifice his own soul to save the whole world, is illogical in all his inferences, collectively. So the social principle is rooted intrinsically in logic.

That being the case, it becomes interesting to inquire how it is with men as a matter of fact. There is a psychological theory that man cannot act without a view to his own pleasure. This theory is based on a falsely assumed subjectivism. Upon our principles of the objectivity of knowledge, it could not be based, and if they are correct it is reduced to an absurdity. It seems to me that the usual opinion of the selfishness of man is based in large measure upon this false theory. I do not think that the facts bear out the usual opinion. The immense self-sacrifices which the most wilful men often make, show that wilfulness is a very different thing from selfishness. The care that men have for what is to happen after they are dead, cannot be selfish. And finally and chiefly, the constant use of the word "*we*"—as when we speak of our possessions on the Pacific—our destiny as a republic—in cases in which no personal interests at all are involved, show conclusively that men do not make their personal interests their only ones, and therefore may, at least, subordinate them to the interests of the community.

But just the revelation of the possibility of this complete self-sacrifice in man, and the belief in its saving power, will serve to redeem the logicality of all men. For he who recognizes the logical necessity of complete self-identification of one's own interests with those of the community, and its potential existence in man, even if he has it not himself, will perceive that only the inferences of that man who has it are logical, and so views his own inferences as being valid only so far as they would be accepted by that man. But so far as he has this belief, he becomes identified with that man. And that ideal perfection of knowledge by which we have seen that reality is constituted must thus belong to a community in which this identification is complete.

This would serve as a complete establishment of private logicality, were it not that the assumption that man or the community (which may be wider than man) shall ever arrive at a state of information greater than some definite finite information, is entirely unsupported by reasons. There cannot be a scintilla of evidence to show that at some time all living beings shall not be annihilated at once, and that forever after there shall be throughout the universe any intelligence whatever. Indeed, this very assumption involves itself a transcendent and supreme interest, and therefore from its very nature is unsusceptible of any support from reasons. This infinite hope which we all have (for even the atheist will constantly betray his calm expectation that what is Best will come about) is something so august and momentous, that all reasoning in reference to it is a trifling impertinence. We do not want to know what are the weights of reasons *pro* and *con*—that is, how much *odds* we should wish to receive on such a venture in the long run—because there is no long run in the case; the question is single and supreme, and ALL is at stake upon it. We are in the condition of a man in a life and death struggle; if he have not sufficient strength, it is wholly indifferent to him how he acts, so that the only assumption upon which he can act rationally is the hope of success. So this sentiment is rigidly demanded by logic. If its object were any determinate fact, any private interest, it might conflict with the results of knowledge and so with itself; but when its object is of a nature as wide as the community can turn out to be, it is always a hypothesis uncontradicted by facts and justified by its indispensableness for making any action rational.

7

■ ■ ■

[Fraser's *The Works of George Berkeley*]

Aside from its interest as a concise history of much of medieval and modern philosophy, Peirce's review of Berkeley is notable for its elaboration of the antinominalist position he had staked out in the Cognition Series. In attacking the position that only individual facts are real, Peirce showed that his semiotic was deeply opposed to the materialism and necessitarianism which, in the nineteenth century, had become nearly synonymous with science. Most scientists were therefore profoundly nominalistic; they accounted for natural phenomena in terms of secondness, or dyadic relations—reactions between pairs of individual objects. But Peirce argued for another kind of real relation—thirdness, or the relation of one object to a second by the representation of a third, a sign. Because the sign relation is real, nominalists err in supposing that there is no such thing as a "general idea."

Source: *Writings of Charles S. Peirce*, 2:462–87.
Originally published in *North American Review* 113
(October 1871): 449–72.

The Works of George Berkeley, D.D., formerly Bishop of Cloyne: including many of his Writings hitherto unpublished. With Prefaces, Annotations, his Life and Letters, and an Account of his Philosophy. By Alexander Campbell Fraser, M.A., Professor of Logic and Metaphysics in the University of Edinburgh. In Four Volumes. Oxford: At the Clarendon Press. 8vo. 1871.

This new edition of Berkeley's works is much superior to any of the former ones. It contains some writings not in any of the other editions, and the rest are given with a more carefully edited text. The editor has done his work well. The introductions to the several pieces contain analyses of their contents which will be found of the greatest service to the reader. On the other hand, the explanatory notes which disfigure every page seem to us altogether unnecessary and useless.

Berkeley's metaphysical theories have at first sight an air of paradox and levity very unbecoming to a bishop. He denies the existence of matter, our ability to see distance, and the possibility of forming the simplest general conception; while he admits the existence of Platonic ideas; and argues the whole with a cleverness which every reader admits, but which few are convinced by. His disciples seem to think the present moment a favorable one for obtaining for their philosophy a more patient hearing than it has yet got. It is true that we of this day are sceptical and not given to metaphysics, but so, say they, was the generation which Berkeley addressed, and for which his style was chosen; while it is hoped that the spirit of calm and thorough inquiry which is now, for once, almost the fashion, will save the theory from the perverse misrepresentations which formerly assailed it, and lead to a fair examination of the arguments which, in the minds of his sectators, put the truth of it beyond all doubt. But above all it is anticipated that the Berkeleyan treatment of that question of the validity of human knowledge and of the inductive process of science, which is now so much studied, is such as to command the attention of scientific men to the idealistic system. To us these hopes seem vain. The truth is that the minds from whom the spirit of the age emanates have now no interest in the only problems that metaphysics ever pretended to solve. The abstract acknowledgment of God, Freedom, and Immortality, apart from those other religious beliefs (which cannot possibly rest on metaphysical grounds) which alone may animate this, is now seen to have no practical consequence whatever. The world is getting to think of these creatures of metaphysics, as Aristotle of the Platonic ideas: τερετίσματα γάρ ἐστι, καὶ εἰ ἔστιν, οὐδὲν πρὸς τὸν λόγον ἐστίν. ["They are mere prattle or twitterings, and even if they exist, they are irrelevant."] The question of the grounds of the validity of induction has, it is true, excited an interest, and may continue to do so (though the argument is now become too difficult for popular apprehension); but whatever interest it has had has been due to a hope that the solution of it would afford the basis for sure and useful maxims concerning the logic of induction,—a hope which would be destroyed so soon as it were shown that the question was a purely metaphysical one. This is the prevalent feeling, among advanced minds. It may not be just; but it exists. And its existence is an effectual bar (if there were no other) to the general acceptance of Berkeley's system. The few who do now care for metaphysics are not of that bold order of minds who delight to hold a position so unsheltered by the prejudices of common sense as that of the good bishop.

As a matter of history, however, philosophy must always be interesting. It is the best representative of the mental development of each age. It is so even of ours, if we think what really is our philosophy. Metaphysical history is one of the chief branches of history, and ought to be expounded side by side with the history of society, of government, and of war; for in its relations with these we trace the significance of events for the human mind. The history of philosophy in the British Isles is a subject possessing more unity and entirety within itself than has usually been recognized in it. The influence of Descartes was never so great in England as that of traditional conceptions, and we can trace a continuity between modern and mediæval thought there, which is wanting in the history of France, and still more, if possible, in that of Germany.

From very early times, it has been the chief intellectual characteristic of the English to wish to effect everything by the plainest and directest means, without unnecessary contrivance. In war, for example, they rely more than any other people in Europe upon sheer hardihood, and rather despise military science. The main peculiarities of their system of law arise from the fact that every evil has been rectified as it became intolerable, without any thoroughgoing measure. The bill for legalizing marriage with a deceased wife's sister is yearly pressed because it supplies a remedy for an inconvenience actually felt; but nobody has proposed a bill to legalize marriage with a deceased husband's brother. In philosophy, this national tendency appears as a strong preference for the simplest theories, and a resistance to any complication of the theory as long as there is the least possibility that the facts can be explained in the simpler way. And, accordingly, British philosophers have always desired to weed out of philosophy all conceptions which could not be made perfectly definite and easily intelligible, and have shown strong nominalistic tendencies since the time of Edward I, or even earlier. Berkeley is an admirable illustration of this national character, as well as of that strange union of nominalism with Platonism, which has repeatedly appeared in history, and has been such a stumbling-block to the historians of philosophy.

The mediæval metaphysic is so entirely forgotten, and has so close a historic connection with modern English philosophy, and so much bearing upon the truth of Berkeley's doctrine, that we may perhaps be pardoned a few pages on the nature of the celebrated controversy concerning universals. And first let us set down a few dates. It was at the very end of the eleventh century that the dispute concerning nominalism and realism, which had existed in a vague way before, began to attain extraordinary proportions. During the twelfth century it was the matter of most interest to logicians, when William of Champeaux, Abélard, John of Salisbury, Gilbert de la Porrée, and many others, defended as many different opinions. But there was no historic connection between this controversy and those of scholasticism proper, the scholasticism of Aquinas, Scotus, and Ockam. For about the end of the twelfth century a great revolution of thought took place in Europe. What the influences were which produced it requires new historical researches to say. No doubt, it was partly due to the Crusades. But a great awakening of intelligence did take place at that time. It requires, it is true, some examination to distinguish this particular movement from a general awakening which had begun a century earlier, and had been growing stronger ever since. But now there was an accelerated impulse. Commerce was attaining new importance, and was inventing some of her chief conveniences and safeguards. Law, which had hitherto been utterly barbaric, began to be a profession. The civil law was adopted in Europe, the canon law was digested; the common law took some form. The Church, under Innocent III, was assuming the sublime functions of a moderator over kings. And those orders of mendicant friars were established, two of which did so much for the development of the scholastic philosophy. Art felt the spirit of a new age, and there could hardly be a greater change than from the highly ornate round-arched architecture of the twelfth century to the comparatively simple Gothic of the thirteenth. Indeed, if any one wishes to know what a scholastic commentary is like, and what the tone of thought in it is, he has only to contemplate a Gothic cathedral. The first quality of either is a religious devotion, truly heroic. One feels that the men who did these works did really believe in religion as we believe in nothing. We cannot easily understand how Thomas Aquinas can speculate so much on the nature of angels, and whether ten thousand of them could dance on a needle's point. But it was simply because he held them for real. If they are real, why are they not more interesting than the bewildering varieties of insects which naturalists study; or why should the orbits of double stars attract more attention than spiritual intelligences? It will be said that we have no means of knowing anything about them. But that is on a par with censuring the schoolmen for referring questions to the authority of the Bible and of the Church. If they really believed in their religion, as they did, what better could they do? And if they found in these authorities testimony concerning angels, how could they avoid admitting it. Indeed, objections of this sort only make it appear still more clearly how much those were the ages of faith. And if the spirit was not altogether admirable, it is only because faith itself has its faults as a foundation for the intellectual character. The men of that time did fully believe and did think that, for the sake of giving themselves up absolutely to their great task of building or of writing, it was well worth while to resign all the joys of life. Think of the spirit in which Duns Scotus must have worked, who wrote his thirteen volumes in folio, in a style as condensed as the most condensed parts of Aristotle, before the age of thirty-four. Nothing is more striking in either of the great intellectual products of that age, than the complete absence of self-conceit on the part of the artist or philosopher. That anything of value can be added to his sacred and catholic work by its having the smack of individuality about it, is what he has never conceived. His work is not designed to embody *his* ideas, but the universal truth; there will not be one thing in it however minute, for which you will not find that he has his authority; and whatever originality emerges is of that inborn kind which so saturates a man that he cannot himself perceive it. The individual feels his own worthlessness in comparison with his task, and does not dare to introduce his vanity into the doing of it. Then there is no machine-work, no unthinking repetition about the thing. Every part is worked out for itself as a separate problem, no matter how analogous it may be in general to another part. And no matter how small and hidden a detail may be, it has been conscientiously studied, as though it were intended for the eye of God. Allied to this character is a detestation of antithesis or the studied balancing of one thing against another, and of a too geometrical grouping,—a hatred of posing which is as much a moral trait as the others. Finally, there is nothing in which the scholastic philosophy and the Gothic architecture resemble one another more than in the gradually increasing sense of immensity which impresses the mind of the student as he learns to appreciate the real dimensions and cost of each. It is very unfortunate that the thirteenth, fourteenth, and fifteenth centuries should, under the name of Middle Ages, be confounded with others, which they are in every respect as unlike as the Renaissance is from modern times. In the history of logic, the break between the twelfth and thirteenth centuries is so great that only one author of the former age is ever quoted in the latter. If this is to be attributed to the fuller acquaintance with the works of Aristotle, to what, we would ask, is this profounder study itself to be attributed, since it is now known that the knowledge of those works was not imported from the Arabs? The thirteenth century was realistic, but the question concerning universals was not as much agitated as several others. Until about the end of the century, scholasticism was somewhat vague, immature, and unconscious of its own power. Its greatest glory was in the first half of the fourteenth century. Then Duns Scotus,[1] a Briton (for whether Scotch, Irish, or English is disputed), first stated the realistic position consistently, and developed it with great fulness and applied it to all the different questions which depend upon it. His theory of "formalities" was the subtlest, except perhaps Hegel's logic, ever broached, and he was separated from nominalism only by the division of a hair. It is not therefore surprising that the nominalistic position was soon adopted by several writers, especially by the celebrated William of Ockam, who took the lead of this party by the thoroughgoing and masterly way in which he treated the theory and combined it with a then rather recent but now forgotten addition to the doctrine of logical terms. With Ockam, who died in 1347, scholasticism may be said to have culminated. After him the scholastic philosophy showed a tendency to separate itself from the religious element which alone could dignify it, and sunk first into extreme formalism and fancifulness, and then into the merited contempt of all men; just as the Gothic architecture had a very similar fate, at about the same time, and for much the same reasons.

The current explanations of the realist-nominalist controversy are equally false and unintelligible. They are said to be derived ultimately from Bayle's *Dictionary*; at any rate, they are not based on a study of the authors. "Few, very few, for a hundred years past," says Hallam, with truth, "have broken the repose of the immense works of the schoolmen." Yet it is perfectly possible so to state the matter that no one shall fail to comprehend what the question was, and how there might be two opinions about it. Are universals real? We have only to stop and consider a moment what was meant by the word *real*, when the whole issue soon becomes apparent. Objects are divided into figments, dreams, etc., on the one hand, and realities on the other. The former are those which exist only inasmuch as you or I or some man imagines them; the latter are those which have an existence independent of your mind or mine or that of any number of persons. The real is that which is not whatever we happen to think it, but is unaffected by what we may think of it. The question, therefore, is whether *man, horse*, and other names of natural classes, correspond with anything which all men, or all horses, really have in common, independent of our thought, or whether these classes are constituted

1. Died 1308.

simply by a likeness in the way in which our minds are affected by individual objects which have in themselves no resemblance or relationship whatsoever. Now that this is a real question which different minds will naturally answer in opposite ways, becomes clear when we think that there are two widely separated points of view, from which *reality*, as just defined, may be regarded. Where is the real, the thing independent of how we think it, to be found? There must be such a thing, for we find our opinions constrained; there is something, therefore, which influences our thoughts, and is not created by them. We have, it is true, nothing immediately present to us but thoughts. Those thoughts, however, have been caused by sensations, and those sensations are constrained by something out of the mind. This thing out of the mind, which directly influences sensation, and through sensation thought, because it *is* out of the mind, is independent of how we think it, and is, in short, the real. Here is one view of reality, a very familiar one. And from this point of view it is clear that the nominalistic answer must be given to the question concerning universals. For, while from this standpoint it may be admitted to be true as a rough statement that one man is like another, the exact sense being that the realities external to the mind produce sensations which may be embraced under one conception, yet it can by no means be admitted that the two real men have really anything in common, for to say that they are both men is only to say that the one mental term or thought-sign "man" stands indifferently for either of the sensible objects caused by the two external realities; so that not even the two sensations have in themselves anything in common, and far less is it to be inferred that the external realities have. This conception of reality is so familiar, that it is unnecessary to dwell upon it; but the other, or realist conception, if less familiar, is even more natural and obvious. All human thought and opinion contains an arbitrary, accidental element, dependent on the limitations in circumstances, power, and bent of the individual; an element of error, in short. But human opinion universally tends in the long run to a definite form, which is the truth. Let any human being have enough information and exert enough thought upon any question, and the result will be that he will arrive at a certain definite conclusion, which is the same that any other mind will reach under sufficiently favorable circumstances. Suppose two men, one deaf, the other blind. One hears a man declare he means to kill another, hears the report of the pistol, and hears the victim cry; the other sees the murder done. Their sensations are affected in the highest degree with their individual peculiarities. The first information that their sensations will give them, their first inferences, will be more nearly alike, but still different; the one having, for example, the idea of a man shouting, the other of a man with a threatening aspect; but their final conclusions, the thought the remotest from sense, will be identical and free from the one-sidedness of their idiosyncrasies. There is, then, to every question a true answer, a final conclusion, to which the opinion of every man is constantly gravitating. He may for a time recede from it, but give him more experience and time for consideration, and he will finally approach it. The individual may not live to reach the truth; there is a residuum of error in every individual's opinions. No matter; it remains that there is a definite opinion to which the mind of man is, on the whole and in the long run, tending. On many questions the final agreement is already reached, on all it will be reached if time enough is given. The arbitrary will or other individual peculiarities of a sufficiently large number of minds may postpone the general agreement in that opinion indefinitely; but it cannot affect what the character of that opinion shall be when it is reached. This final opinion, then, is independent, not indeed of thought in general, but of all that is arbitrary and individual in thought; is quite independent of how you, or I, or any number of men think. Everything, therefore, which will be thought to exist in the final opinion is real, and nothing else. What is the POWER of external things, to affect the senses? To say that people sleep after taking opium because it has a soporific *power*, is that to say anything in the world but that people sleep after taking opium because they sleep after taking opium? To assert the existence of a power or potency, is it to assert the existence of anything actual? Or to say that a thing has a potential existence, is it to say that it has an actual existence? In other words, is the present existence of a power anything in the world but a regularity in future events relating to a certain thing regarded as an element which is to be taken account of beforehand, in the conception of that thing? If not, to assert that there are external things which can be known only as exerting a power on our sense, is nothing different from asserting that there is a general *drift* in the history of human thought which will lead it to one general agreement, one catholic consent. And any truth more perfect than this destined conclusion, any reality more absolute than what is thought in it, is a fiction of metaphysics. It is obvious how this way of thinking harmonizes with a belief in an infallible Church, and how much more natural it would be in the Middle Ages than in Protestant or positivist times.

This theory of reality is instantly fatal to the idea of a thing in itself,—a thing existing independent of all relation to the mind's conception of it. Yet it would by no means forbid, but rather encourage us, to regard the appearances of sense as only signs of the realities. Only, the realities which they represent would not be the unknowable cause of sensation, but *noumena*, or intelligible conceptions which are the last products of the mental action which is set in motion by sensation. The matter of sensation is altogether accidental; precisely the same information, practically, being capable of communication through different senses. And the catholic consent which constitutes the truth is by no means to be limited to men in this earthly life or to the human race, but extends to the whole communion of minds to which we belong, including some probably whose senses are very different from ours, so that in that consent no predication of a sensible quality can enter, except as an admission that so certain sorts of senses are affected. This theory is also highly favorable to a belief in external realities. It will, to be sure, deny that there is any reality which is absolutely incognizable in itself, so that it cannot be taken into the mind. But observing that "the external" means simply that which is independent of what phenomenon is immediately present, that is of how we may think or feel; just as "the real" means that which is independent of how we may think or feel *about it*; it must be granted that there are many objects of true science which are external, because there are many objects of thought which, if they are independent of that thinking whereby they are thought (that is, if they are real), are indisputably independent of all *other* thoughts and feelings.

It is plain that this view of reality is inevitably realistic; because general conceptions enter into all judgments, and therefore into true opinions. Consequently a thing in the general is as real as in the concrete. It is perfectly true that all white things have whiteness in them, for that is only saying, in another form of words, that all white things are white; but since it is true that real things possess whiteness, whiteness is real. It is a real which only exists by virtue of an act of thought knowing it, but that thought is not an arbitrary or accidental one dependent on any idiosyncrasies, but one which will hold in the final opinion.

This theory involves a phenomenalism. But it is the phenomenalism of Kant, and not that of Hume. Indeed, what Kant called his Copernican step was precisely the passage from the nominalistic to the realistic view of reality. It was the essence of his philosophy to regard the real object as determined by the mind. That was nothing else than to consider every conception and intuition which enters necessarily into the experience of an object, and which is not transitory and accidental, as having objective validity. In short, it was to regard the reality as the normal product of mental action, and not as the incognizable cause of it.

This realistic theory is thus a highly practical and common-sense position. Wherever universal agreement prevails, the realist will not be the one to disturb the general belief by idle and fictitious doubts. For according to him it is a consensus or common confession which constitutes reality. What he wants, therefore, is to see questions put to rest. And if a general belief, which is perfectly stable and immovable, can in any way be produced, though it be by the fagot and the rack, to talk of any error in such belief is utterly absurd. The realist will hold that the very same objects which are immediately present in our minds in experience really exist just as they are experienced out of the mind; that is, he will maintain a doctrine of immediate perception. He will not, therefore, sunder existence out of the mind and being in the mind as two wholly improportionable modes. When a thing is in such relation to the individual mind that that mind cognizes it, it is in the mind; and its being so in the mind will not in the least diminish its external existence. For he does not think of the mind as a receptacle, which if a thing is in, it ceases to be out of. To make a distinction between the true conception of a thing and the thing itself is, he will say, only to regard one and the same thing from two different points of view; for the immediate object of thought in a true judgment *is* the reality. The realist will, therefore, believe in the objectivity of all necessary conceptions, space, time, relation, cause, and the like.

No realist or nominalist ever expressed so definitely, perhaps, as is here done, his conception of reality. It is difficult to give a clear notion of an opinion of a past age, without exaggerating its distinctness. But careful examination of the works of the schoolmen will show that the distinction between these two views of the real—one as the fountain of the current of human thought, the other as the unmoving form to which it is flowing—is what really occasions their disagreement on the question concerning universals. The gist of all the nominalist's arguments will be found to relate to a *res extra animam*, while the realist defends his position only by assuming that the immediate object of thought in a true judgment is real. The notion that the controversy between realism and nominalism had anything to do with Platonic ideas is a mere product of the imagination, which the slightest examination of the books would suffice to disprove. But to prove that the statement here given of the essence of these positions is historically true and not a fancy sketch, it will be well to add a brief analysis of the opinions of Scotus and Ockam.

Scotus sees several questions confounded together under the usual *utrum universale est aliquid in rebus*. In the first place, there is the question concerning the Platonic forms. But putting Platonism aside as at least incapable of proof, and as a self-contradictory opinion if the archetypes are supposed to be strictly universal, there is the celebrated dispute among Aristotelians as to whether the universal is really in things or only derives its existence from the mind. Universality is a relation of a predicate to the subjects of which it is predicated. That can exist only in the mind, wherein alone the coupling of subject and predicate takes place. But the word *universal* is also used to denote what are named by such terms as *a man* or *a horse*; these are called universals, because a man is not necessarily this man, nor a horse this horse. In such a sense it is plain universals are real; there really is a man and there really is a horse. The whole difficulty is with the actually indeterminate universal, that which not only is not necessarily *this*, but which, being one single object of thought, is predicable of many things. In regard to this it may be asked, first, is it necessary to its existence that it should be in the mind; and, second, does it exist *in re*? There are two ways in which a thing may be in the mind,—*habitualiter* and *actualiter*. A notion is in the mind *actualiter* when it is actually conceived; it is in the mind *habitualiter* when it can directly produce a conception. It is by virtue of mental association (we moderns should say), that things are in the mind *habitualiter*. In the Aristotelian philosophy, the intellect is regarded as being to the soul what the eye is to the body. The mind *perceives* likenesses and other relations in the objects of sense, and thus just as sense affords sensible images of things, so the intellect affords intelligible images of them. It is as such a *species intelligibilis* that Scotus supposes that a conception exists which is in the mind *habitualiter*, not *actualiter*. This *species* is in the mind, in the sense of being the immediate object of knowledge, but its existence in the mind is independent of *consciousness*. Now that the *actual* cognition of the universal is necessary to its existence, Scotus denies. The subject of science is universal; and if the existence of universal were dependent upon what we happened to be thinking, science would not relate to anything real. On the other hand, he admits that the universal must be in the mind *habitualiter*, so that if a thing be considered as it is independent of its being cognized, there is no universality in it. For there is *in re extra* no one intelligible object attributed to different things. He holds, therefore, that such natures (i.e. sorts of things) as a *man* and a *horse*, which are real, and are not of themselves necessarily *this* man or *this* horse, though they cannot exist *in re* without being some particular man or horse, are in the *species intelligibilis* always represented positively indeterminate, it being the nature of the mind so to represent things. Accordingly any such nature is to be regarded as something which is of itself neither universal nor singular, but is universal in the mind, singular in things out of the mind. If there were nothing in the different men or horses which was not of itself singular, there would be no real unity except the numerical unity of the singulars; which would involve such absurd consequences as that the only real difference would be a numerical difference, and that there would be no real likenesses among things. If, therefore, it is asked whether the universal is in things, the answer is, that the nature which in the mind is universal, and is not in itself singular, exists in things. It is the very same nature which in the mind is universal and *in re* is singular; for if it were not, in knowing anything of a universal we should be knowing nothing of things, but only of our own thoughts, and our opinion would not be converted from true to false by a change in things. This nature is actually indeterminate only so far as it is in the mind. But to say that an object is in the mind is only a metaphorical way of saying that it stands to the intellect in the relation of known to knower. The truth is, therefore, that that real nature which exists *in re*, apart from all action of the intellect, though in itself, apart from its relations, it be singular, yet is actually universal as it exists in relation to the mind. But this universal only differs from the singular in the manner of its being conceived (*formaliter*), but not in the manner of its existence (*realiter*).

Though this is the slightest possible sketch of the realism of Scotus, and leaves a number of important points unnoticed, yet it is sufficient to show the general manner of his thought and how subtle and difficult his doctrine is. That about one and the same nature being in the grade of singularity in existence, and in the grade of universality in the mind, gave rise to an extensive doctrine concerning the various kinds of identity and difference, called the doctrine of the *formalitates*; and this is the point against which Ockam directed his attack.

Ockam's nominalism may be said to be the next stage in English opinion. As Scotus's mind is always running on forms, so Ockam's is on logical terms; and all the subtle distinctions which Scotus effects by his *formalitates*, Ockam explains by implied syncategorematics (or adverbial expressions, such as *per se*, etc.) in terms. Ockam always thinks of a mental conception as a logical term, which, instead of existing on paper, or in the voice, is in the mind, but is of the same general nature, namely, a *sign*. The conception and the word differ in two respects: first, a word is arbitrarily imposed, while a conception is a natural sign; second, a word signfies whatever it signifies only indirectly, through the conception which signfies the same thing directly. Ockam enunciates his nominalism as follows:

> It should be known that *singular* may be taken in two senses. In one sense, it signifies that which is one and not many; and in this sense those who hold that the universal is a quality of mind predicable of many, standing however in this predication, not for itself, but for those many (i.e. the nominalists), have to say that every universal is truly and really singular; because as every word, however general we may agree to consider it, is truly and really singular and one in number, because it is one and not many, so every universal is singular. In another sense, the name *singular* is used to denote whatever is one and not many, is a sign of something which is singular in the first sense, and is not fit to be the sign of many. Whence, using the word *universal* for that which is not one in number,—an acceptation many attribute to it,—I say that there is no universal; unless perchance you abuse the word and say that *people* is not one in number and is universal. But that would be puerile. It is to be maintained, therefore, that every universal is one singular thing, and therefore there is no universal except by signification, that is, by its being the sign of many.

The arguments by which he supports this position present nothing of interest.[2] Against Scotus's doctrine that universals are without the mind in individuals, but are not really distinct from the individuals, but only formally so, he objects that it is impossible there should be any distinction existing out of the mind except between things really distinct. Yet he does not think of denying that an individual consists of matter and form, for these, though inseparable, are really distinct things; though a modern nominalist might ask in what sense things could be said to be distinct independently of any action of the mind, which are so inseparable as matter and form. But as to *relation*, he most emphatically and clearly denies that it exists as anything different from the things related; and this denial he expressly extends to relations of agreement and likeness as well as to those of opposition. While, therefore, he admits the real existence of qualities, he denies that these real qualities are respects in

2. The *entia non sunt multiplicanda præter necessitatem* ["entities are not to be multiplied beyond necessity"] is the argument of Durand de St. Pourçain. But any given piece of popular information about scholasticism may be safely assumed to be wrong.

which things agree or differ; but things which agree or differ agree or differ in themselves and in no respect *extra animam*. He allows that things without the mind are similar, but this similarity consists merely in the fact that the mind can abstract one notion from the contemplation of them. A resemblance, therefore, consists solely in the property of the mind by which it naturally imposes one mental sign upon the resembling things. Yet he allows there is something in the things to which this mental sign corresponds.

This is the nominalism of Ockam so far as it can be sketched in a single paragraph, and without entering into the complexities of the Aristotelian psychology nor of the *parva logicalia*. He is not so thoroughgoing as he might be, yet compared with Durandus and other contemporary nominalists he seems very radical and profound. He is truly the *venerabilis inceptor* of a new way of philosophizing which has now broadened, perhaps deepened also, into English empiricism.

England never forgot these teachings. During that Renaissance period when men could think that human knowledge was to be advanced by the use of Cicero's *Commonplaces*, we naturally see little effect from them; but one of the earliest prominent figures in modern philosophy is a man who carried the nominalistic spirit into everything,—religion, ethics, psychology, and physics, the *plusquam nominalis*, Thomas Hobbes of Malmesbury. His razor cuts off, not merely substantial forms, but every incorporeal substance. As for universals, he not only denies their real existence, but even that there are any universal conceptions except so far as we conceive names. In every part of his logic, names and speech play an extraordinarily important part. Truth and falsity, he says, have no place but among such creatures as use speech, for a true proposition is simply one whose predicate is the name of everything of which the subject is the name. "From hence, also, this may be deduced, that the first truths were arbitrarily made by those that first of all imposed names upon things, or received them from the imposition of others. For it is true (for example), that *man is a living creature*, but it is for this *reason* that it pleased men to impose both those names on the same thing." The difference between true religion and superstition is simply that the state recognizes the former and not the latter.

The nominalistic love of simple theories is seen also in his opinion, that every event is a movement, and that the sensible qualities exist only in sensible beings, and in his doctrine that man is at bottom purely selfish in his actions.

His views concerning matter are worthy of notice, because Berkeley is known to have been a student of Hobbes, as Hobbes confesses himself to have been of Ockam. The following paragraph gives his opinion:—

And as for that matter which is common to all things, and which philosophers, following Aristotle, usually call *materia prima*, that is, *first matter*, it is not a body distinct from all other bodies, nor is it one of them. What then is it? A mere name; yet a name which is not of vain use; for it signfies a conception of body without the consideration of any form or other accident except only magnitude or extension, and aptness to receive form and other accident. So that whensoever we have use of the name *body in general*, if we use that of *materia prima*, we do well. For when a man, not knowing which was first, water or ice, would find out which of the two were the matter of both, he would be fain to suppose some third matter which were neither of these two; so he that would find out what is the matter of all things ought to suppose such as is not the matter of anything that exists. Wherefore *materia prima* is nothing; and therefore they do not attribute to it form or any other accident, besides quantity; whereas all singular things have their forms and accidents certain.

Materia prima therefore is body in general, that is, body considered universally, not as having neither form nor any accident, but in which no form nor any other accident but quantity are at all considered, that is, they are not drawn into argumentation. (p. 118)

The next great name in English philosophy is Locke's. His philosophy is nominalistic, but does not regard things from a logical point of view at all. Nominalism, however, appears in psychology as sensationalism; for nominalism arises from taking that view of reality which regards whatever is in thought as caused by something in sense, and whatever is in sense as caused by something without the mind. But everybody knows that this is the character of Locke's philosophy. He believed that every idea springs from sensation and from his (vaguely explained) reflection.

Berkeley is undoubtedly more the offspring of Locke than of any other philosopher. Yet the influence of Hobbes with him is very evident and great; and Malebranche doubtless contributed to his thought. But he was by nature a radical and a nominalist. His whole philosophy rests upon an extreme nominalism of a sensationalistic type. He sets out with the proposition (supposed to have been already proved by Locke), that all the ideas in our minds are simply reproductions of sensations, external and internal. He maintains, moreover, that sensations can only be thus reproduced in such combinations as might have been given in immediate perception. We can conceive a man without a head, because there is nothing in the nature of sense to prevent our seeing such a thing; but we cannot conceive a sound without any pitch, because the two things are necessarily united in perception. On this principle he denies that we can have any abstract general ideas, that is, that universals can exist in the mind; if I think of a man it must be either of a short or a long or a middle-sized man, because if I see a man he must be one or the other of these. In the first draft of the Introduction of the *Principles of Human Knowledge*, which is now for the first time printed, he even goes so far as to censure Ockam for admitting that we can have general terms in our mind; Ockam's opinion being that we have in our minds conceptions, which are singular themselves, but are *signs* of many things.[3] But Berkeley probably knew only of Ockam from hearsay, and perhaps thought he occupied a position like that of Locke. Locke had a very singular opinion on the subject of general conceptions. He says:—

If we nicely reflect upon them, we shall find that general ideas are fictions, and contrivances of the mind, that carry difficulty with them, and do not so easily offer themselves as we are apt to imagine. For example, does it not require some pains and skill to form the general idea of a triangle (which is none of the most abstract, comprehensive, and difficult); for it must be neither oblique nor rectangle, neither equilateral, equicrural, nor scalenon, but all and none of these at once? In effect, is something imperfect that cannot exist, an idea wherein some parts of several different and inconsistent ideas are put together.

To this Berkeley replies:—

Much is here said of the difficulty that abstract ideas carry with them, and the pains and skill requisite in forming them. And it is on all hands

3. The sole difference between Ockam and Hobbes is that the former admits the universal signs in the mind to be natural, while the latter thinks they only follow instituted language. The consequence of this difference is that, while Ockam regards all truth as depending on the mind's naturally imposing the same sign on two things, Hobbes will have it that the first truths were established by convention. But both would doubtles allow that there is something *in re* to which such truths corresponded. But the sense of Berkeley's implication would be that there are no universal thought-signs at all. Whence it would follow that there is no truth and no judgments but propositions spoken or on paper.

agreed that there is need of great toil and labor of the mind to emancipate our thoughts from particular objects, and raise them to those sublime speculations that are conversant about abstract ideas. From all which the natural consequence should seem to be, that so difficult a thing as the forming of abstract ideas was not necessary to communication, which is so easy and familiar to all sort of men. But we are told, if they seem obvious and easy to grown men, it is only because by constant and familiar use they are made so. Now, I would fain know at what time it is men are employed in surmounting that difficulty. It cannot be when they are grown up, for then it seems they are not conscious of such painstaking; it remains, therefore, to be the business of their childhood. And surely the great and multiplied labor of framing abstract notions will be found a hard task at that tender age. Is it not a hard thing to imagine that a couple of children cannot prate together of their sugar-plums and rattles, and the rest of their little trinkets, till they have first tacked together numberless inconsistencies, and so formed in their minds abstract general ideas, and annexed them to every common name they make use of?

In his private note-book Berkeley has the following:—"*Mem.* To bring the killing blow at the last, e.g. in the matter of abstraction to bring Locke's general triangle in the last."

There was certainly an opportunity for a splendid blow here, and he gave it.

From this nominalism he deduces his idealistic doctrine. And he puts it beyond any doubt that, if this principle be admitted, the existence of matter must be denied. Nothing that we can know or even think can exist without the mind, for we can only think reproductions of sensations, and the *esse* of these is *percipi*. To put it another way, we cannot think of a thing as existing unperceived, for we cannot separate in thought what cannot be separated in perception. It is true, I can think of a tree in a park without anybody by to see it; but I cannot think of it without anybody to imagine it; for I am aware that I am imagining it all the time. Syllogistically: trees, mountains, rivers, and all sensible things are perceived; and anything which is perceived is a sensation; now for a sensation to exist without being perceived is impossible; therefore, for any sensible thing to exist out of perception is impossible. Nor can there be anything out of the mind which *resembles* a sensible object, for the conception of likeness cannot be separated from likeness between ideas, because that is the only likeness which can be given in perception. An idea can be nothing but an idea, and it is absurd to say that anything inaudible can resemble a sound, or that anything invisible can resemble a color. But what exists without the mind can neither be heard nor seen; for we perceive only sensations within the mind. It is said that *Matter* exists without the mind. But what is meant by matter? It is acknowledged to be known only as *supporting* the accidents of bodies; and this word 'supporting' in this connection is a word without meaning. Nor is there any necessity for the hypothesis of external bodies. What we observe is that we have ideas. Were there any use in supposing external things it would be to account for this fact. But grant that bodies exist, and no one can say how they can possibly affect the mind; so that instead of removing a difficulty, the hypothesis only makes a new one.

But though Berkeley thinks we know nothing out of the mind, he by no means holds that all our experience is of a merely phantasmagoric character. It is not all a dream; for there are two things which distinguish experience from imagination: one is the superior vividness of experience; the other and most important is its connected character. Its parts hang together in the most intimate and intricate conjunction, in consequence of which we can infer the future from the past. "These two things it is," says Berkeley, in effect, "which constitute reality. I do not, therefore, deny the reality of common experience, although I deny its externality." Here we seem to have a third new conception of reality, different from either of those which we have insisted are characteristic of the nominalist and realist respectively, or if this is to be identified with either of those, it is with the realist view. Is not this something quite unexpected from so extreme a nominalist? To us, at least, it seems that this conception is indeed required to give an air of common sense to Berkeley's theory, but that it is of a totally different complexion from the rest. It seems to be something imported into his philosophy from without. We shall glance at this point again presently. He goes on to say that ideas are perfectly inert and passive. One idea does not make another and there is no power or agency in it. Hence, as there must be some cause of the succession of ideas, it must be *Spirit*. There is no *idea* of a spirit. But I have a consciousness of the operations of my spirit, what he calls a *notion* of my activity in calling up ideas at pleasure, and so have a relative knowledge of myself as an active being. But there is a succession of ideas not dependent on my will, the ideas of perception. Real things do not depend on my thought, but have an existence distinct from being perceived by me; but the *esse* of everything is *percipi*; therefore, *there must be some other mind wherein they exist*. "As sure, therefore, as the sensible world really exists, so sure do there an infinite omnipotent Spirit who contains and supports it." This puts the keystone into the arch of Berkeleyan idealism, and gives a theory of the relation of the mind to external nature which, compared with the Cartesian Divine Assistance, is very satisfactory. It has been well remarked that, if the Cartesian dualism be admitted, no divine *assistance* can enable things to affect the mind or the mind things, but divine power must do the whole work. Berkeley's philosophy, like so many others, has partly originated in an attempt to escape the inconveniences of Cartesian dualism. God, who has created our spirits, has the power immediately to raise ideas in them; and out of his wisdom and benevolence, he does this with such regularity that these ideas may serve as signs of one another. Hence, the laws of nature. Berkeley does not explain how our wills act on our bodies, but perhaps he would say that to a certain limited extent we can produce ideas in the mind of God as he does in ours. But a material thing being only an idea, exists only so long as it is in some mind. Should every mind cease to think it for a while, for so long it ceases to exist. Its permanent existence is kept up by its being an idea in the mind of God. Here we see how superficially the just-mentioned theory of reality is laid over the body of his thought. If the reality of a thing consists in its harmony with the body of realities, it is a quite needless extravagance to say that it ceases to exist as soon as it is no longer thought of. For the coherence of an idea with experience in general does not depend at all upon its being actually present to the mind all the time. But it is clear that when Berkeley says that reality consists in the connection of experience, he is simply using the word *reality* in a sense of his own. That *an object's independence of our thought about it* is constituted by its connection with experience in general, he has never conceived. On the contrary, that, according to him, is effected by its being in the mind of God. In the usual sense of the word *reality*, therefore, Berkeley's doctrine is that the reality of sensible things resides only in their archetypes in the divine mind. This is Platonistic, but it is not realistic. On the contrary, since it places reality wholly out of the mind in the cause of sensations, and since it denies reality (in the true sense of the word) to sensible things in so far as they are sensible, it is distinctly nominalistic. Historically there have been prominent examples of an alliance between nominalism and Platonism. Abélard and John of Salisbury, the only two defenders of nominalism of the time of the great controversy whose works remain to us, are both Platonists; and Roscellin, the famous author of the *sententia de flatu vocis*, the first man in the Middle Ages who carried attention to nominalism, is said and believed (all his writings are lost) to have been a follower of Scotus

Erigena, the great Platonist of the ninth century. The reason of this odd conjunction of doctrines may perhaps be guessed at. The nominalist, by isolating his reality so entirely from mental influence as he has done, has made it something which the mind cannot conceive; he has created the so often talked of "improportion between the mind and the thing in itself." And it is to overcome the various difficulties to which this gives rise, that he supposes this *noumenon*, which, being totally unknown, the imagination can play about as it pleases, to be the emanation of archetypal ideas. The reality thus receives an intelligible nature again, and the peculiar inconveniences of nominalism are to some degree avoided.

It does not seem to us strange that Berkeley's idealistic writings have not been received with much favor. They contain a great deal of argumentation of doubtful soundness, the dazzling character of which puts us more on our guard against it. They appear to be the productions of a most brilliant, original, powerful, but not thoroughly disciplined mind. He is apt to set out with wildly radical propositions, which he qualifies when they lead him to consequences he is not prepared to accept, without seeing how great the importance of his admissions is. He plainly begins his principles of human knowledge with the assumption that we have nothing in our minds but sensations, external and internal, and reproductions of them in the imagination. This goes far beyond Locke; it can be maintained only by the help of that "mental chemistry" started by Hartley. But soon we find him admitting various *notions* which are not *ideas*, or reproductions of sensations, the most striking of which is the notion of a cause, which he leaves himself no way of accounting for experientially. Again, he lays down the principle that we can have no ideas in which the sensations are reproduced in an order or combination different from what could have occurred in experience; and that therefore we have no abstract conceptions. But he very soon grants that we can consider a triangle, without attending to whether it is equilateral, isosceles, or scalene; and does not reflect that such exclusive attention constitutes a species of abstraction. His want of profound study is also shown in his so wholly mistaking, as he does, the function of the hypothesis of matter. He thinks its only purpose is to account for the production of ideas in our minds, so occupied is he with the Cartesian problem. But the real part that material substance has to play is to account for (or formulate) the constant connection between the accidents. In his theory, this office is performed by the wisdom and benevolence of God in exciting ideas with such regularity that we can know what to expect. This makes the unity of accidents a rational unity, the material theory makes it a unity not of a *directly* intellectual origin. The question is, then, which does experience, which does science decide for? Does it appear that in nature all regularities are directly rational, all causes final causes; or does it appear that regularities extend beyond the requirement of a rational purpose, and are brought about by mechanical causes? Now science, as we all know, is generally hostile to the final causes, the operation of which it would restrict within certain spheres, and it finds decidedly an other than directly intellectual regularity in the universe. Accordingly the claim which Mr. Collyns Simon, Professor Fraser, and Mr. Archer Butler make for Berkeleyanism, that it is especially fit to harmonize with scientific thought, is as far as possible from the truth. The sort of science that his idealism would foster would be one which should consist in saying what each natural production was made for. Berkeley's own remarks about natural philosophy show how little he sympathized with physicists. They should all be read; we have only room to quote a detached sentence or two:—

> To endeavor to explain the production of colors or sound by figure, motion, magnitude, and the like, must needs be labor in vain. . . . In the business of gravitation or mutual attraction, because it appears in many instances, some are straightway for pronouncing it *universal*; and that to attract and be attracted by every body is an essential quality inherent in all bodies whatever. . . . There is nothing necessary or essential in the case, but it depends entirely on the will of the Governing Spirit, who causes certain bodies to cleave together or tend towards each other according to various laws, whilst he keeps others at a fixed distance; and to some he gives a quite contrary tendency, to fly asunder just as he sees convenient. . . . First, it is plain philosophers amuse themselves in vain, when they inquire for any natural efficient cause, distinct from *mind* or *spirit*. Secondly, considering the whole creation is the workmanship of a *wise and good Agent*, it should seem to become philosophers to employ their thoughts (contrary to what some hold) about the final causes of things; and I must confess I see no reason why pointing out the various ends to which natural things are adapted, and for which they were originally with unspeakable wisdom contrived, should not be thought one good way of accounting for them, and altogether worthy of a philosopher. (Vol. I, p. 466)

After this how can his disciples say "*that the true logic of physics is the first conclusion from his system!*"

As for that argument which is so much used by Berkeley and others, that such and such a thing cannot exist because we cannot so much as frame the idea of a thing,—that matter, for example, is impossible because it is an abstract idea, and we have no abstract ideas,—it appears to us to be a mode of reasoning which is to be used with extreme caution. Are the facts such, that if we could have an idea of the thing in question, we should infer its existence, or are they not? If not, no argument is necessary against its existence, until something is found out to make us suspect it exists. But if we ought to infer that it exists, if we only could frame the idea of it, why should we allow our mental incapacity to prevent us from adopting the proposition which logic requires? If such arguments had prevailed in mathematics (and Berkeley was equally strenuous in advocating them there), and if everything about negative quantities, the square root of *minus*, and infinitesimals, had been excluded from the subject on the ground that we can form no idea of such things, the science would have been simplified no doubt, simplified by never advancing to the more difficult matters. A better rule for avoiding the deceits of language is this: Do things fulfil the same function practically? Then let them be signified by the same word. Do they not? Then let them be distinguished. If I have learned a formula in gibberish which in any way jogs my memory so as to enable me in each single case to act as though I had a general idea, what possible utility is there in distinguishing between such a gibberish and formula and an idea? Why use the term *a general idea* in such a sense as to separate things which, for all experiential purposes, are the same?

The great inconsistency of the Berkeleyan theory, which prevents his nominalistic principles from appearing in their true colors, is that he has not treated mind and matter in the same way. All that he has said against the existence of matter might be said against the existence of mind; and the only thing which prevented his seeing that, was the vagueness of the Lockian *reflection*, or faculty of internal perception. It was not until after he had published his systematic exposition of his doctrine, that this objection ever occurred to him. He alludes to it in one of his dialogues, but his answer to it is very lame. Hume seized upon this point, and, developing it, equally denied the existence of mind and matter, maintaining that only appearances exist. Hume's philosophy is nothing but Berkeley's, with this change made in it, and written by a mind of a more sceptical tendency. The innocent bishop generated Hume; and as no one disputes that Hume gave rise to all modern philosophy of every kind, Berkeley ought to have a far more important place in the history of philosophy than has usually been assigned to him. His doctrine was the half-way station, or necessary resting-place between Locke's and Hume's.

Hume's greatness consists in the fact that he was the man who had the courage to carry out his principles to their utmost consequences, without regard to the character of the conclusions he reached. But neither he nor any other one has set forth nominalism in an absolutely thoroughgoing manner; and it is safe to say that no one ever will, unless it be to reduce it to absurdity.

We ought to say one word about Berkeley's theory of vision. It was undoubtedly an extraordinary piece of reasoning, and might have served for the basis of the modern science. Historically it has not had that fortune, because the modern science has been chiefly created in Germany, where Berkeley is little known and greatly misunderstood. We may fairly say that Berkeley taught the English some of the most essential principles of that hypothesis of sight which is now getting to prevail, more than a century before they were known to the rest of the world. This is much; but what is claimed by some of his advocates is astounding. One writer says that Berkeley's theory has been accepted by the leaders of all schools of thought! Professor Fraser admits that it has attracted no attention in Germany, but thinks the German mind too *a priori* to like Berkeley's reasoning. But Helmholtz, who has done more than any other man to bring the empiricist theory into favor, says: "Our knowledge of the phenomena of vision is not so complete as to allow only one theory and exclude every other. It seems to me that the choice which different *savans* make between different theories of vision has thus far been governed more by their metaphysical inclinations than by any constraining power which the facts have had." The best authorities, however, prefer the empiricist hypothesis; the fundamental proposition of which, as it is of Berkeley's, is that the sensations which we have in seeing are signs of the relations of things whose interpretation has to be discovered inductively. In the enumeration of the signs and of their uses, Berkeley shows considerable power in that sort of investigation, though there is naturally no very close resemblance between his and the modern accounts of the matter. There is no modern physiologist who would not think that Berkeley had greatly exaggerated the part that the muscular sense plays in vision.

Berkeley's theory of vision was an important step in the development of the associationist psychology. He thought all our conceptions of body and of space were simply reproductions in the imagination of sensations of touch (including the muscular sense). This, if it were true, would be a most surprising case of mental chemistry, that is of a sensation being felt and yet so mixed with others that we cannot by an act of simple attention recognize it. Doubt-less this theory had its influence in the production of Hartley's system.

Hume's phenomenalism and Hartley's associationism were put forth almost contemporaneously about 1750. They contain the fundamental positions of the current English "positivism." From 1750 down to 1830—eighty years—nothing of particular importance was added to the nominalistic doctrine. At the beginning of this period Hume was toning down his earlier radicalism, and Smith's theory of Moral Sentiments appeared. Later came Priestley's ma-terialism, but there was nothing new in that; and just at the end of the period, Brown's *Lectures on the Human Mind*. The great body of the philosophy of those eighty years is of the Scotch common-sense school. It is a weak sort of realistic reaction, for which there is no adequate explanation within the sphere of the history of philosophy. It would be curious to inquire whether anything in the history of society could account for it. In 1829 appeared James Mill's *Analysis of the Human Mind*, a really great nominalistic book again. This was followed by Stuart Mill's *Logic* in 1843. Since then, the school has produced nothing of the first importance; and it will very likely lose its distinctive char-acter now for a time, by being merged in an empiricism of a less metaphysical and more working kind. Already in Stuart Mill the nominalism is less salient than in the classical writers; though it is quite unmistakable.

Thus we see how large a part of the metaphysical ideas of to-day have come to us by inheritance from very early times, Berkeley being one of the intellec-tual ancestors whose labors did as much as any one's to enhance the value of the bequest. The realistic philosophy of the last century has now lost all its popularity, except with the most conservative minds. And science as well as philosophy is nominalistic. The doctrine of the correlation of forces, the dis-coveries of Helmholtz, and the hypotheses of Liebig and of Darwin, have all that character of explaining familiar phenomena apparently of a peculiar kind by extending the operation of simple mechanical principles, which belongs to nominalism. Or if the nominalistic character of these doctrines themselves cannot be detected, it will at least be admitted that they are observed to carry along with them those daughters of nominalism,—sensationalism, phenome-nalism, individualism, and materialism. That physical science is necessarily connected with doctrines of a debasing moral tendency will be believed by few. But if we hold that such an effect will not be produced by these doctrines on a mind which really understands them, we are accepting this belief, not on experience, which is rather against it, but on the strength of our general faith that what is really true it is good to believe and evil to reject. On the other hand, it is allowable to suppose that science has no essential affinity with the philosophical views with which it seems to be every year more associated. History cannot be held to exclude this supposition; and science as it exists is certainly much less nominalistic than the nominalists think it should be. Whewell represents it quite as well as Mill. Yet a man who enters into the scientific thought of the day and has not materialistic tendencies, is getting to be an impossibility. So long as there is a dispute between nominalism and realism, so long as the position we hold on the question is not determined by any proof *indisputable,* but is more or less a matter of inclination, a man as he gradually comes to feel the profound hostility of the two tendencies will, if he is not less than man, become engaged with one or other and can no more obey both than he can serve God and Mammon. If the two impulses are neutralized within him, the result simply is that he is left without any great intellectual motive. There is, indeed, no reason to suppose the logical question is in its own nature unsusceptible of solution. But that path out of the difficulty lies through the thorniest mazes of a science as dry as mathematics. Now there is a demand for mathematics; it helps to build bridges and drive engines, and therefore it becomes somebody's business to study it severely. But to have a philosophy is a matter of luxury; the only use of that is to make us feel comfortable and easy. It is a study for leisure hours; and we want it supplied in an elegant, an agreeable, an interesting form. The law of natural selection, which is the precise analogue in another realm of the law of supply and demand, has the most immediate effect in fostering the other faculties of the understanding, for the men of mental power succeed in the struggle for life; but the faculty of philosophizing, except in the literary way, is not called for; and therefore a difficult question cannot be expected to reach solution until it takes some practical form. If anybody should have the good luck to find out the solution, nobody else would take the trouble to understand it. But though the question of realism and nominalism has its roots in the technicalities of logic, its branches reach about our life. The question whether the *genus homo* has any existence except as individuals, is the question whether there is anything of any more dignity, worth, and importance than individual happiness, individual aspirations, and individual life. Whether men really have anything in common, so that the *community* is to be considered as an end in itself, and if so, what the relative value of the two factors is, is the most fundamental practical question in regard to every public institution the constitution of which we have it in our power to influence.

On the Nature of Signs

In the following brief manuscript, written in 1873, Peirce makes it as clear as anywhere in his writings that he is not one of those semioticians who emphasize the arbitrariness of signs. Every sign, even a prediction of a future event, has a "physical connection" to the object it represents. The three characters—material quality, pure demonstrative application, and appeal to a mind—that he here attributes to signs also correspond to the three categories in his "New List" of 1867 that he eventually generalized into firstness, secondness, and thirdness. The manuscript concludes with a reaffirmation of the main point of Peirce's 1868 essay "Questions concerning Certain Faculties Claimed for Man," in which he held that even our thoughts ("ideas") have the characters of signs.

Source: *Writings of Charles S. Peirce*, 3:66–68.

A sign is an object which stands for another to some mind. I propose to describe the characters of a sign. In the first place like any other thing it must have qualities which belong to it whether it be regarded as a sign or not. Thus a printed word is black, has a certain number of letters and those letters have certain shapes. Such characters of a sign I call its material quality. In the next place a sign must have some real connection with the thing it signifies so that when the object is present or is so as the sign signifies it to be, the sign shall so signify it and otherwise not. What I mean will best be understood by illustration. A weathercock is a sign of the direction of the wind. It would not be so unless the wind made it turn round. There is to be such a physical connection between every sign and its object. Take a painted portrait. It is the sign of the person for whom it is intended. It is a sign of that person in virtue of its likeness to that person: but this is not enough—it cannot be said of any two things that are alike one is a sign of the other but the portrait is a sign of that person because it was painted after that person and represents him. The connection here is an indirect one. The appearance of the person made a certain impression upon the painter's mind and that acted to cause the painter to make such a picture as he did do so that the appearance of the portrait is really an effect of the appearance of the person for whom it was intended. The one caused the other through the medium of the painter's mind. Take any statement which is made concerning a matter of fact. It is caused or determined by the fact. The fact has been observed & the perception of the fact which was caused by it in its turn causes the statement to be made. Perhaps however the fact was not directly perceived. The statement may be a prediction. In that case it cannot be said that that which follows after has caused that which precedes it, the prediction, but if the event has been predicted it has been through some knowledge of its cause and this same cause which precedes the event also precedes some cognition of the mind which gave rise to the prediction so that there is a real causal connection between the sign and the thing signified although it does not consist in one's being the effect of the other but in both being the effect of the same cause. I shall term this character of signs their pure demonstrative application. In the 3rd place it is necessary for a sign to be a sign that it should be regarded as a sign for it is only a sign to that mind which so considers and if it is not a sign to any mind it is not a sign at all. It must be known to the mind first in its material qualities but also in its pure demonstrative application. That mind must conceive it to be connected with its object so that it is possible to reason from the sign to the thing. Let us now see what the appeal of a sign to the mind amounts to. It produces a certain idea in the mind which is the idea that it is a sign of the thing it signifies and an idea is itself a sign, for an idea is an object and it represents an object. The idea itself has its material quality which is the feeling which there is in thinking. Thus the red and blue are different in the mere sensation. This difference in no way resembles the distinction which there is between those things in the outward world which are called red and those things which are called blue. Those things differ only in the rapidity with which their particles vibrate. In order that the senses discriminate between the two cases it is necessary that there should be some differences in the sensation but it is entirely indifferent so far as the difference of sensation is concerned whether it be a shorter or a longer vibration which produces that peculiar sensation which red things do. Whatever looks red might look blue or vice versa and the representation would be equally true to the facts. Thus our mere sensations are only the material quality of our ideas considered as signs. Our ideas have also a causal connection with the things that they represent without which there would be no real knowledge. It is not so clear at first sight that our ideas resemble their signs in necessarily appealing to some mind. That appeal could amount to nothing except the production of certain other ideas in which the first one should be virtually reproduced and according to the ordinary conception of the mind when the idea has once reached consciousness the correlation is complete. Nevertheless I regard this as an error of a very important character.

The Fixation of Belief

This essay is one of Peirce's most famous. The first of a series of six "Illustrations of the Logic of Science," it does not directly mention signs. Yet the essay is based on semiotic. Writing for a popular audience, Peirce did not go deeply into the reasons for his opinions. A reader unacquainted with Peirce's other writings might well think that Peirce's motive for here rejecting the "interior light of reason" as a method of fixing belief is simply its poor record in the history of science. Yet Peirce had doubted not merely the usefulness but the very possibility of introspection a decade earlier in his youthful writings on semiotic and philosophy of mind. Peirce believed that the method of science, of testing hypotheses by external fact, had proven successful because it was consistent with the semiotic realism that he had worked out apart from the history of science. That is, thought or the sign relation is objectively real and can validly be used to understand nature because it possesses a real unity with nature.

Source: *Writings of Charles S. Peirce*, 3:242–57.
Originally published in *Popular Science Monthly* 12
(November 1877): 1–15.

I

Few persons care to study logic, because everybody conceives himself to be proficient enough in the art of reasoning already. But I observe that this satisfaction is limited to one's own ratiocination, and does not extend to that of other men.

We come to the full possession of our power of drawing inferences the last of all our faculties, for it is not so much a natural gift as a long and difficult art. The history of its practice would make a grand subject for a book. The mediæval schoolmen, following the Romans, made logic the earliest of a boy's studies after grammar, as being very easy. So it was, as they understood it. Its fundamental principle, according to them, was, that all knowledge rests on either authority or reason; but that whatever is deduced by reason depends ultimately on a premise derived from authority. Accordingly, as soon as a boy was perfect in the syllogistic procedure, his intellectual kit of tools was held to be complete.

To Roger Bacon, that remarkable mind who in the middle of the thirteenth century was almost a scientific man, the schoolmen's conception of reasoning appeared only an obstacle to truth. He saw that experience alone teaches anything—a proposition which to us seems easy to understand, because a distinct conception of experience has been handed down to us from former generations; which to him also seemed perfectly clear, because its difficulties had not yet unfolded themselves. Of all kinds of experience, the best, he thought, was interior illumination, which teaches many things about Nature which the external senses could never discover, such as the transubstantiation of bread.

Four centuries later, the more celebrated Bacon, in the first book of his *Novum Organum*, gave his clear account of experience as something which must be open to verification and reëxamination. But, superior as Lord Bacon's conception is to earlier notions, a modern reader who is not in awe of his grandiloquence is chiefly struck by the inadequacy of his view of scientific procedure. That we have only to make some crude experiments, to draw up briefs of the results in certain blank forms, to go through these by rule, checking off everything disproved and setting down the alternatives, and that thus in a few years physical science would be finished up—what an idea! "He wrote on science like a Lord Chancellor," indeed.

The early scientists, Copernicus, Tycho Brahe, Kepler, Galileo, and Gilbert, had methods more like those of their modern brethren. Kepler undertook to draw a curve through the places of Mars;[1] and his greatest service to science was in impressing on men's minds that this was the thing to be done if they wished to improve astronomy; that they were not to content themselves with inquiring whether one system of epicycles was better than another, but

---

1. Not quite so, but as nearly so as can be told in a few words.

that they were to sit down to the figures and find out what the curve, in truth, was. He accomplished this by his incomparable energy and courage, blundering along in the most inconceivable way (to us), from one irrational hypothesis to another, until, after trying twenty-two of these, he fell, by the mere exhaustion of his invention, upon the orbit which a mind well furnished with the weapons of modern logic would have tried almost at the outset.

In the same way, every work of science great enough to be remembered for a few generations affords some exemplification of the defective state of the art of reasoning of the time when it was written; and each chief step in science has been a lesson in logic. It was so when Lavoisier and his contemporaries took up the study of chemistry. The old chemist's maxim had been, "*Lege, lege, lege, labora, ora, et relege.*" Lavoisier's method was not to read and pray, not to dream that some long and complicated chemical process would have a certain effect, to put it into practice with dull patience, after its inevitable failure to dream that with some modification it would have another result, and to end by publishing the last dream as a fact: his way was to carry his mind into his laboratory, and to make of his alembics and cucurbits instruments of thought, giving a new conception of reasoning, as something which was to be done with one's eyes open, by manipulating real things instead of words and fancies.

The Darwinian controversy is, in large part, a question of logic. Mr. Darwin proposed to apply the statistical method to biology. The same thing had been done in a widely different branch of science, the theory of gases. Though unable to say what the movements of any particular molecule of gas would be on a certain hypothesis regarding the constitution of this class of bodies, Clausius and Maxwell were yet able, by the application of the doctrine of probabilities, to predict that in the long run such and such a proportion of the molecules would, under given circumstances, acquire such and such velocities; that there would take place, every second, such and such a number of collisions, etc.; and from these propositions were able to deduce certain properties of gases, especially in regard to their heat-relations. In like manner, Darwin, while unable to say what the operation of variation and natural selection in any individual case will be, demonstrates that in the long run they will adapt animals to their circumstances. Whether or not existing animal forms are due to such action, or what position the theory ought to take, forms the subject of a discussion in which questions of fact and questions of logic are curiously interlaced.

II

The object of reasoning is to find out, from the consideration of what we already know, something else which we do not know. Consequently, reasoning is good if it be such as to give a true conclusion from true premises, and not otherwise. Thus, the question of its validity is purely one of fact and not of thinking. A being the premises and B the conclusion, the question is, whether these facts are really so related that if A is B is. If so, the inference is valid; if not, not. It is not in the least the question whether, when the premises are accepted by the mind, we feel an impulse to accept the conclusion also. It is true that we do generally reason correctly by nature. But that is an accident; the true conclusion would remain true if we had no impulse to accept it; and the false one would remain false, though we could not resist the tendency to believe in it.

We are, doubtless, in the main logical animals, but we are not perfectly so. Most of us, for example, are naturally more sanguine and hopeful than logic would justify. We seem to be so constituted that in the absence of any facts to go upon we are happy and self-satisfied; so that the effect of experience is continually to contract our hopes and aspirations. Yet a lifetime of the application of this corrective does not usually eradicate our sanguine disposition. Where hope is unchecked by any experience, it is likely that our optimism is extravagant. Logicality in regard to practical matters is the most useful quality an animal can possess, and might, therefore, result from the action of natural selection; but outside of these it is probably of more advantage to the animal to have his mind filled with pleasing and encouraging visions, independently of their truth; and thus, upon unpractical subjects, natural selection might occasion a fallacious tendency of thought.

That which determines us, from given premises, to draw one inference rather than another, is some habit of mind, whether it be constitutional or acquired. The habit is good or otherwise, according as it produces true conclusions from true premises or not; and an inference is regarded as valid or not, without reference to the truth or falsity of its conclusion specially, but according as the habit which determines it is such as to produce true conclusions in general or not. The particular habit of mind which governs this or that inference may be formulated in a proposition whose truth depends on the validity of the inferences which the habit determines; and such a formula is called a *guiding principle* of inference. Suppose, for example, that we observe that a rotating disk of copper quickly comes to rest when placed between the poles of a magnet, and we infer that this will happen with every disk of copper. The guiding principle is, that what is true of one piece of copper is true of another. Such a guiding principle with regard to copper would be much safer than with regard to many other substances—brass, for example.

A book might be written to signalize all the most important of these guiding principles of reasoning. It would probably be, we must confess, of no service to a person whose thought is directed wholly to practical subjects, and whose activity moves along thoroughly-beaten paths. The problems which present themselves to such a mind are matters of routine which he has learned once for all to handle in learning his business. But let a man venture into an unfamiliar field, or where his results are not continually checked by experience, and all history shows that the most masculine intellect will ofttimes lose his orientation and waste his efforts in directions which bring him no nearer to his goal, or even carry him entirely astray. He is like a ship in the open sea, with no one on board who understands the rules of navigation. And in such a case some general study of the guiding principles of reasoning would be sure to be found useful.

The subject could hardly be treated, however, without being first limited; since almost any fact may serve as a guiding principle. But it so happens that there exists a division among facts, such that in one class are all those which are absolutely essential as guiding principles, while in the others are all which have any other interest as objects of research. This division is between those which are necessarily taken for granted in asking whether a certain conclusion follows from certain premises, and those which are not implied in that question. A moment's thought will show that a variety of facts are already assumed when the logical question is first asked. It is implied, for instance, that there are such states of mind as doubt and belief—that a passage from one to the other is possible, the object of thought remaining the same, and that this transition is subject to some rules which all minds are alike bound by. As these are facts which we must already know before we can have any clear conception of reasoning at all, it cannot be supposed to be any longer of much interest to inquire into their truth or falsity. On the other hand, it is easy to believe that those rules of reasoning which are deduced from the very idea of the process are the ones which are the most essential; and, indeed, that so long as it conforms to these it will, at least, not lead to false conclusions from true premises. In point of fact, the importance of what may be deduced from the assumptions involved in the logical question turns out to be greater than might be supposed, and this for reasons which it is difficult to exhibit at the outset. The only one which I shall here mention is, that conceptions which are really products of logical reflection, without being readily seen to be so, mingle with our ordinary thoughts, and are frequently the causes of great confusion. This is the case, for example, with the conception of quality. A quality as such is never an object of observation. We can see that a thing is blue or green, but the quality of being blue and the quality of being green are not things which we see; they are products of logical reflection. The truth is, that common-sense, or thought as it first emerges above the level of the narrowly practical, is deeply imbued with that bad logical quality to which the epithet *metaphysical* is commonly applied; and nothing can clear it up but a severe course of logic.

III

We generally know when we wish to ask a question and when we wish to pronounce a judgment, for there is a dissimilarity between the sensation of doubting and that of believing.

But this is not all which distinguishes doubt from belief. There is a practical difference. Our beliefs guide our desires and shape our actions. The Assassins, or followers of the Old Man of the Mountain, used to rush into death at his least command, because they believed that obedience to him would insure everlasting felicity. Had they doubted this, they would not have acted as they did. So it is with every belief, according to its degree. The feeling of believing is a more or less sure indication of there being established in our nature some habit which will determine our actions. Doubt never has such an effect.

Nor must we overlook a third point of difference. Doubt is an uneasy and dissatisfied state from which we struggle to free ourselves and pass into the state of belief; while the latter is a calm and satisfactory state which we do not wish to avoid, or to change to a belief in anything else.[2] On the contrary, we cling tenaciously, not merely to believing, but to believing just what we do believe.

Thus, both doubt and belief have positive effects upon us, though very different ones. Belief does not make us act at once, but puts us into such a

2. I am not speaking of secondary effects occasionally produced by the interference of other impulses.

condition that we shall behave in a certain way, when the occasion arises. Doubt has not the least effect of this sort, but stimulates us to action until it is destroyed. This reminds us of the irritation of a nerve and the reflex action produced thereby; while for the analogue of belief, in the nervous system, we must look to what are called nervous associations—for example, to that habit of the nerves in consequence of which the smell of a peach will make the mouth water.

IV

The irritation of doubt causes a struggle to attain a state of belief. I shall term this struggle *inquiry*, though it must be admitted that this is sometimes not a very apt designation.

The irritation of doubt is the only immediate motive for the struggle to attain belief. It is certainly best for us that our beliefs should be such as may truly guide our actions so as to satisfy our desires; and this reflection will make us reject any belief which does not seem to have been so formed as to insure this result. But it will only do so by creating a doubt in the place of that belief. With the doubt, therefore, the struggle begins, and with the cessation of doubt it ends. Hence, the sole object of inquiry is the settlement of opinion. We may fancy that this is not enough for us, and that we seek, not merely an opinion, but a true opinion. But put this fancy to the test, and it proves groundless; for as soon as a firm belief is reached we are entirely satisfied, whether the belief be true or false. And it is clear that nothing out of the sphere of our knowledge can be our object, for nothing which does not affect the mind can be the motive for a mental effort. The most that can be maintained is, that we seek for a belief that we shall *think* to be true. But we think each one of our beliefs to be true, and, indeed, it is mere tautology to say so.

That the settlement of opinion is the sole end of inquiry is a very important proposition. It sweeps away, at once, various vague and erroneous conceptions of proof. A few of these may be noticed here.

1. Some philosophers have imagined that to start an inquiry it was only necessary to utter a question or set it down upon paper, and have even recommended us to begin our studies with questioning everything! But the mere putting of a proposition into the interrogative form does not stimulate the

mind to any struggle after belief. There must be a real and living doubt, and without this all discussion is idle.

2. It is a very common idea that a demonstration must rest on some ultimate and absolutely indubitable propositions. These, according to one school, are first principles of a general nature; according to another, are first sensations. But, in point of fact, an inquiry, to have that completely satisfactory result called demonstration, has only to start with propositions perfectly free from all actual doubt. If the premises are not in fact doubted at all, they cannot be more satisfactory than they are.

3. Some people seem to love to argue a point after all the world is fully convinced of it. But no further advance can be made. When doubt ceases, mental action on the subject comes to an end; and, if it did go on, it would be without a purpose.

V

If the settlement of opinion is the sole object of inquiry, and if belief is of the nature of a habit, why should we not attain the desired end, by taking any answer to a question which we may fancy, and constantly reiterating it to ourselves, dwelling on all which may conduce to that belief, and learning to turn with contempt and hatred from anything which might disturb it? This simple and direct method is really pursued by many men. I remember once being entreated not to read a certain newspaper lest it might change my opinion upon free-trade. "Lest I might be entrapped by its fallacies and misstatements," was the form of expression. "You are not," my friend said, "a special student of political economy. You might, therefore, easily be deceived by fallacious arguments upon the subject. You might, then, if you read this paper, be led to believe in protection. But you admit that free-trade is the true doctrine; and you do not wish to believe what is not true." I have often known this system to be deliberately adopted. Still oftener, the instinctive dislike of an undecided state of mind, exaggerated into a vague dread of doubt, makes men cling spasmodically to the views they already take. The man feels that, if he only holds to his belief without wavering, it will be entirely satisfactory. Nor can it be denied that a steady and immovable faith yields great peace of mind. It may, indeed, give rise to inconveniences, as if a man should resolutely continue to believe that fire would not burn him, or that he would be eternally damned if he received his *ingesta* otherwise than through a stomach-pump. But then the man who adopts this method will not allow that its inconveniences are greater than its advantages. He will say, "I hold steadfastly to the truth, and the truth is always wholesome." And in many cases it may very well be that the pleasure he derives from his calm faith overbalances any inconveniences resulting from its deceptive character. Thus, if it be true that death is annihilation, then the man who believes that he will certainly go straight to heaven when he dies, provided he have fulfilled certain simple observances in this life, has a cheap pleasure which will not be followed by the least disappointment. A similar consideration seems to have weight with many persons in religious topics, for we frequently hear it said, "Oh, I could not believe so-and-so, because I should be wretched if I did." When an ostrich buries its head in the sand as danger approaches, it very likely takes the happiest course. It hides the danger, and then calmly says there is no danger; and, if it feels perfectly sure there is none, why should it raise its head to see? A man may go through life, systematically keeping out of view all that might cause a change in his opinions, and if he only succeeds—basing his method, as he does, on two fundamental psychological laws—I do not see what can be said against his doing so. It would be an egotistical impertinence to object that his procedure is irrational, for that only amounts to saying that his method of settling belief is not ours. He does not propose to himself to be rational, and, indeed, will often talk with scorn of man's weak and illusive reason. So let him think as he pleases.

But this method of fixing belief, which may be called the method of tenacity, will be unable to hold its ground in practice. The social impulse is against it. The man who adopts it will find that other men think differently from him, and it will be apt to occur to him, in some saner moment, that their opinions are quite as good as his own, and this will shake his confidence in his belief. This conception, that another man's thought or sentiment may be equivalent to one's own, is a distinctly new step, and a highly important one. It arises from an impulse too strong in man to be suppressed, without danger of destroying the human species. Unless we make ourselves hermits, we shall necessarily influence each other's opinions; so that the problem becomes how to fix belief, not in the individual merely, but in the community.

Let the will of the state act, then, instead of that of the individual. Let an institution be created which shall have for its object to keep correct doctrines before the attention of the people, to reiterate them perpetually, and to teach them to the young; having at the same time power to prevent contrary doctrines from being taught, advocated, or expressed. Let all possible causes of a change of mind be removed from men's apprehensions. Let them be kept ignorant, lest they should learn of some reason to think otherwise than they do. Let their passions be enlisted, so that they may regard private and unusual opinions with hatred and horror. Then, let all men who reject the established belief be terrified into silence. Let the people turn out and tar-and-feather such men, or let inquisitions be made into the manner of thinking of suspected persons, and, when they are found guilty of forbidden beliefs, let them be subjected to some signal punishment. When complete agreement could not otherwise be reached, a general massacre of all who have not thought in a certain way has proved a very effective means of settling opinion in a country. If the power to do this be wanting, let a list of opinions be drawn up, to which no man of the least independence of thought can assent, and let the faithful be required to accept all these propositions, in order to segregate them as radically as possible from the influence of the rest of the world.

This method has, from the earliest times, been one of the chief means of upholding correct theological and political doctrines, and of preserving their universal or catholic character. In Rome, especially, it has been practised from the days of Numa Pompilius to those of Pius Nonus. This is the most perfect example in history; but wherever there is a priesthood—and no religion has been without one—this method has been more or less made use of. Wherever there is an aristocracy, or a guild, or any association of a class of men whose interests depend or are supposed to depend on certain propositions, there will be inevitably found some traces of this natural product of social feeling. Cruelties always accompany this system; and when it is consistently carried out, they become atrocities of the most horrible kind in the eyes of any rational man. Nor should this occasion surprise, for the officer of a society does not feel justified in surrendering the interests of that society for the sake of mercy, as he might his own private interests. It is natural, therefore, that sympathy and fellowship should thus produce a most ruthless power.

In judging this method of fixing belief, which may be called the method of authority, we must, in the first place, allow its immeasurable mental and moral superiority to the method of tenacity. Its success is proportionately greater; and, in fact, it has over and over again worked the most majestic results. The mere structures of stone which it has caused to be put together—in Siam, for example, in Egypt, and in Europe—have many of them a sublimity hardly more than rivaled by the greatest works of Nature. And, except the geological epochs, there are no periods of time so vast as those which are measured by some of these organized faiths. If we scrutinize the matter closely, we shall find that there has not been one of their creeds which has remained always the same; yet the change is so slow as to be imperceptible during one person's life, so that individual belief remains sensibly fixed. For the mass of mankind, then, there is perhaps no better method than this. If it is their highest impulse to be intellectual slaves, then slaves they ought to remain.

But no institution can undertake to regulate opinions upon every subject. Only the most important ones can be attended to, and on the rest men's minds must be left to the action of natural causes. This imperfection will be no source of weakness so long as men are in such a state of culture that one opinion does not influence another—that is, so long as they cannot put two and two together. But in the most priestridden states some individuals will be found who are raised above that condition. These men possess a wider sort of social feeling; they see that men in other countries and in other ages have held to very different doctrines from those which they themselves have been brought up to believe; and they cannot help seeing that it is the mere accident of their having been taught as they have, and of their having been surrounded with the manners and associations they have, that has caused them to believe as they do and not far differently. And their candour cannot resist the reflection that there is no reason to rate their own views at a higher value than those of other nations and other centuries; and this gives rise to doubts in their minds.

They will further perceive that such doubts as these must exist in their minds with reference to every belief which seems to be determined by the caprice either of themselves or of those who originated the popular opinions. The willful adherence to a belief, and the arbitrary forcing of it upon others, must, therefore, both be given up, and a new method of settling opinions must be adopted, which shall not only produce an impulse to believe, but shall also decide what proposition it is which is to be believed. Let the action of natural preferences be unimpeded, then, and under their influence let men, conversing together and regarding matters in different lights, gradually develop beliefs in harmony with natural causes. This method resembles that by which conceptions of art have been brought to maturity. The most perfect example of it is to be found in the history of metaphysical philosophy. Systems of this sort have not usually rested upon any observed facts, at least not in any great degree. They have been chiefly adopted because their fundamental propositions seemed "agreeable to reason." This is an apt expression; it does not mean that which agrees with experience, but that which we find ourselves inclined to believe. Plato, for example, finds it agreeable to reason that the distances of the celestial spheres from one another should be proportional to the different lengths of strings which produce harmonious chords. Many philosophers have been led to their main conclusions by considerations like this; but this is the lowest and least developed form which the method takes, for it is clear that another man might find Kepler's theory, that the celestial spheres are proportional to the inscribed and circumscribed spheres of the different regular solids, more agreeable to *his* reason. But the shock of opinions will soon lead men to rest on preferences of a far more universal nature. Take, for example, the doctrine that man only acts selfishly—that is, from the consideration that acting in one way will afford him more pleasure than acting in another. This rests on no fact in the world, but it has had a wide acceptance as being the only reasonable theory.

This method is far more intellectual and respectable from the point of view of reason than either of the others which we have noticed. But its failure has been the most manifest. It makes of inquiry something similar to the development of taste; but taste, unfortunately, is always more or less a matter of fashion, and accordingly metaphysicians have never come to any fixed agreement, but the pendulum has swung backward and forward between a more material and a more spiritual philosophy, from the earliest times to the latest. And so from this, which has been called the *a priori* method, we are driven, in Lord Bacon's phrase, to a true induction. We have examined into this *a priori* method as something which promised to deliver our opinions from their accidental and capricious element. But development, while it is a process which eliminates the effect of some casual circumstances, only magnifies that of others. This method, therefore, does not differ in a very essential way from that of authority. The government may not have lifted its finger to influence my convictions; I may have been left outwardly quite free to choose, we will say, between monogamy and polygamy, and, appealing to my conscience only, I may have concluded that the latter practice is in itself licentious. But when I come to see that the chief obstacle to the spread of Christianity among a people of as high culture as the Hindoos has been a conviction of the immorality of our way of treating women, I cannot help seeing that, though governments do not interfere, sentiments in their development will be very greatly determined by accidental causes. Now, there are some people, among whom I must suppose that my reader is to be found, who, when they see that any belief of theirs is determined by any circumstance extraneous to the facts, will from that moment not merely admit in words that that belief is doubtful, but will experience a real doubt of it, so that it ceases to be a belief.

To satisfy our doubts, therefore, it is necessary that a method should be found by which our beliefs may be caused by nothing human, but by some external permanency—by something upon which our thinking has no effect. Some mystics imagine that they have such a method in a private inspiration from on high. But that is only a form of the method of tenacity, in which the conception of truth as something public is not yet developed. Our external permanency would not be external, in our sense, if it was restricted in its influence to one individual. It must be something which affects, or might affect, every man. And, though these affections are necessarily as various as are individual conditions, yet the method must be such that the ultimate conclusion of every man shall be the same. Such is the method of science. Its fundamental hypothesis, restated in more familiar language, is this: There are real things, whose characters are entirely independent of our opinions about them; those realities affect our senses according to regular laws, and, though our sensations are as different as our relations to the objects, yet, by taking advantage of the laws of perception, we can ascertain by reasoning how things really are, and any man, if he have sufficient experience and reason enough about it, will be led to the one true conclusion. The new conception here involved is that of reality. It may be asked how I know that there are any realities. If this hypothesis is the sole support of my method of inquiry, my method of inquiry must not be used to support my hypothesis. The reply is this: 1. If investigation cannot be regarded as proving that there are real things, it at least does not lead to a contrary conclusion; but the method and the conception on which it is based remain ever in harmony. No doubts of the method, therefore, necessarily arise from its practice, as is the case with all the others. 2. The feeling which gives rise to any method of fixing belief is a dissatisfaction at two repugnant propositions. But here already is a vague concession that there is some *one* thing to which a proposition should conform. Nobody, therefore, can really doubt that there are realities, or, if he did, doubt would not be a source of dissatisfaction. The hypothesis, therefore, is one which every mind admits. So that the social impulse does not cause me to doubt it. 3. Everybody uses the scientific method about a great many things, and only ceases to use it when he does not know how to apply it. 4. Experience of the method has not led me to doubt it, but, on the contrary, scientific investigation has had the most wonderful triumphs in the way of settling opinion. These afford the explanation of my not doubting the method or the hypothesis which it supposes; and not having any doubt, nor believing that anybody else whom I could influence has, it would be the merest babble for me to say more about it. If there be anybody with a living doubt upon the subject, let him consider it.

To describe the method of scientific investigation is the object of this series of papers. At present I have only room to notice some points of contrast between it and other methods of fixing belief.

This is the only one of the four methods which presents any distinction of a right and a wrong way. If I adopt the method of tenacity and shut myself out from all influences, whatever I think necessary to doing this is necessary according to that method. So with the method of authority: the state may try to put down heresy by means which, from a scientific point of view, seem very ill-calculated to accomplish its purposes; but the only test *on that method* is what the state thinks, so that it cannot pursue the method wrongly. So with the *a priori* method. The very essence of it is to think as one is inclined to think. All metaphysicians will be sure to do that, however they may be inclined to judge each other to be perversely wrong. The Hegelian system recognizes every natural tendency of thought as logical, although it be certain to be abolished by counter-tendencies. Hegel thinks there is a regular system in the succession of these tendencies, in consequence of which, after drifting one way and the other for a long time, opinion will at last go right. And it is true that metaphysicians get the right ideas at last; Hegel's system of Nature represents tolerably the science of that day; and one may be sure that whatever scientific investigation has put out of doubt will presently receive *a priori* demonstration on the part of the metaphysicians. But with the scientific method the case is different. I may start with known and observed facts to proceed to the unknown; and yet the rules which I follow in doing so may not be such as investigation would approve. The test of whether I am truly following the method is not an immediate appeal to my feelings and purposes, but, on the contrary, itself involves the application of the method. Hence it is that bad reasoning as well as good reasoning is possible; and this fact is the foundation of the practical side of logic.

It is not to be supposed that the first three methods of settling opinion present no advantage whatever over the scientific method. On the contrary, each has some peculiar convenience of its own. The *a priori* method is distinguished for its comfortable conclusions. It is the nature of the process to adopt whatever belief we are inclined to, and there are certain flatteries to the vanity of man which we all believe by nature, until we are awakened from our pleasing dream by some rough facts. The method of authority will always govern the mass of mankind; and those who wield the various forms of organized force in the state will never be convinced that dangerous reasoning ought not to be suppressed in some way. If liberty of speech is to be untrammelled from the grosser forms of constraint, then uniformity of opinion will be secured by a moral terrorism to which the respectability of society will give its thorough approval. Following the method of authority is the path of peace. Certain non-conformities are permitted; certain others (considered unsafe) are forbidden. These are different in different countries and in different ages; but, wherever you are, let it be known that you seriously hold a tabooed belief, and you may be perfectly sure of being treated with a cruelty less brutal but more refined than hunting you like a wolf. Thus, the greatest intellectual benefactors of mankind have never dared, and dare not now, to utter the whole of their thought; and thus a shade of *prima facie* doubt is cast upon every proposition which is considered essential to the security of society. Singularly enough, the persecution does not all come from without; but a man torments himself and is oftentimes most distressed at finding himself believing propositions which he has been brought up to regard with aversion. The peaceful and sympathetic man will, therefore, find it hard to resist the temptation to submit his opinions to authority. But most of all I admire the method of tenacity for its strength, simplicity, and directness. Men who pursue it are distinguished for their decision of character, which becomes very easy with such a mental rule. They do not waste time in trying to make up their minds what they want, but, fastening like lightning upon whatever alternative comes first, they hold to it to the end, whatever happens, without an instant's irresolution. This is one of the splendid qualities which generally accompany brilliant, unlasting success. It is impossible not to envy the man who can dismiss reason, although we know how it must turn out at last.

Such are the advantages which the other methods of settling opinion have over scientific investigation. A man should consider well of them; and then he should consider that, after all, he wishes his opinions to coincide with the fact, and that there is no reason why the results of these three methods should do so. To bring about this effect is the prerogative of the method of science. Upon such considerations he has to make his choice—a choice which is far more than the adoption of any intellectual opinion, which is one of the ruling decisions of his life, to which, when once made, he is bound to adhere. The force of habit will sometimes cause a man to hold on to old beliefs, after he is in a condition to see that they have no sound basis. But reflection upon the state of the case will overcome these habits, and he ought to allow reflection its full weight. People sometimes shrink from doing this, having an idea that beliefs are wholesome which they cannot help feeling rest on nothing. But let such persons suppose an analogous though different case from their own. Let them ask themselves what they would say to a reformed Mussulman who should hesitate to give up his old notions in regard to the relations of the sexes; or to a reformed Catholic who should still shrink from reading the Bible. Would they not say that these persons ought to consider the matter fully, and clearly understand the new doctrine, and then ought to embrace it, in its entirety? But, above all, let it be considered that what is more wholesome than any particular belief is integrity of belief, and that to avoid looking into the support of any belief from a fear that it may turn out rotten is quite as immoral as it is disadvantageous. The person who confesses that there is such a thing as truth, which is distinguished from falsehood simply by this, that if acted on it will carry us to the point we aim at and not astray, and then, though convinced of this, dares not know the truth and seeks to avoid it, is in a sorry state of mind indeed.

Yes, the other methods do have their merits: a clear logical conscience does cost something—just as any virtue, just as all that we cherish, costs us dear. But we should not desire it to be otherwise. The genius of a man's logical method should be loved and reverenced as his bride, whom he has chosen from all the world. He need not contemn the others; on the contrary, he may honor them deeply, and in doing so he only honors her the more. But she is the one that he has chosen, and he knows that he was right in making that choice. And having made it, he will work and fight for her, and will not complain that there are blows to take, hoping that there may be as many and as hard to give, and will strive to be the worthy knight and champion of her from the blaze of whose splendors he draws his inspiration and his courage.

How to Make Our Ideas Clear

In this second essay of the six "Illustrations of the Logic of Science" (the third through the sixth are available in *The Writings of Charles S. Peirce*, 3:276–338), Peirce stated his eventually famous pragmatic maxim: the meaning of a thought could be made clear only by considering the conceivably practical effects of the thought. As with the previous essay, the word "sign" does not appear, but the argument is nevertheless dependent on his semiotic realism, his notion that all thought is in visceral signs requiring inferential interpretation rather than in bodiless Cartesian ideas whose meaning was immediately known, provided only that they were sufficiently "clear and distinct" in the mind. Thus Peirce compares thinking to a musical tune composed of a sequence of notes, each one of which is immediately present to consciousness for a brief time. But the melody is known mediately. The melody is not present all at once but depends on the interpretation of a relation between notes no longer present to consciousness. As the separate notes are to music, bodily sensations are to thought. Sensations, of which most are past and therefore not immediately present to consciousness, achieve meaning by an interpretive relation.

Source: *Writings of Charles S. Peirce*, 3:257–76.
Originally published in *Popular Science Monthly* 12
(January 1878): 286–302.

I

Whoever has looked into a modern treatise on logic of the common sort, will doubtless remember the two distinctions between *clear* and *obscure* conceptions, and between *distinct* and *confused* conceptions. They have lain in the books now for nigh two centuries, unimproved and unmodified, and are generally reckoned by logicians as among the gems of their doctrine.

A clear idea is defined as one which is so apprehended that it will be recognized wherever it is met with, and so that no other will be mistaken for it. If it fails of this clearness, it is said to be obscure.

This is rather a neat bit of philosophical terminology; yet, since it is clearness that they were defining, I wish the logicians had made their definition a little more plain. Never to fail to recognize an idea, and under no circumstances to mistake another for it, let it come in how recondite a form it may, would indeed imply such prodigious force and clearness of intellect as is seldom met with in this world. On the other hand, merely to have such an acquaintance with the idea as to have become familiar with it, and to have lost all hesitancy in recognizing it in ordinary cases, hardly seems to deserve the name of clearness of apprehension, since after all it only amounts to a subjective feeling of mastery which may be entirely mistaken. I take it, however, that when the logicians speak of "clearness," they mean nothing more than such a familiarity with an idea, since they regard the quality as but a small merit, which needs to be supplemented by another, which they call *distinctness*.

A distinct idea is defined as one which contains nothing which is not clear. This is technical language; by the *contents* of an idea logicians understand whatever is contained in its definition. So that an idea is *distinctly* apprehended, according to them, when we can give a precise definition of it, in abstract terms. Here the professional logicians leave the subject; and I would not have troubled the reader with what they have to say, if it were not such a striking example of how they have been slumbering through ages of intellectual activity, listlessly disregarding the enginery of modern thought, and never dreaming of applying its lessons to the improvement of logic. It is easy to show that the doctrine that familiar use and abstract distinctness make the perfection of apprehension has its only true place in philosophies which have long been extinct; and it is now time to formulate the method of attaining to a more perfect clearness of thought, such as we see and admire in the thinkers of our own time.

When Descartes set about the reconstruction of philosophy, his first step was to (theoretically) permit scepticism and to discard the practice of the schoolmen of looking to authority as the ultimate source of truth. That done, he sought a more natural fountain of true principles, and professed to find it in the human mind; thus passing, in the directest way, from the method of authority to that of apriority, as described in my first paper. Self-conscious-ness was to furnish us with our fundamental truths, and to decide what was agreeable to reason. But since, evidently, not all ideas are true, he was led to note, as the first condition of infallibility, that they must be clear. The distinc-tion between an idea *seeming* clear and really being so, never occurred to him. Trusting to introspection, as he did, even for a knowledge of external things, why should he question its testimony in respect to the contents of our own minds? But then, I suppose, seeing men, who seemed to be quite clear and positive, holding opposite opinions upon fundamental principles, he was further led to say that clearness of ideas is not sufficient, but that they need also to be distinct, i.e., to have nothing unclear about them. What he probably meant by this (for he did not explain himself with precision) was, that they must sustain the test of dialectical examination; that they must not only seem clear at the outset, but that discussion must never be able to bring to light points of obscurity connected with them.

Such was the distinction of Descartes, and one sees that it was precisely on the level of his philosophy. It was somewhat developed by Leibnitz. This great and singular genius was as remarkable for what he failed to see as for what he saw. That a piece of mechanism could not do work perpetually with-out being fed with power in some form, was a thing perfectly apparent to him; yet he did not understand that the machinery of the mind can only transform knowledge, but never originate it, unless it be fed with facts of observation. He thus missed the most essential point of the Cartesian philosophy, which is, that to accept propositions which seem perfectly evident to us is a thing which, whether it be logical or illogical, we cannot help doing. Instead of regarding the matter in this way, he sought to reduce the first principles of science to formulas which cannot be denied without self-contradiction, and was apparently unaware of the great difference between his position and that of Descartes. So he reverted to the old formalities of logic, and, above all, abstract definitions played a great part in his philosophy. It was quite natural, therefore, that on observing that the method of Descartes labored under the difficulty that we may seem to ourselves to have clear apprehensions of ideas which in truth are very hazy, no better remedy occurred to him than to require an abstract definition of every important term. Accordingly, in adopting the distinction of *clear* and *distinct* notions, he described the latter quality as the clear apprehension of everything contained in the definition; and the books have ever since copied his words. There is no danger that his chimerical scheme will ever again be over-valued. Nothing new can ever be learned by analyzing definitions. Nevertheless, our existing beliefs can be set in order by this process, and order is an essential element of intellectual economy, as of every other. It may be acknowledged, therefore, that the books are right in making familiarity with a notion the first step toward clearness of apprehension, and the defining of it the second. But in omitting all mention of any higher perspicuity of thought, they simply mirror a philosophy which was exploded a hundred years ago. That much-admired "ornament of logic"—the doctrine of clearness and distinctness—may be pretty enough, but it is high time to relegate to our cabinet of curiosities the antique *bijou*, and to wear about us something better adapted to modern uses.

The very first lesson that we have a right to demand that logic shall teach us is, how to make our ideas clear; and a most important one it is, depreciated only by minds who stand in need of it. To know what we think, to be masters of our own meaning, will make a solid foundation for great and weighty thought. It is most easily learned by those whose ideas are meagre and restricted; and far happier they than such as wallow helplessly in a rich mud of conceptions. A nation, it is true, may, in the course of generations, overcome the disadvantage of an excessive wealth of language and its natural concomitant, a vast, unfathomable deep of ideas. We may see it in history, slowly perfecting its literary forms, sloughing at length its metaphysics, and, by virtue of the untirable patience which is often a compensation, attaining great excellence in every branch of mental acquirement. The page of history is not yet unrolled which is to tell us whether such a people will or will not in the long-run prevail over one whose ideas (like the words of their language) are few, but which possesses a wonderful mastery over those which it has. For an individual, however, there can be no question that a few clear ideas are worth more than many confused ones. A young man would hardly be persuaded to sacrifice the greater part of his thoughts to save the rest; and the muddled head is the least apt to see the necessity of such a sacrifice. Him we can usually only commiserate, as a person with a congenital defect. Time will help him, but intellectual maturity with regard to clearness comes rather late, an unfortunate arrangement of Nature, inasmuch as clearness is of less use to a man settled in life, whose errors have in great measure had their effect, than it would be to one whose path lies before him. It is terrible to see how a single unclear idea, a single formula without meaning, lurking in a young man's head, will sometimes act like an obstruction of inert matter in an artery, hindering the nutrition of the brain, and condemning its victim to pine away in the fullness of his intellectual vigor and in the midst of intellectual plenty.

Many a man has cherished for years as his hobby some vague shadow of an idea, too meaningless to be positively false; he has, nevertheless, passionately loved it, has made it his companion by day and by night, and has given to it his strength and his life, leaving all other occupations for its sake, and in short has lived with it and for it, until it has become, as it were, flesh of his flesh and bone of his bone; and then he has waked up some bright morning to find it gone, clean vanished away like the beautiful Melusina of the fable, and the essence of his life gone with it. I have myself known such a man; and who can tell how many histories of circle-squarers, metaphysicians, astrologers, and what not, may not be told in the old German story?

II

The principles set forth in the first of these papers lead, at once, to a method of reaching a clearness of thought of a far higher grade than the "distinctness" of the logicians. We have there found that the action of thought is excited by the irritation of doubt, and ceases when belief is attained; so that the production of belief is the sole function of thought. All these words, however, are too strong for my purpose. It is as if I had described the phenomena as they appear under a mental microscope. Doubt and Belief, as the words are commonly employed, relate to religious or other grave discussions. But here I use them to designate the starting of any question, no matter how small or how great, and the resolution of it. If, for instance, in a horse-car, I pull out my purse and find a five-cent nickel and five coppers, I decide, while my hand is going to the purse, in which way I will pay my fare. To call such a question Doubt, and my decision Belief, is certainly to use words very disproportionate to the occasion. To speak of such a doubt as causing an irritation which needs to be appeased, suggests a temper which is uncomfortable to the verge of insanity. Yet, looking at the matter minutely, it must be admitted that, if there is the least hesitation as to whether I shall pay the five coppers or the nickel (as there will be sure to be, unless I act from some previously contracted habit in the matter), though irritation is too strong a word, yet I am excited to such small mental activity as may be necessary to deciding how I shall act. Most frequently doubts arise from some indecision, however momentary, in our action. Sometimes it is not so. I have, for example, to wait in a railway-station, and to pass the time I read the advertisements on the walls, I compare the advantages of different trains and different routes which I never expect to take, merely fancying myself to be in a state of hesitancy, because I am bored with having nothing to trouble me. Feigned hesitancy, whether feigned for mere amusement or with a lofty purpose, plays a great part in the production of scientific inquiry. However the doubt may originate, it stimulates the mind to an activity which may be slight or energetic, calm or turbulent. Images pass rapidly through consciousness, one incessantly melting into another, until at last, when all is over—it may be in a fraction of a second, in an hour, or after long years—we find ourselves decided as to how we should act under such circumstances as those which occasioned our hesitation. In other words, we have attained belief.

In this process we observe two sorts of elements of consciousness, the distinction between which may best be made clear by means of an illustration. In a piece of music there are the separate notes, and there is the air. A single tone may be prolonged for an hour or a day, and it exists as perfectly in each second of that time as in the whole taken together; so that, as long as it is sounding, it might be present to a sense from which everything in the past was as completely absent as the future itself. But it is different with the air, the performance of which occupies a certain time, during the portions of which only portions of it are played. It consists in an orderliness in the succession of sounds which strike the ear at different times; and to perceive it there must be some continuity of consciousness which makes the events of a lapse of time present to us. We certainly only perceive the air by hearing the separate notes; yet we cannot be said to directly hear it, for we hear only what is present at the instant, and an orderliness of succession cannot exist in an instant. These two sorts of objects, what we are *immediately* conscious of and what we are *mediately* conscious of, are found in all consciousness. Some elements (the sensations) are completely present at every instant so long as they last, while others (like thought) are actions having beginning, middle, and end, and consist in a congruence in the succession of sensations which flow through the mind. They cannot be immediately present to us, but must cover some portion of the past or future. Thought is a thread of melody running through the succession of our sensations.

We may add that just as a piece of music may be written in parts, each part having its own air, so various systems of relationship of succession subsist together between the same sensations. These different systems are distinguished by having different motives, ideas, or functions. Thought is only one such system, for its sole motive, idea, and function, is to produce belief, and whatever does not concern that purpose belongs to some other system of relations. The action of thinking may incidentally have other results; it may serve to amuse us, for example, and among *dilettanti* it is not rare to find those who have so perverted thought to the purposes of pleasure that it seems to vex them to think that the questions upon which they delight to exercise it may ever get finally settled; and a positive discovery which takes a favorite subject out of the arena of literary debate is met with ill-concealed dislike. This disposition is the very debauchery of thought. But the soul and meaning of thought, abstracted from the other elements which accompany it, though it may be voluntarily thwarted, can never be made to direct itself toward anything but the production of belief. Thought in action has for its only possible motive the attainment of thought at rest; and whatever does not refer to belief is no part of the thought itself.

And what, then, is belief? It is the demi-cadence which closes a musical phrase in the symphony of our intellectual life. We have seen that it has just three properties: First, it is something that we are aware of; second, it appeases the irritation of doubt; and, third, it involves the establishment in our nature of a rule of action, or, say for short, a *habit*. As it appeases the irritation of doubt, which is the motive for thinking, thought relaxes, and comes to rest for a moment when belief is reached. But, since belief is a rule for action, the application of which involves further doubt and further thought, at the same time that it is a stopping-place, it is also a new starting-place for thought. That is why I have permitted myself to call it thought at rest, although thought is essentially an action. The *final* upshot of thinking is the exercise of volition, and of this thought no longer forms a part; but belief is only a stadium of mental action, an effect upon our nature due to thought, which will influence future thinking.

The essence of belief is the establishment of a habit, and different beliefs are distinguished by the different modes of action to which they give rise. If beliefs do not differ in this respect, if they appease the same doubt by producing the same rule of action, then no mere differences in the manner of consciousness of them can make them different beliefs, any more than playing a tune in different keys is playing different tunes. Imaginary distinctions are often drawn between beliefs which differ only in their mode of expression;—the wrangling which ensues is real enough, however. To believe that any objects are arranged as in Fig. 1, and to believe that they are arranged in Fig. 2, are one and the same belief; yet it is conceivable that a man should assert one proposition and deny the other. Such false distinctions do as much harm as the confusion of beliefs really different, and are among the pitfalls of

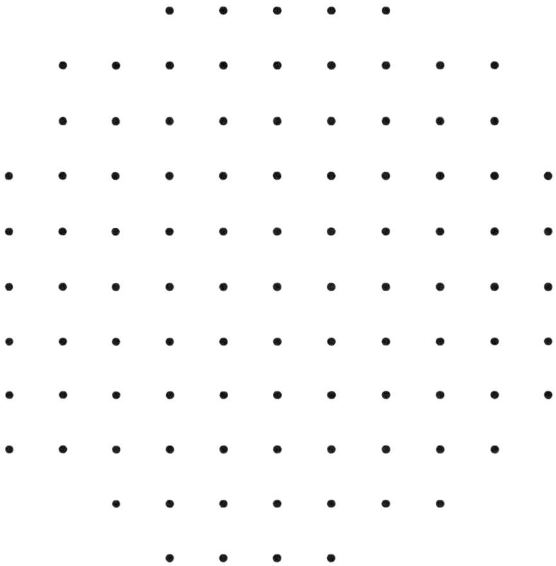

Figure 1.

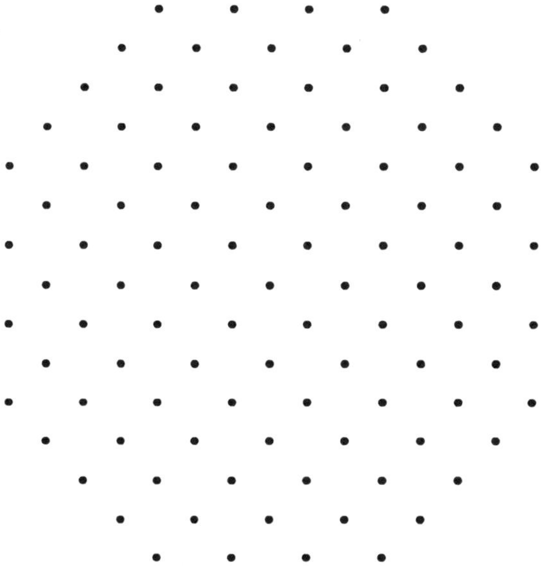

Figure 2.

which we ought constantly to beware, especially when we are upon meta-physical ground. One singular deception of this sort, which often occurs, is to mistake the sensation produced by our own unclearness of thought for a character of the object we are thinking. Instead of perceiving that the obscurity is purely subjective, we fancy that we contemplate a quality of the object which is essentially mysterious; and if our conception be afterward presented to us in a clear form we do not recognize it as the same, owing to the absence of the feeling of unintelligibility. So long as this deception lasts, it obviously puts an impassable barrier in the way of perspicuous thinking; so that it equally interests the opponents of rational thought to perpetuate it, and its adherents to guard against it.

Another such deception is to mistake a mere difference in the grammatical construction of two words for a distinction between the ideas they express. In this pedantic age, when the general mob of writers attend so much more to words than to things, this error is common enough. When I just said that thought is an *action*, and that it consists in a *relation*, although a person performs an action but not a relation, which can only be the result of an action, yet there was no inconsistency in what I said, but only a grammatical vagueness.

From all these sophisms we shall be perfectly safe so long as we reflect that the whole function of thought is to produce habits of action; and that whatever there is connected with a thought, but irrelevant to its purpose, is an accretion to it, but no part of it. If there be a unity among our sensations which has no reference to how we shall act on a given occasion, as when we listen to a piece of music, why we do not call that thinking. To develop its meaning, we have, therefore, simply to determine what habits it produces, for what a thing means is simply what habits it involves. Now, the identity of a habit depends on how it might lead us to act, not merely under such circumstances as are likely to arise, but under such as might possibly occur, no matter how improbable they may be. What the habit is depends on *when* and *how* it causes us to act. As for the *when*, every stimulus to action is derived from perception; as for the *how*, every purpose of action is to produce some sensible result. Thus, we come down to what is tangible and practical, as the root of every real distinction of thought, no matter how subtle it may be; and there is no distinction of meaning so fine as to consist in anything but a possible difference of practice.

To see what this principle leads to, consider in the light of it such a doctrine as that of transubstantiation. The Protestant churches generally hold that the elements of the sacrament are flesh and blood only in a tropical sense; they nourish our souls as meat and the juice of it would our bodies. But the Catholics maintain that they are literally just that; although they possess all the sensible qualities of wafer-cakes and diluted wine. But we can have no conception of wine except what may enter into a belief, either—

1. That this, that, or the other, is wine; or,
2. That wine possesses certain properties.

Such beliefs are nothing but self-notifications that we should, upon occasion, act in regard to such things as we believe to be wine according to the qualities which we believe wine to possess. The occasion of such action would be some sensible perception, the motive of it to produce some sensible result. Thus our action has exclusive reference to what affects the senses, our habit has the same bearing as our action, our belief the same as our habit, our conception the same as our belief; and we can consequently mean nothing by wine but what has certain effects, direct or indirect, upon our senses; and to talk of something as having all the sensible characters of wine, yet being in reality blood, is senseless jargon. Now, it is not my object to pursue the theological question; and having used it as a logical example I drop it, without caring to anticipate the theologian's reply. I only desire to point out how impossible it is that we should have an idea in our minds which relates to anything but conceived sensible effects of things. Our idea of anything *is* our idea of its sensible effects; and if we fancy that we have any other we deceive ourselves, and mistake a mere sensation accompanying the thought for a part of the thought itself. It is absurd to say that thought has any meaning unrelated to its only function. It is foolish for Catholics and Protestants to fancy themselves in disagreement about the elements of the sacrament, if they agree in regard to all their sensible effects, here or hereafter.

It appears, then, that the rule for attaining the third grade of clearness of apprehension is as follows: Consider what effects, which might conceivably have practical bearings, we conceive the object of our conception to have. Then, our conception of these effects is the whole of our conception of the object.

III

Let us illustrate this rule by some examples; and, to begin with the simplest one possible, let us ask what we mean by calling a thing *hard*. Evidently that it will not be scratched by many other substances. The whole conception of this quality, as of every other, lies in its conceived effects. There is absolutely no difference between a hard thing and a soft thing so long as they are not brought to the test. Suppose, then, that a diamond could be crystallized in the midst of a cushion of soft cotton, and should remain there until it was finally burned up. Would it be false to say that that diamond was soft? This seems a foolish question, and would be so, in fact, except in the realm of logic. There such questions are often of the greatest utility as serving to bring logical principles into sharper relief than real discussions ever could. In studying logic we must not put them aside with hasty answers, but must consider them with attentive care, in order to make out the principles involved. We may, in the present case, modify our question, and ask what prevents us from saying that all hard bodies remain perfectly soft until they are touched, when their hardness increases with the pressure until they are scratched. Reflection will show that the reply is this: there would be no *falsity* in such modes of speech. They would involve a modification of our present usage of speech with regard to the words hard and soft, but not of their meanings. For they represent no fact to be different from what it is; only they involve arrangements of facts which would be exceedingly maladroit. This leads us to remark that the question of what would occur under circumstances which do not actually arise is not a question of fact, but only of the most perspicuous arrangement of them. For example, the question of free-will and fate in its simplest form, stripped of verbiage, is something like this: I have done something of which I am ashamed; could I, by an effort of the will, have resisted the temptation, and done otherwise? The philosophical reply is, that this is not a question of fact, but only of the arrangement of facts. Arranging them so as to exhibit what is particularly pertinent to my question—namely, that I ought to blame myself for having done wrong—it is perfectly true to say that, if I had willed to do otherwise than I did, I should have done otherwise. On the other hand, arranging the facts so as to exhibit another important consideration, it is equally true that, when a temptation has once been allowed to work, it will, if it has a certain force, produce its effect, let me struggle how I may. There is no objection to a contradiction in what would result from a false supposition. The *reductio ad absurdum* consists in showing that contradictory results would follow from a hypothesis which is consequently judged to be false. Many questions are involved in the free-will discussion, and I am far from desiring to say that both sides are equally right. On the contrary, I am of opinion that one side denies important facts, and that the other does not. But what I do say is, that the above single question was the origin of the whole doubt; that, had it not been for this question, the controversy would never have arisen; and that this question is perfectly solved in the manner which I have indicated.

Let us next seek a clear idea of Weight. This is another very easy case. To say that a body is heavy means simply that, in the absence of opposing force, it will fall. This (neglecting certain specifications of how it will fall, etc., which exist in the mind of the physicist who uses the word) is evidently the whole conception of weight. It is a fair question whether some particular facts may not *account* for gravity; but what we mean by the force itself is completely involved in its effects.

This leads us to undertake an account of the idea of Force in general. This is the great conception which, developed in the early part of the seventeenth century from the rude idea of a cause, and constantly improved upon since, has shown us how to explain all the changes of motion which bodies experience, and how to think about all physical phenomena; which has given birth to modern science, and changed the face of the globe; and which, aside from its more special uses, has played a principal part in directing the course of modern thought, and in furthering modern social development. It is, therefore, worth some pains to comprehend it. According to our rule, we must begin by asking what is the immediate use of thinking about force; and the answer is, that we thus account for changes of motion. If bodies were left to themselves, without the intervention of forces, every motion would continue unchanged both in velocity and in direction. Furthermore, change of motion never takes place abruptly; if its direction is changed, it is always through a curve without angles; if its velocity alters, it is by degrees. The gradual changes which are constantly taking place are conceived by geometers to be compounded together according to the rules of the parallelogram of forces. If the reader does not already know what this is, he will find it, I hope, to his advantage to endeavor to follow the following explanation; but if mathematics are insupportable to him, pray let him skip three paragraphs rather than that we should part company here.

A *path* is a line whose beginning and end are distinguished. Two paths are considered to be equivalent, which, beginning at the same point, lead to the same point. Thus the two paths, *A B C D E* and *A F G H E*, are equivalent. Paths which do *not* begin at the same point are considered to be equivalent, provided that, on moving either of them without turning it, but keeping it always parallel to its original position, when its beginning coincides with that

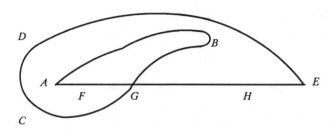

Figure 3.

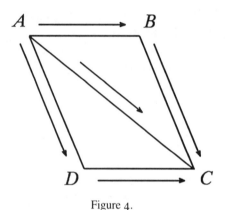

Figure 4.

of the other path, the ends also coincide. Paths are considered as geometrically added together, when one begins where the other ends; thus the path *AE* is conceived to be a sum of *AB, BC, CD,* and *DE.* In the parallelogram of Fig. 4 the diagonal *AC* is the sum of *AB* and *BC*; or, since *AD* is geometrically equivalent to *BC, AC* is the geometrical sum of *AB* and *AD.*

All this is purely conventional. It simply amounts to this: that we choose to call paths having the relations I have described equal or added. But, though it is a convention, it is a convention with a good reason. The rule for geometrical addition may be applied not only to paths, but to any other things which can be represented by paths. Now, as a path is determined by the varying direction and distance of the point which moves over it from the starting-point, it follows that anything which from its beginning to its end is determined by a varying direction and a varying magnitude is capable of being represented by a line. Accordingly, *velocities* may be represented by lines, for they have only directions and rates. The same thing is true of *accelerations*, or changes of velocities. This is evident enough in the case of velocities;

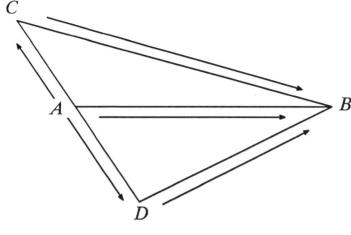

Figure 5.

and it becomes evident for accelerations if we consider that precisely what velocities are to positions—namely, states of change of them—that accelerations are to velocities.

The so-called "parallelogram of forces" is simply a rule for compounding accelerations. The rule is, to represent the accelerations by paths, and then to geometrically add the paths. The geometers, however, not only use the "parallelogram of forces" to compound different accelerations, but also to resolve one acceleration into a sum of several. Let *AB* (Fig. 5) be the path which represents a certain acceleration—say, such a change in the motion of a body that at the end of one second the body will, under the influence of that change, be in a position different from what it would have had if its motion had continued unchanged such that a path equivalent to *AB* would lead from the latter position to the former. This acceleration may be considered as the sum of the accelerations represented by *AC* and *CB*. It may also be considered as the sum of the very different accelerations represented by *AD* and *DB*, where *AD* is almost the opposite of *AC*. And it is clear that there is an immense variety of ways in which *AB* might be resolved into the sum of two accelerations.

After this tedious explanation, which I hope, in view of the extraordinary interest of the conception of force, may not have exhausted the reader's patience, we are prepared at last to state the grand fact which this conception embodies. This fact is that if the actual changes of motion which the different particles of bodies experience are each resolved in its appropriate way, each component acceleration is precisely such as is prescribed by a certain law of

Nature, according to which bodies in the relative positions which the bodies in question actually have at the moment,[1] always receive certain accelerations, which, being compounded by geometrical addition, give the acceleration which the body actually experiences.

This is the only fact which the idea of force represents, and whoever will take the trouble clearly to apprehend what this fact is, perfectly comprehends what force is. Whether we ought to say that a force *is* an acceleration, or that it *causes* an acceleration, is a mere question of propriety of language, which has no more to do with our real meaning than the difference between the French idiom *"Il fait froid"* and its English equivalent *"It is cold."* Yet it is surprising to see how this simple affair has muddled men's minds. In how many profound treatises is not force spoken of as a "mysterious entity," which seems to be only a way of confessing that the author despairs of ever getting a clear notion of what the word means! In a recent admired work on "Analytic Mechanics" it is stated that we understand precisely the effect of force, but what force itself is we do not understand! This is simply a self-contradiction. The idea which the word force excites in our minds has no other function than to affect our actions, and these actions can have no reference to force otherwise than through its effects. Consequently, if we know what the effects of force are, we are acquainted with every fact which is implied in saying that a force exists, and there is nothing more to know. The truth is, there is some vague notion afloat that a question may mean something which the mind cannot conceive; and when some hair-splitting philosophers have been confronted with the absurdity of such a view, they have invented an empty distinction between positive and negative conceptions, in the attempt to give their non-idea a form not obviously nonsensical. The nullity of it is sufficiently plain from the considerations given a few pages back; and, apart from those considerations, the quibbling character of the distinction must have struck every mind accustomed to real thinking.

IV

Let us now approach the subject of logic, and consider a conception which particularly concerns it, that of *reality*. Taking clearness in the sense of familiarity, no idea could be clearer than this. Every child uses it with perfect

---

1. Possibly the velocities also have to be taken into account.

confidence, never dreaming that he does not understand it. As for clearness in its second grade, however, it would probably puzzle most men, even among those of a reflective turn of mind, to give an abstract definition of the real. Yet such a definition may perhaps be reached by considering the points of difference between reality and its opposite, fiction. A figment is a product of somebody's imagination; it has such characters as his thought impresses upon it. That those characters are independent of how you or I think is an external reality. There are, however, phenomena within our own minds, dependent upon our thought, which are at the same time real in the sense that we really think them. But though their characters depend on how we think, they do not depend on what we think those characters to be. Thus, a dream has a real existence as a mental phenomenon, if somebody has really dreamt it; that he dreamt so and so, does not depend on what anybody thinks was dreamt, but is completely independent of all opinion on the subject. On the other hand, considering, not the fact of dreaming, but the thing dreamt, it retains its peculiarities by virtue of no other fact than that it was dreamt to possess them. Thus we may define the real as that whose characters are independent of what anybody may think them to be.

But, however satisfactory such a definition may be found, it would be a great mistake to suppose that it makes the idea of reality perfectly clear. Here, then, let us apply our rules. According to them, reality, like every other quality, consists in the peculiar sensible effects which things partaking of it produce. The only effect which real things have is to cause belief, for all the sensations which they excite emerge into consciousness in the form of beliefs. The question therefore is, how is true belief (or belief in the real) distinguished from false belief (or belief in fiction). Now, as we have seen in the former paper, the ideas of truth and falsehood, in their full development, appertain exclusively to the scientific method of settling opinion. A person who arbitrarily chooses the propositions which he will adopt can use the word truth only to emphasize the expression of his determination to hold on to his choice. Of course, the method of tenacity never prevailed exclusively; reason is too natural to men for that. But in the literature of the dark ages we find some fine examples of it. When Scotus Erigena is commenting upon a poetical passage in which hellebore is spoken of as having caused the death of Socrates, he does not hesitate to inform the inquiring reader that Helleborus and Socrates were two eminent Greek philosophers, and that the latter having been overcome in argument by the former took the matter to heart and died of it! What sort of an idea of truth could a man have who could adopt and teach, without the qualification of a perhaps, an opinion taken so entirely at random? The real spirit of Socrates, who I hope would have been delighted to have been "overcome in argument," because he would have learned something by it, is in curious contrast with the naïve idea of the glossist, for whom discussion would seem to have been simply a struggle. When philosophy began to awake from its long slumber, and before theology completely dominated it, the practice seems to have been for each professor to seize upon any philosophical position he found unoccupied and which seemed a strong one, to intrench himself in it, and to sally forth from time to time to give battle to the others. Thus, even the scanty records we possess of those disputes enable us to make out a dozen or more opinions held by different teachers at one time concerning the question of nominalism and realism. Read the opening part of the "Historia Calamitatum" of Abelard, who was certainly as philosophical as any of his contemporaries, and see the spirit of combat which it breathes. For him, the truth is simply his particular stronghold. When the method of authority prevailed, the truth meant little more than the Catholic faith. All the efforts of the scholastic doctors are directed toward harmonizing their faith in Aristotle and their faith in the Church, and one may search their ponderous folios through without finding an argument which goes any further. It is noticeable that where different faiths flourish side by side, renegades are looked upon with contempt even by the party whose belief they adopt; so completely has the idea of loyalty replaced that of truth-seeking. Since the time of Descartes, the defect in the conception of truth has been less apparent. Still, it will sometimes strike a scientific man that the philosophers have been less intent on finding out what the facts are, than on inquiring what belief is most in harmony with their system. It is hard to convince a follower of the *a priori* method by adducing facts; but show him that an opinion he is defending is inconsistent with what he has laid down elsewhere, and he will be very apt to retract it. These minds do not seem to believe that disputation is ever to cease; they seem to think that the opinion which is natural for one man is not so for another, and that belief will, consequently, never be settled. In contenting themselves with fixing their own opinions by a method which would lead another man to a different result, they betray their feeble hold of the conception of what truth is.

On the other hand, all the followers of science are fully persuaded that the processes of investigation, if only pushed far enough, will give one certain solution to every question to which they can be applied. One man may investigate the velocity of light by studying the transits of Venus and the aberration of the stars; another by the oppositions of Mars and the eclipses of Jupiter's satellites; a third by the method of Fizeau; a fourth by that of Foucault; a fifth by the motions of the curves of Lissajoux; a sixth, a seventh, an eighth, and a ninth, may follow the different methods of comparing the measures of statical and dynamical electricity. They may at first obtain different results, but, as each perfects his method and his processes, the results will move steadily together toward a destined centre. So with all scientific research. Different minds may set out with the most antagonistic views, but the progress of investigation carries them by a force outside of themselves to one and the same conclusion. This activity of thought by which we are carried, not where we wish, but to a foreordained goal, is like the operation of destiny. No modification of the point of view taken, no selection of other facts for study, no natural bent of mind even, can enable a man to escape the predestinate opinion. This great law is embodied in the conception of truth and reality. The opinion which is fated[2] to be ultimately agreed to by all who investigate, is what we mean by the truth, and the object represented in this opinion is the real. That is the way I would explain reality.

But it may be said that this view is directly opposed to the abstract definition which we have given of reality, inasmuch as it makes the characters of the real to depend on what is ultimately thought about them. But the answer to this is that, on the one hand, reality is independent, not necessarily of thought in general, but only of what you or I or any finite number of men may think about it; and that, on the other hand, though the object of the final opinion depends on what that opinion is, yet what that opinion is does not depend on what you or I or any man thinks. Our perversity and that of others may indefinitely postpone the settlement of opinion; it might even conceivably cause an arbitrary proposition to be universally accepted as long as the human race should last. Yet even that would not change the nature of the belief, which alone could be the result of investigation carried sufficiently far; and if, after the extinction of our race, another should arise with faculties and disposition for investigation, that true opinion must be the one which they would ultimately come to. "Truth crushed to earth shall rise again," and the opinion which would finally result from investigation does not depend on how

2. Fate means merely that which is sure to come true, and can nohow be avoided. It is a superstition to suppose that a certain sort of events are ever fated, and it is another to suppose that the word fate can never be freed from its superstitious taint. We are all fated to die.

anybody may actually think. But the reality of that which is real does depend on the real fact that investigation is destined to lead, at last, if continued long enough, to a belief in it.

But I may be asked what I have to say to all the minute facts of history, forgotten never to be recovered, to the lost books of the ancients, to the buried secrets.

> Full many a gem of purest ray serene
>> The dark, unfathomed caves of ocean bear;
> Full many a flower is born to blush unseen,
>> And waste its sweetness on the desert air.

Do these things not really exist because they are hopelessly beyond the reach of our knowledge? And then, after the universe is dead (according to the prediction of some scientists), and all life has ceased forever, will not the shock of atoms continue though there will be no mind to know it? To this I reply that, though in no possible state of knowledge can any number be great enough to express the relation between the amount of what rests unknown to the amount of the known, yet it is unphilosophical to suppose that, with regard to any given question (which has any clear meaning), investigation would not bring forth a solution of it, if it were carried far enough. Who would have said, a few years ago, that we could ever know of what substances stars are made whose light may have been longer in reaching us than the human race has existed? Who can be sure of what we shall not know in a few hundred years? Who can guess what would be the result of continuing the pursuit of science for ten thousand years, with the activity of the last hundred? And if it were to go on for a million, or a billion, or any number of years you please, how is it possible to say that there is any question which might not ultimately be solved?

But it may be objected, "Why make so much of these remote considerations, especially when it is your principle that only practical distinctions have a meaning?" Well, I must confess that it makes very little difference whether we say that a stone on the bottom of the ocean, in complete darkness, is brilliant or not—that is to say, that it *probably* makes no difference, remembering always that that stone *may* be fished up to-morrow. But that there are gems at the bottom of the sea, flowers in the untraveled desert, etc., are propositions which, like that about a diamond being hard when it is not pressed, concern much more the arrangement of our language than they do the meaning of our ideas.

It seems to me, however, that we have, by the application of our rule, reached so clear an apprehension of what we mean by reality, and of the fact which the idea rests on, that we should not, perhaps, be making a pretension so presumptuous as it would be singular, if we were to offer a metaphysical theory of existence for universal acceptance among those who employ the scientific method of fixing belief. However, as metaphysics is a subject much more curious than useful, the knowledge of which, like that of a sunken reef, serves chiefly to enable us to keep clear of it, I will not trouble the reader with any more Ontology at this moment. I have already been led much further into that path than I should have desired; and I have given the reader such a dose of mathematics, psychology, and all that is most abstruse, that I fear he may already have left me, and that what I am now writing is for the compositor and proof-reader exclusively. I trusted to the importance of the subject. There is no royal road to logic, and really valuable ideas can only be had at the price of close attention. But I know that in the matter of ideas the public prefer the cheap and nasty; and in my next paper I am going to return to the easily intelligible, and not wander from it again. The reader who has been at the pains of wading through this month's paper, shall be rewarded in the next one by seeing how beautifully what has been developed in this tedious way can be applied to the ascertainment of the rules of scientific reasoning.

We have, hitherto, not crossed the threshold of scientific logic. It is certainly important to know how to make our ideas clear, but they may be ever so clear without being true. How to make them so, we have next to study. How to give birth to those vital and procreative ideas which multiply into a thousand forms and diffuse themselves everywhere, advancing civilization and making the dignity of man, is an art not yet reduced to rules, but of the secret of which the history of science affords some hints.

One, Two, Three:

Fundamental Categories

of Thought and of Nature

This selection and the following one were unpublished in Peirce's lifetime. They develop related themes and will repay joint study. This piece, the less developed of the two, was written first (in 1885) and is therefore printed first here. But if the reader is not certain that he or she understands the categories of firstness, secondness, and thirdness, it may be best to read chapter 1 of the following selection before reading this essay. Peirce here explains the categorical relation between his logic and his typology of signs. He then supports his monism by explaining logic and semiotic in terms of "consciousness," or psychological phenomena, and then psychological phenomena in terms of cognition, and cognition in terms of neurology. The neurological discussion is here omitted because Peirce pursues the question more clearly and in more detail in the next selection.

Source: MS 901.

Kant, the King of modern thought, it was who first remarked the frequency in logical analytics of *trichotomies* or three-fold distinctions. It really is so; I have tried hard and long to persuade myself that it is only fanciful, but the facts will not countenance that way of disposing of the phenomenon. Take any ordinary syllogism:

> All men are mortal,
> Elijah was a man;
> Therefore, Elijah was mortal.

There are here three propositions, namely, two premises and a conclusion; there are also three terms, *man, mortal*, and *Elijah*. If we transpose one of the premises with the conclusion, denying both, we obtain what are called the indirect figures of syllogism; for example

> All men are mortal,
> But Elijah was not mortal;
> Therefore, Elijah was not a man.

> Elijah was not mortal,
> But Elijah was a man;
> Therefore, some men are not mortal.

Thus, there are three figures of ordinary syllogism. It is true there are other modes of inference which do not come under any of these heads; but that does not annul the fact that we have here a trichotomy. Indeed, if we examine by itself what is by some logicians called the fourth figure we find that it also has three varieties related to one another as the three figures of ordinary syllogism. There is an entirely different way of conceiving the relations of the figures of syllogism; namely by means of the conversion of propositions. But from that point of view also the same classes are preserved. DeMorgan has added a large number of new syllogistic moods which do not find places in this classification. The reasoning in these is of a peculiar character and introduces the principle of dilemma. Still, regarding these dilemmatic reasonings by themselves, they fall into three classes in a precisely similar manner. Again, I have shown that the probable and approximate inferences of science must be classified on the very same principles, being either Deductions, Inductions, or Hypotheses. Other examples of threes in logic are statements of what is actual, what is possible, and what is necessary; the three kinds of forms, Names, Propositions, and Inferences; affirmative, negative, and uncertain answers to a question. One very important triad is this: it has been found that there are three kinds of signs which are all indispensible in all reasoning; the first is the diagrammatic sign or *icon*, which exhibits a similarity or analogy to the subject of discourse; the second is the *index*, which like a pronoun demonstrative or relative, forces the attention to the particular object intended without describing it; the third is the general name or description which signifies its object by means of an association of ideas or habitual connection between the name and the character signified. But there is one triad in particular which throws a strong light on the nature of all the others.

Namely, we find it necessary to recognize in logic three kinds of characters, three kinds of facts. First there are *singular* characters which are predicable of single objects, as when we say that anything is white, large, etc. Secondly, there are dual characters which appertain to pairs of objects; these are implied by all relative terms as 'lover,' 'similar,' 'other,' etc. Thirdly, there are plural characters, which can all be reduced to triple characters but not to dual characters. Thus, we cannot express the fact that A is a benefactor of B by any descriptions of A and B separately; we must introduce a relative term. This is requisite, not merely in English, but in every language which might be invented. This is true even of such a fact as A is taller than B. If we say, 'A is tall, but B is short,' the conjugation 'but' has a relative force, and if we omit this word the mere collocation of the two sentences is a relative or dual mode of signifying. We must, however, recognize two kinds of relative characters, those which can be implied in such a mere collocation and those, like A's benefitting B, which cannot. The mathematicians say that two straight lines constitute a *degenerate* conic. To borrow this expression we may say that the mere collocation of two facts about A and B constitutes a degenerate relation. In this case, the two facts are seen by the mind to be in relation to one another. As the old logicians said, relations are divisible into real relations or relations of reason. Let us now consider a triple character, say that A gives B to C. This is not a mere congeries of dual characters. It is not enough to say that A parts with C, and that B receives C. A synthesis of these two facts must be made to bring them into a single fact; we must express that C in being parted with by A is received by B. If, on the other hand, we take a quadruple fact, it is easy to express as a compound of two triple facts. Thus, suppose A gives B to C in exchange for D. Then, if we take the word 'sale' to include the parting with a thing in exchange not merely for money but for any object in barter, we may express the fact in question thus: 'A makes a sale, E, to C, and E is a sale of B in exchange for D.' We are here able to express the synthesis of the two facts into one, because a triple character involves the conception of synthesis. Analysis involves the same relations as synthesis; so that we may explain the fact that all plural facts can be reduced to triple facts in this way. A road with a fork in it is the analogue of a triple fact, because it brings three termini into relation with one another. A dual fact is like a road without a fork; it only connects two termini. Now, no combination of roads without forks can have more than two termini; but any number of termini can be connected by roads which nowhere have a knot of more than three ways. See the figure, where I have drawn the termini as self-returning roads, in order

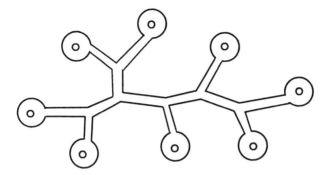

to introduce nothing beyond the road itself. Thus, the three essential elements of a network of roads are *road about a terminus, roadway-connection,* and *branching*; and in like manner, the three fundamental categories of fact are, fact about an object, fact about two objects (relation), fact about several objects (synthetic fact).

We have seen that the mere coexistence of two singular facts constitutes a degenerate form of dual fact; and in like manner there are two orders of degeneracy in plural facts, for either they may consist in a mere synthesis of facts of which the highest is dual, or they may consist in a mere synthesis of singular facts. This explains why there should be three classes of *signs*; for there is a triple connection of *sign, thing signified, cognition produced in the mind.* There may be a mere relation of reason between the sign and the thing signified; in that case the sign is an *icon.* Or there may be a direct physical connection; in that case, the sign is an *index.* Or there may be a relation which consists in the fact that the mind associates the sign with its object; in that case the sign is a *name.* Now consider the difference between a logical *term,* a *proposition,* and an *inference.* A term is a mere general description, and as neither *icon* nor *index* possess generality, it must be a name; and it is nothing more. A proposition is also a general description, but it differs from a term in that it purports to be in a real relation to the fact, to be really determined by it; thus, a proposition can only be formed of the conjunction of a name and an index. An inference, too, contains a general description and purports to really represent the fact; but it does more, it professes to give in its premises such a representation of the fact that by the contemplation of them something else may be learned about the thing; this it can only do by presenting an analogue or *icon* of the fact; and thus we see why all three kinds of signs are requisite for inference.

By such sort of synthesis, the whole organism of logic may be mentally evolved from the three conceptions of first, second, and third, or more precisely, An, Other, Medium.

But if these three conceptions enter as we find they do as elements of all conceptions connected with reasoning, they must be virtually in the mind when reasoning first commences. In that sense, at least, they must be innate ideas; and consequently they must be capable of explanation, psychologically;—there must be in the consciousness three faculties corresponding to these three categories of logic. Now, we know that the introspective psychologists have for a long time told us that the mind has three fundamental faculties, the feeling of pleasure and pain, volition and desire, and cognition. Let us see, then, if we cannot modify this statement so that without being less true to the phenomena of introspective consciousness,—even more true, if possible,—it may be put into a form in which it will serve as the psychological explanation, which must surely lie somewhere, of the new facts which we bring from the study of logic.

The ordinary doctrine is open to a variety of objections from the very point of view from which it was first delineated. 1st. Desire certainly includes an element of pleasure quite as much as of will. Wishing is not willing; it is a speculative variation of willing mingled with a speculative and anticipatory feeling of pleasure. Desire should therefore be struck out of the definition of the second faculty leaving it mere volition. But volition without desire is not voluntary; it is mere activity. Consequently, all activity, voluntary or not, should be brought under the second faculty. Thus attention is a kind of activity which is sometimes voluntary and sometimes not so. 2nd. Pleasure and pain can only be recognized as such in a judgment; they are general predicates which are attached to feelings rather than true feelings. But mere passive feeling, which does not act and does not judge, which has all sorts of qualities but does not itself recognize these qualities, because it does not analyze nor compare,—this is an element of all consciousness to which a distinct title ought to be given. 3rd. Every phenomenon of our mental life is more or less like cognition. Every emotion, every burst of passion, every exercise of will is like cognition. But modifications of consciousness which are alike have some element in common. Cognition, therefore, has nothing distinctive and cannot be regarded as a fundamental faculty. If, however, we ask whether there be not an element in cognition which is neither feeling, sense, nor activity, we do find something; the faculty of learning, acquisition, memory-and-inference, synthesis. 4th. Looking once more at activity, we observe that the only consciousness we have of it is the sense of resistance. We are conscious of hitting or of getting hit, of meeting with a *fact*. But whether the activity is within or without we know only by secondary signs and not by our original faculty of recognizing fact.

It seems, then, that the true categories of consciousness are, 1st, Feeling, the consciousness which can be included with an instant of time, passive consciousness of quality, without recognition or analysis; 2nd, Consciousness of an interruption into the field of consciousness, sense of resistance, of an external fact, of another something; 3rd, synthetic consciousness binding time together, sense of learning, thought.

If we accept these are the fundamental elementary modes of consciousness, they afford a psychological explanation of the three logical conceptions of quality, relation, and synthesis or mediation. The conception of quality, which is absolutely simple in itself and yet viewed in its relations is seen to be full of variety, would arise whenever feeling or the singular consciousness becomes prominent. The conception of relation comes from the dual consciousness or sense of action and reaction. The conception of mediation springs out of the plural consciousness or sense of learning.

12

. . .

A Guess at the Riddle

The following is extracted from notes that Peirce wrote in preparation for a never-completed book that would have defended his metaphysical categories—firstness, secondness, and thirdness—by showing how they might explain the basic principles of logic, psychology, physiology, biology, physics, sociology, and theology. Had the book been written, it would have been, as Peirce says below, "one of the births of time" and certainly the preeminent achievement of nineteenth-century American philosophy. Nevertheless, Peirce did cover many of the planned topics in articles published during his lifetime, some of which are reprinted in this volume.

Printed in the selection below is Peirce's outline for the entire book, all of what he wrote of chapter 1, and part of what he wrote of chapter 5. Chapter 1 is a clear description of his categories, especially of thirdness. In the fifth chapter Peirce strives for a neurological account of thought as thirdness. This was a radical alternative to conventional neurological accounts of thought, which were usually written from the traditional perspective of either Cartesian dualism or simple materialism. Dualists allowed for neurological descriptions of thought as the physical side of psychophysical parallelism. Materialists viewed thought as an entirely neurological process but described the process in terms of dyadic relations or brute force, the action of one object in striking a second. This unrealistically denied, Peirce believed, the element of spontaneity in thought. The assertion that the process involved a mediating third object enabled Peirce to describe thought as a process of triadic relations involving representation of the first object by the sign (third) and interpretation of the sign by the interpretant (second). The superiority of this model, in Peirce's view, was that it allowed for realistic recognition that although thinking is a material, neurological process, it cannot be explained in terms of dyadic relations, that is, as a mechanical process of action and reaction.

The part of chapter 5 that is omitted moves to a still more basic physiological level by explaining thought in terms of the properties of protoplasm, a topic dealt with in selection 14, "Man's Glassy Essence."

Source: MS 909.

Chapter 1. One, Two, Three. Already written.

Chapter 2. The triad in reasoning. Not touched. It is to be made as follows. 1. Three kinds of signs; as best shown in my last paper in the *Am. Jour. Math.* 2. Term, proposition, and argument, mentioned in my paper on a new list of categories. 3. Three kinds of argument, deduction, induction, hypothesis, as shown in my paper in *Studies in Logic.* Also three figures of syllogism, as shown there and in my paper on the classification of arguments. 4. Three kinds of terms, absolute, relative, and conjugative, as shown in my first paper on Logic of Relatives. There are various other triads which may be alluded to. The dual divisions of logic result from a false way of looking at things absolutely. Thus, besides affirmative and negative, there are really probable enunciations, which are intermediate. So besides universal and particular there are all sorts of propositions of numerical quantity. For example, the particular proposition Some *A* is *B*, means At least one *A* is *B*. But we can also say At least 2 *A*'s are *B*'s. Also, All the *A*'s but one are *B*'s, etc. etc. ad infinitum. We pass from dual quantity, or a system of quantity such as that of Boolian algebra, where there are only two values, to plural quantity.

Chapter 3. The triad in metaphysics. This chapter, one of the best, is to treat of the theory of cognition.

Chapter 4. The triad in psychology. The greater part is written.

Chapter 5. The triad in physiology. The greater part is written.

Chapter 6. The triad in biology. This is to show the true nature of the Darwinian hypothesis.

Chapter 7. The triad in physics. The germinal chapter. 1. The necessity of a natural history of the laws of nature, so that we may get some notion of what to expect. 2. The logical postulate for explanation forbids the assumption of any absolute. That is, it calls for the introduction of thirdness. 3. Metaphysics is an imitation of geometry; and mathematicians having declared against axioms, the metaphysical axioms are destined to fall too. 4. Absolute chance. 5. The universality of the principle of habit. 6. The whole theory stated. 7. Consequences.

Chapter 8. The triad in sociology or shall I say pneumatology. That the consciousness is a sort of public spirit among the nerve-cells. Man as a community of cells; compound animals and composite plants; society; nature. Feeling implied in firstness.

Chapter 9. The triad in theology. Faith requires [us] to be materialists without flinching.

NOTES FOR A BOOK, TO BE ENTITLED: *A GUESS AT THE RIDDLE,* WITH A VIGNETTE OF THE SPHYNX BELOW THE TITLE. And this book if ever written, as it soon will be if I am in a situation to do it, will be one of the births of time.

CHAPTER I. *Trichotomy.*

Perhaps I might begin by noticing how different numbers have found their champions. Two was extolled by Peter Ramus, Four by Pythagoras, Five by Sir Thomas Browne, and so on. For my part, I am a determined foe of no innocent number; I respect and esteem them all their several ways; but I am forced to confess to a leaning to the number three in philosophy. In fact, I make so much use of three-fold divisions in my speculations, that it seems best to commence by making a slight preliminary study of the conceptions upon which all such divisions must rest. I mean no more than the ideas of First, Second, Third,—ideas so broad that they may be looked upon rather as moods or tones of thought, than as definite notions, but which have great significance for all that. Viewed as numerals, to be applied to what objects we like, they are indeed thin skeletons of thought, if not mere words. If we only wanted to make enumerations, it would be out of place to ask for the significations of the numbers we should have to use; but then the distinctions of philosophy are supposed to attempt something far more than that; they are intended to go down to the very essence of things, and if we are to make one single three-fold philosophical distinction, it behooves us to ask beforehand what are the kinds of objects that are first, second, and third, not as being so counted, but in their own true characters. That there are such ideas of the really First, Second, and Third, we shall presently find reason to admit.

The First is that whose being is simply in itself, not referring to anything nor lying behind anything. The Second is that which is what it is by force of something to which it is second. The Third is that which is what it is owing to things between which it mediates and which it brings into relation to each other.

The idea of the absolutely First must be entirely separated from all conception of or reference to anything else; for what involves a second is itself a second to that second. The First must therefore be present and immediate, so as not to be second to a representation. It must be fresh and new, for if old it is second to its former state. It must be initiative, original, spontaneous, and free; otherwise it is second to a determining cause. It is also something vivid and conscious; so only it avoids being the object of some sensation. It precedes all synthesis and all differentiation: it has no unity and no parts. It cannot be articulately thought: assert it, and it has already lost its characteristic innocence; for assertion always implies a denial of something else. Stop to think of it, and it has flown! What the world was to Adam on the day he opened his eyes to it, before he had drawn any distinctions, or had become conscious of his own existence,—that is first, present, immediate, fresh, new, initiative, original, spontaneous, free, vivid, conscious, and evanescent. Only, remember that every description of it must be false to it.

Just as the first is not absolutely first if thought along with a second, so likewise to think the Second in its perfection we must banish every third. The Second is therefore the absolute last. But we need not, and must not, banish the idea of the first from the second; on the contrary, the Second is precisely that which cannot be without the first. It meets us in such facts as Another, Relation, Compulsion, Effect, Dependence, Independence, Negation, Occurrence, Reality, Result. A thing cannot be other, negative, or independent, without a first to or of which it shall be other, negative, or independent. Still, this is not a very deep kind of secondness; for the first might in these cases be destroyed yet leave the real character of the second absolutely unchanged. When the second suffers some change from the action of the first, and is dependent upon it, the secondness is more genuine. But the dependence must not go so far that the second is a mere accident or incident of the first; otherwise the secondness again degenerates. The genuine second suffers and yet resists, like dead matter, whose existence consists in its inertia. Note, too, that for the Second to have the Finality that we have seen belongs to it, it must be determined by the first immoveably, and thenceforth be fixed; so that unalterable fixity becomes one of its attributes. We find secondness in occurrence, because an occurrence is something whose existence consists in our knocking up against it. A hard fact is of the same sort; that is to say, it is something which is there, and which I cannot think away, but am forced to acknowledge as an object or second beside myself, the subject or number one, and which forms material for the exercise of my will.

The idea of second must be reckoned as an easy one to comprehend. That of first is so tender that you cannot touch it without spoiling it; but that of second is eminently hard and tangible. It is very familiar, too; it is forced upon us daily: it is the main lesson of life. In youth, the world is fresh and we seem free; but limitation, conflict, constraint, and secondness generally, make up the teaching of experience. With what firstness

> The scarfed bark puts from her native bay;

with what secondness

> doth she return,
> With overweathered ribs and ragged sails.

But familiar as the notion is, and compelled as we are to acknowledge it at every turn, still we never can realize it; we never can be immediately conscious of finiteness, or of anything but a divine freedom that in its own original firstness knows no bounds.

First and Second, Agent and Patient, Yes and No, are categories which enable us roughly to describe the facts of experience, and they satisfy the mind for a very long time. But at last they are found inadequate, and the Third is the conception which is then called for. The Third is that which bridges over the chasm between the absolute first and last, and brings them into relationship. We are told that every science has its Qualitative and its Quantitative stage; now its qualitative stage is when dual distinctions,—whether a given subject has a given predicate or not,—suffice; the quantitative stage comes when, no longer content with such rough distinctions, we require to insert a possible half-way between every two possible conditions of the subject in regard to its possession of the quality indicated by the predicate. Ancient mechanics recognized forces as causes which produced motions as their immediate effects, looking no further than the essentially dual relation of cause and effect. That was why it could make no progress with dynamics. The work of Galileo and his successors lay in showing that forces are accelerations by which a state of velocity is gradually brought about. The words "cause" and "effect" still linger, but the old conceptions have been dropped from mechanical philosophy; for the fact now known is that in certain relative positions bodies undergo certain accelerations. Now an acceleration, instead of being like a velocity a relation between two successive positions, is a relation between three; so that the new doctrine has consisted in the suitable introduction of the conception of Threeness. On this idea, the whole of modern physics is built. The superiority of modern geometry, too, has certainly been due to nothing so much as to the bridging over of the innumerable distinct cases with which the ancient science was encumbered; and we may go so far as to say that all the great steps in the method of science in every department have consisted in bringing into relation cases previously discrete.

We can easily recognize the man whose thought is mainly in the dual stage by his unmeasured use of language. In former days, when he was natural, everything with him was unmitigated, absolute, ineffable, utter, matchless, supreme, unqualified, root and branch; but now that it is the fashion to be depreciatory, he is just as plainly marked by the ridiculous inadequacy of his expressions. The principle of contradiction is a shibboleth for such minds; to disprove a proposition they will always try to prove there lurks a contradiction in it, notwithstanding that it may be as clear and comprehensible as the day. Remark for your amusement the grand unconcern with which mathematics, since the invention of the calculus, has pursued its way, caring no more for the peppering of contradiction-mongers than an ironclad for an American fort.

We have seen that it is the immediate consciousness that is preeminently first, the external dead thing that is preeminently second. In like manner, it is evidently the representation mediating between these two that is preeminently third. Other examples, however, should not be neglected. The first is agent, the second patient, the third is the action by which the former influences the latter. Between the beginning as first, and the end as last, comes the process which leads from first to last.

According to the mathematicians, when we measure along a line, were our yardstick replaced by a yard marked off on an infinitely long rigid bar, then in all the shiftings of it which we make for the purpose of applying it to successive portions of the line to be measured, two points on that bar would remain fixed and unmoved. To that pair of points, the mathematicians accord the title of the absolute; they are the points that are at an infinite distance one way and the other as measured by that yard. These points are either really distinct, coincident, or imaginary (in which case there is but a finite distance completely round the line), according to the relation of the mode of measurement to the nature of the line upon which the measurement is made. These two points are the absolute first and the absolute last or second, while every measurable point on the line is of the nature of a third. We have seen that the conception of the absolute first eludes every attempt to grasp it; and so in another sense does that of the absolute second; but there is no absolute third, for the third is of its own nature relative, and this is what we are always thinking, even when we aim at the first or second. The starting-point of the universe, God the Creator, is the Absolute First; the terminus of the universe, God completely revealed, is the Absolute Second; every state of the universe at a measurable point of time is the third. If you think the measurable is all there is, and deny it any definite tendency whence or whither, then you are considering the pair of points that makes the absolute to be imaginary and are an Epicurean. If you hold that there is a definite drift to the course of nature as a whole, but yet believe its absolute end is nothing but the nirvana from which it set out, you make the two points of the absolute to be coincident, and are a pessimist. But if your creed is that the whole universe is approaching in the infinitely distant future a state having a general character different from that toward which we look back in the infinitely distant past, you make the absolute to consist in two distinct real points and are an evolutionist.[1]

This is one of the matters concerning which a man can only learn from his own reflections, but I believe that if my suggestions are followed out, the reader will grant that One, Two, Three, are more than mere count-words like "eeny, meeny, miny, mo," but carry vast, though vague ideas.

But it will be asked, why stop at three? Why not go on to find a new conception in Four, Five, and so on indefinitely? The reason is that while it is impossible to form a genuine three by any modification of the pair, without introducing something of a different nature from the unit and the pair, four, five, and every higher number can be formed by mere complications of threes. To make this clear, I will first show it in an example. The fact that A presents B with a gift C, is a triple relation, and as such cannot possibly be resolved into any combination of dual relations. Indeed, the very idea of a combination involves that of thirdness, for a combination is something which is what it is owing to the parts which it brings into mutual relationship. But we may waive that consideration, and still we cannot build up the fact that A presents C to

1. The last view is essentially that of Christian theology, too. The theologians hold the physical universe to be finite, but considering that universe which they will admit to have existed from all time, it would appear to be in a different condition in the end from what it was in the beginning, the whole spiritual creation having been accomplished, and abiding.

B by any aggregate of dual relations between *A* and *B*, *B* and *C*, and *C* and *A*. *A* may enrich *B*, *B* may receive *C*, and *A* may part with *C*, and yet *A* need not necessarily give *C* to *B*. For that, it would be necessary that these three dual relations should not only coexist, but be welded into one fact. Thus, we see that a triad cannot be analyzed into dyads. But now I will show by an example that a four can be analyzed into threes. Take the quadruple fact that *A* sells *C* to *B* for the price *D*. This is a compound of two facts: 1st, that *A* makes with *C* a certain transaction, which we may name *E*; and 2nd, that this transaction *E* is a sale of *B* for the price *D*. Each of these two facts is a triple fact, and their combination makes up [as] genuine [a] quadruple fact as can be found. The explanation of this striking difference is not far to seek. A dual relative term, such as "lover" or "Tservaut," is a sort of blank form, where there are two places left blank. I mean that in building a sentence round lover, as the principal word of the predicate, we are at liberty to make anything we see fit the subject, and then, besides that, anything we please the object of the action of loving. But a triple relative term such as "giver" has two correlates, and is thus a blank form with three places left blank. Consequently, we can take two of these triple relatives and fill up one blank place in each with the same letter, *X*, which has only the force of a pronoun or identifying index, and then the two taken together will form a whole having four blank places; and from that we can go on in a similar way to any higher number. But when we attempt to imitate this proceeding with dual relatives, and combine two of them by means of an X, we find we only have two blank places in the combination, just as we had in either of the relatives taken by itself. A road with only three-way forkings may have any number of termini, but no number of straight roads put end on end will give more than two termini. Thus any number, however large, can be built out of triads; and consequently no idea can be involved in such a number, radically different from the idea of three. I do not mean to deny that the higher numbers may present interesting special configurations from which notions may be derived of more or less general applicability; but these cannot rise to the height of philosophical categories so fundamental as those that have been considered.

The argument of this book has been developed in the mind of the author, substantially as it is presented, as a following out of these three conceptions, in a sort of game of follow my leader from one field of thought into another. Their importance was originally brought home to me in the study of logic, where they play so remarkable a part that I was led to look for them in psychology. Finding them there again, I could not help asking myself whether they did not enter into the physiology of the nervous system. By drawing a little on hypothesis, I succeeded in detecting them there; and then the question naturally came how they would appear in the theory of protoplasm in general. Here I seemed to break into an interesting avenue of reflections giving instructive aperçus both into the nature of protoplasm and into the conceptions themselves; though it was not till later that I mapped out my thoughts on the subject as they are presented in Chapter IV. I had no difficulty in following the lead into the domain of natural selection; and once arrived at that point, I was irresistibly carried on to speculations concerning physics. One bold saltus landed me in a garden of fruitful and beautiful suggestions, the exploration of which long prevented my looking further. As soon, however, as I was induced to look further, and to examine the application of the three ideas to the deepest problems of the soul, nature, and God, I saw at once that they must carry me far into the heart of those primeval mysteries. That is the way the book has grown in my mind: it is also the order in which I have written it; and only this first chapter is more or less an afterthought, since at an earlier stage of my studies I should have looked upon the matter here set down as too vague to have any value. I should have discerned in it too strong a resemblance to many a crack-brained book that I had laughed over. A deeper study has taught me that even out of the mouths of babes and sucklings strength may be brought forth, and that weak metaphysical trash has sometimes contained the germs of conceptions capable of growing up into important and positive doctrines.

Thus, the whole book being nothing but a continual exemplification of the triad of ideas, we need linger no longer upon this preliminary exposition of them. There is, however, one feature of them upon which it is quite indispensable to dwell. It is that there are two distinct grades of secondness and three grades of thirdness. There is a close analogy to this in geometry. Conic sections are either the curves usually so called, or they are pairs of straight lines. A pair of straight lines is called a degenerate conic. So plane cubic curves are either the genuine curves of the third order, or they are conics paired with straight lines, or they consist of three straight lines; so that there are the two orders of degenerate cubics. Nearly in this same way, besides genuine secondness, there is a degenerate sort which does not exist as such, but is only so conceived. The medieval logicians (following a hint of Aristotle) distinguished between real relations and relations of reason. A real relation subsists in virtue of a fact which would be totally impossible were either of the related objects destroyed; while a relation of reason subsists in virtue of two facts, one only of which would disappear on the annihilation of either of the relates. Such are all resemblances: for any two objects in nature resemble each other, and indeed in themselves just as much as any other two; it is only with reference to our senses and needs that one resemblance counts for more than another. Rumford and Franklin resembled each other by virtue of being both Americans; but either would have been just as much an American if the other had never lived. On the other hand, the fact that Cain killed Abel cannot be stated as a mere aggregate of two facts one concerning Cain and the other concerning Abel. Resemblances are not the only relations of reason, though they have that character in an eminent degree. Contrasts and comparisons are of the same sort. Resemblance is an identity of characters; and this is the same as to say that the mind gathers the resembling ideas together into one conception. Other relations of reason arise from ideas being connected by the mind in other ways; they consist in the relation between two parts of one complex concept, or, as we may say, in the relation of a complex concept to itself, in respect to two of its parts. This brings us to consider a sort of degenerate secondness that does not fulfill the definition of a relation of reason. Identity is the relation that everything bears to itself: Lucullus dines with Lucullus. Again, we speak of allurements and motives in the language of forces, as though a man suffered compulsion from within. So with the voice of conscience: and we observe our own feelings by a reflective sense. An echo is my own voice coming back to answer itself. So also, we speak of the abstract quality of a thing as if it were some second thing that the first thing possesses. But the relations of reason and these self-relations are alike in this, that they arise from the mind setting one part of a notion into relation to another. All degenerate seconds may be conveniently termed Internal, in contrast to External seconds, which are constituted by external fact, and are true actions of one thing upon another.

Among thirds, there are two degrees of degeneracy. The first is where there is in the fact itself no thirdness or mediation, but where there is true duality; the second degree is where there is not even true secondness in the fact itself.

Consider, first, the thirds degenerate in the first degree. A pin fastens two things together by sticking through one and also through the other: either might be annihilated, and the pin would continue to stick through the one which remained. A mixture brings its ingredients together by containing each. We may term these accidental thirds. "How did I slay thy son?" asked the merchant, and the genie replied, "When thou threwest away the date-stone, it smote my son who was passing at the time, on the breast, and he died forthright." Here there were two independent facts, first that the merchant threw away the date-stone, and second that the date-stone struck and killed the genie's son. Had it been aimed at him, the case would have been different; for then there would have been a relation of aiming which would have connected together the aimer, the thing aimed, and the object aimed at, in one fact. What monstrous injustice and inhumanity on the part of that genie to hold that poor merchant responsible for such an accident! I remember how I wept at it, as I lay in my father's arms and he first told me the story. It is certainly just that a man, even though he had no evil intention, should be held responsible for the immediate effects of his actions; but not for such as might result from them in a sporadic case here and there, but only for such as might have been guarded against by a reasonable rule of prudence. Nature herself often supplies the place of the intention of a rational agent in making a thirdness genuine and not merely accidental; as when a spark, as third, falling into a barrel of gunpowder, as first, causes an explosion, as second. But how does nature do this? By virtue of an intelligible law according to which she acts. If two forces are combined according to the parallelogram of forces, their resultant is a real third. Yet any force may, by the parallelogram of forces, be mathematically resolved into the sum of two others, in an infinity of different ways. Such components, however, are mere creations of the mind. What is the difference? As far as one isolated event goes, there is none; the real forces are no more present in the resultant than any components that the mathematician may imagine. But what makes the real forces really there is the general law of nature which calls for them, and not for any other components of the resultant. Thus, intelligibility, or reason objectified, is what makes thirdness genuine.

We now come to thirds degenerate in the second degree. The dramatist Marlowe had something of that character of diction in which Shakespeare and Bacon agree. This is a trivial example; but the mode of relation is important. In natural history, intermediate types serve to bring out the resemblance between forms whose similarity might otherwise escape attention, or not be duly appreciated. In portraiture, photographs mediate between the original and the likeness. In science, a diagram or analogue of the observed fact leads on to a further analogy. The relations of reason which go to the formation of such a triple relation need not be all resemblances. Washington was eminently free from the faults in which most great soldiers resemble one another. A centaur is a mixture of a man and a horse. Philadelphia lies between New York and Washington. Such thirds may be called Intermediate thirds or Thirds of comparison.

Nobody will suppose that I wish to claim any originality in reckoning the triad important in philosophy. Since Hegel, almost every fanciful thinker has done the same. Originality is the last of recommendations for fundamental conceptions. On the contrary, the fact that the minds of men have ever been inclined to threefold divisions is one of the considerations in favor of them. Other numbers have been objects of predilection to this philosopher and that, but three has been prominent at all times and with all schools. My whole method will be found to be in profound contrast with that of Hegel; I reject his philosophy *in toto*. Nevertheless, I have a certain sympathy with it, and fancy that if its author had only noticed a very few circumstances he would himself have been led to revolutionize his system. One of these is the double division or dichotomy of the second idea of the triad. He has usually overlooked external secondness, altogether. In other words, he has committed the trifling oversight of forgetting that there is a real world with real actions and reactions. Rather a serious oversight that. Then Hegel had the misfortune to be unusually deficient in mathematics. He shows this in the very elementary character of his reasoning. Worse still, while the whole burden of his song is that philosophers have neglected to take thirdness into account, which is true enough of the theological kind, with whom alone he was acquainted (for I do not call it acquaintance to look into a book without comprehending it), he unfortunately did not know, what it would have been of the utmost consequence for him to know, that the mathematical analysts had in great measure escaped this great fault, and that the thorough-going pursuit of the ideas and methods of the differential calculus would be sure to cure it altogether. Hegel's dialectical method is only a feeble and rudimentary application of the principles of the calculus to metaphysics. Finally Hegel's plan of evolving everything out of the abstractest conception by a dialectical procedure, though far from being so absurd as the experientialists think, but on the contrary representing one of the indispensable parts of the course of science, overlooks the weakness of individual man, who wants the strength to wield such a weapon as that.

CHAPTER V. *The Triad in Physiology.*

Granted that there are three fundamentally different kinds of consciousness, it follows as a matter of course that there must be something threefold in the physiology of the nervous system to account for them. No materialism is implied in this, further than that intimate dependence of the action of the mind upon the body, which every student of the subject must and does now acknowledge. Once more a prediction, as it were, is made by the theory; that is to say, certain consequences, not contemplated in the construction thereof, necessarily result from it; and these are of such a character that their truth or falsehood can be independently investigated. Were we to find them strikingly and certainly true, a remarkable confirmation of the theory would be afforded. So much as this, however, I cannot promise; I can only say that they are not certainly false; and we must be content to trace out these consequences, and see what they are, and leave them to the future judgment of physiologists.

Two of the three kinds of consciousness, indeed, the simple and dual, receive an instant physiological explanation. We know that the protoplasmic content of every nerve-cell has its active and passive conditions, and argument is unnecessary to show that Feeling, or immediate consciousness, arises in an active state of nerve-cells. Experiments on the effects of cutting the nerves show that there is no feeling after communication with the central nerve-cells is severed, so that the phenomenon has certainly some connection with the nerve-cells; and feeling is excited by just such stimuli as would be likely to throw protoplasm into an active condition. Thus, though we cannot say that every nerve-cell in its active condition has feeling (which we cannot deny, however) there is scarce room to doubt that the activity of nerve-cells is the main physiological requisite for consciousness. On the other hand, the sense of action and reaction, or the polar sense, as we agreed to call it, is plainly connected with the discharge of nervous energy through the nerve-fibres. External volition, the most typical case of it, involves such a discharge into muscle cells. In external sensation, where the polar sense enters in a lower intensity, there is a discharge from the terminal nerve-cell through the afferent nerve upon a cell or cells in the brain. In internal volition, or self-control, there is some inhibitory action of the nerves, which is also known to involve the movement of nervous force; and in internal observation, or visceral sensation, there are doubtless transfers of energy from one central cell to another. Remembering that the polar sense is the sense of the difference between what was before and what is after a dividing instant, or the sense of an instant as having sides, we see clearly that the physiological concomitant of it must be some event which happens very quickly and leaves a more abiding effect, and this description suits the passage of a nervous discharge over a nerve-fibre so perfectly, that I do not think we need hesitate to set this phenomenon down as the condition of dual consciousness.

Synthetic consciousness offers a more difficult problem. Yet the explanation of the genuine form of that consciousness, the sense of learning, is easy enough; it is only the degenerate modes, the sense of similarity, and the sense of real connection, which oblige us to hesitate. With regard to these two degenerate forms, I am driven to make hypotheses.

When two ideas resemble one another, we say that they have something in common; a part of the one is said to be identical with a part of the other. In what does that identity consist? Having closed both eyes, I open first one and then shut it and open the other, and I say that the two sensations are alike. How can the impressions of two nerves be judged to be alike? It appears to me that in order that that should become possible, the two nerve-cells must probably discharge themselves into one common nerve-cell. In any case, it seems to me that the first supposition to make, for scientific observation to confirm or reject, is that two ideas are alike so far as the same nerve-cells have been concerned in the production of them. In short, the hypothesis is that resemblance consists in the identity of a common element, and that that identity lies in a part of the one idea and a part of the other idea being the feeling peculiar to the excitation of one or more nerve-cells.

When we find ourselves under a compulsion to think that two elements of experience which do not particularly resemble one another are, nevertheless, really connected, that connection must, I think, be due in some way, to a discharge of nerve-energy; for the whole sense of reality is a determination of polar consciousness, which is itself due to such discharges. For example, I recognize that a certain surface, on one side of a certain boundary is red, and on the other side is blue; or that any two qualities are immediately contiguous in space or time. If the contiguity is in time, it is by the polar sense directly that we are conscious of a dividing instant with its difference on the two sides. If the contiguity is in space, I think we have at first a completely confused feeling of the whole, as yet unanalyzed and unsynthesized, but afterward, when the analysis has been made, we find ourselves compelled, in recomposing the elements, to pass directly from what is on one side of the boundary to what is on the other. I suppose then that we are compelled to think the two feelings as contiguous because the nerve-cell whose excitation produces the feeling of one recalled sensation discharges itself into the nerve-cell whose excitation makes the feeling of the other recalled sensation.

The genuine synthetic consciousness, or the sense of the process of learning, which is the preeminent ingredient and quintessence of reason, has its physiological basis quite evidently in the most characteristic property of the nervous system, the power of taking habits. This depends on five principles, as follows. 1st, when a stimulus or irritation is continued for some time, the excitation spreads from the cells directly affected to those that are associated with it, and from those to others, and so on, and at the same time increases in intensity. 2nd, after a time, fatigue begins to set in. Now besides the utter fatigue which consists in the cell's losing all excitability, and the nervous system refusing to react to the stimulus at all, there is a gentler fatigue, which plays a very important part in adapting the brain to serving as an organ of reason, this form of fatigue consisting in the reflex action or discharge of the nerve-cell ceasing to go on one path and either beginning on a path where there had been no discharge, or increasing the intensity of the discharge along a path on which there had been previously only a slight discharge. For example, one may sometimes see a frog whose cerebrum or brain has been removed, and whose hind leg has been irritated by putting a drop of acid upon it, after repeatedly rubbing the place with the other foot, as if to wipe off the acid, may at length be observed to give several hops, the first avenue of nervous discharge having become fatigued. 3rd, when, from any cause the stimulus to a nerve-cell is removed, the excitation quickly subsides. That it does not do so instantly is well-known, and the phenomenon goes among physicists by the name of persistence of sensation. All noticeable feeling subsides in a fraction of a second, but a very small remnant continues for a much longer time. 4th, if the same cell which was once excited, and which by some chance had happened to discharge itself along a certain path or paths, comes to get excited a second time, it is more likely to discharge itself the second time along some or all of those paths along which it had previously discharged itself than it would have been had it not so discharged itself before. This is the central principle of habit; and the striking contrast of its modality to that of any mechanical law is most significant. The laws of physics know nothing of tendencies or probabilities; whatever they require at all they require absolutely and without fail, and they are never disobeyed. Were the tendency to take habits replaced by an absolute requirement that the cell should discharge itself always in the same way, or according to any rigidly fixed condition whatever, all possibility of habit developing into intelligence would be cut off at the outset; the virtue of thirdness would be absent. It is essential that there should be an element of chance in some sense as to how the cell shall discharge itself; and then that this chance or uncertainty shall not be entirely obliterated by the principle of habit, but only somewhat affected. 5th, when a considerable time has elapsed without a nerve having reacted in any particu-

lar way, there comes in a principle of forgetfulness or negative habit rendering
it the less likely to react in that way. Now let us see what will be the result of
these five principles taken in combination. When a nerve is stimulated, if the
reflex activity is not at first of the right sort to remove the source of irritation,
it will change its character again and again until the cause of irritation is
removed, when the activity will quickly subside. When the nerve comes to be
stimulated a second time in the same way, probably some of the other movements which had been made on the first occasion will be repeated; but, however this may be, one of them must ultimately be repeated, for the activity
will continue until this does occur, I mean that movement which removes the
source of irritation. On a third occasion, the process of forgetfulness will have
been begun in regard to any tendency to repeat any of the actions of the first
occasion which were not repeated on the second. Of those which were repeated, some will probably be repeated again, and some not; but always there
remains that one which must be repeated before the activity comes to an end.
The ultimate effect of this will inevitably be that a habit gets established of at
once reacting in the way which removes the source of irritation; for this habit
alone will be strengthened at each repetition of the experiment, while every
other will tend to become weakened at an accelerated rate.

I have invented a little game or experiment with playing-cards to illustrate
the working of these principles; and I can promise the reader that if he will
try it half a dozen times he will be better able to estimate the value of the
account of habit here proposed. The rules of this game are as follows. Take a
good many cards of four suits, say a pack of 52, though fewer will do. The
four suits are supposed to represent four modes in which a cell may react. Let
one suit, say spades, represent that mode of reaction which removes the
source of irritation and brings the activity to an end. In order readily to find a
card of any suit as wanted, you had better lay all the cards down face up and
distributed into four packets, each containing the cards of one suit only. Now
take 2 spades, 2 diamonds, 2 clubs, and 2 hearts, to represent the original
disposition of the nerve-cell, which is supposed to be equally likely to react
in any of the four ways. You turn these 8 cards face down and shuffle them
with extreme thoroughness.[2] Then turn up cards from the top of this pack,

2. Cards are almost never shuffled enough to illustrate fairly the principles of
probabilities; but if after being shuffled in any of the usual ways, they are dealt into
three packs and taken up again, and then passed from one hand into the other one by
one, every other one going to the top and every other to the bottom of the pack that
thus accumulates in the second hand, and finally cut, the shuffling may be considered

one by one until a spade is reached. This process represents the reaction of the cell. Take up the cards just dealt off, and add to the pack held in the hand one card of each of those suits that have just been turned up (for habit) and remove from the pack one card of each suit not turned up (for forgetfulness). Shuffle, and go through with this operation 13 times or until the spades are exhausted. It will then generally be found that you hold nothing but spades in your hand.

Thus we see how these principles not only lead to the establishment of habits, but to habits directed to definite ends, namely the removal of sources of irritation. Now it is precisely action according to final causes which distinguishes mental from mechanical action; and the general formula of all our desires may be taken as this: to remove a stimulus. Every man is busily working to bring to an end that state of things which now excites him to work.

---

as sufficient for the purpose of this game. Whenever the direction is to shuffle, shuffling as thorough as this is meant.

James's Psychology

Peirce and William James were lifelong friends, but Peirce believed that James's pragmatism was flawed by a simplistic empiricism. The basis of this difference between them lay in Peirce's semiotic and was made clear in his review of James's famous book *The Principles of Psychology* (1890). James argued that perception was a fundamentally empirical, or experiential, process. Consciousness, therefore, was just what it seemed to be—according to James, the perception of a continuous stream of thought. James therefore attacked as unempirical and unscientific both the Lockean description of thinking as a process of associating atomistic ideas and also later descriptions of perception as a process of unconscious inference. These arguments were fundamentally antagonistic to the view that Peirce had held ever since his 1868 essay "Questions concerning Certain Faculties Claimed for Man," where he argued that knowledge of the meaning of our thoughts is as indirect and mediated as our perception of external objects. A thought is a sign requiring interpretation by a subsequent thought in order to achieve meaning. Therefore, perception which, unlike sensation, has form or meaning must involve inference. To the degree that perception does not appear to be inference, it must be unconscious inference. Because Peirce associated the view that thinking could be nothing other than what it appeared to be with Descartes's belief in the mind's immediate knowledge of its thoughts, Peirce called James a Cartesian.

Source: *The Nation* 53 (July 2 and 9, 1891): 15 and 32–33.

   Upon this vast work no definitive judgment can be passed for a long time; yet it is probably safe to say that it is the most important contribution that has been made to the subject for many years. Certainly it is one of the most weighty productions of American thought. The directness and sharpness with which we shall state some objections to it must be understood as a tribute of respect.

Beginning with the most external and insignificant characters, we cannot much admire it as a piece of bookmaking; for it misses the unity of an essay, and almost that of a connected series of essays, while not attaining the completeness of a thorough treatise. It is a large assortment of somewhat heterogeneous articles loosely tied up in one bag, with tendencies towards sprawling.

With an extraordinarily racy and forcible style, Prof. James is continually wresting words and phrases of exact import to unauthorized and unsuitable uses. He indulges himself with idiosyncrasies of diction and tricks of language such as usually spring up in households of great talent. To illustrate what we mean, we will open one of the volumes at random, and we come upon this: "A statement *ad hominem* meant as part of a reduction to the absurd." Now a *reductio ad absurdum* is a species of demonstration, and as such can contain no *argumentum ad hominem*, which is merely something a man is obliged by his personal interests to admit. On the next page, we read: "This dynamic (we had almost written dynamitic) way of representing knowledge." On the next page: "They talk as if, with this miraculous tying or 'relating,' the Ego's duties were done." It is the same with the technical terms of psychology. Speaking of certain theories, our author says they "carry us back to times when the soul as vehicle of consciousness was not discriminated, as it now is, from the vital principle presiding over the formation of the body." How can anybody write so who knows the technical meaning of *vehicle*? On the same page occurs this phrase, "If unextended, it is absurd to speak of its having space relations at all," which sounds like a general attack on the geometry of points.

Prof. James's thought is highly original, or at least novel; but it is originality of the destructive kind. To prove that we do not know what it has been generally supposed that we did know, that given premises do not justify the conclusions which all other thinkers hold they do justify, is his peculiar function. For this reason the book should have been preceded by an introduction discussing the strange positions in logic upon which all its arguments turn. Even when new theories are proposed, they are based on similar negative or sceptical considerations, and the one thing upon which Prof. James seems to pin his faith is the general incomprehensibility of things. He clings as passionately to that as the old lady of the anecdote did to her total depravity. Of course, he is materialistic to the core—that is to say, in a methodical sense, but not religiously, since he does not deny a separable soul nor a future life; for materialism is that form of philosophy which may safely be relied upon to leave the universe as incomprehensible as it finds it. It is possible that Prof. James would protest against this characterization of his cast of mind. Brought up under the guidance of an eloquent apostle of a form of Swedenborgianism, which is materialism driven deep and clinched on the inside, and educated to the materialistic profession, it can only be by great natural breadth of mind that he can know what materialism is, by having experienced some thoughts that are not materialistic. He inclines towards Cartesian dualism, which is of the true strain of the incomprehensibles and modern materialism's own mother. There is no form of idealism with which he will condescend to argue. Even evolutionism, which has idealistic affinities, seems to be held for suspect. It is his *métier* to subject to severe investigation any doctrine whatever which smells of intelligibility.

The keynote of this is struck in the preface, in these words:

"I have kept close to the point of view of natural science throughout the book. Every natural science assumes certain data uncritically, and declines to challenge the elements between which its own 'laws' obtain, and from which its deductions are carried on. Psychology, the science of finite individual minds, assumes as its data (1) *thoughts and feelings*, and (2) a *physical world* in time and space with which they coexist and which (3) *they know*. Of course these data themselves are discussable; but the discussion of them (as of other elements) is called metaphysics, and falls outside the province of this book. This book, assuming that thoughts and feelings exist, and are the vehicles of knowledge, thereupon contends that Psychology, when she has ascertained the empirical correlation of the various sorts of thought and feeling with definite conditions of the brain, can go no farther—can go no farther, that is, as a natural science. If she goes farther, she becomes metaphysical. All attempts to explain our phenomenally given thoughts as products of deeper-lying entities (whether the latter be named 'Soul,' 'Transcendental Ego,' 'Ideas,' or 'Elementary Units of Consciousness') are metaphysical. This book consequently rejects both the associationist and the spiritualist theories; and in this strictly positivistic point of view consists the only feature of it for which I feel tempted to claim originality."

This is certainly well put—considered as prestigiation. But when we remember that a natural science is not a person, and consequently does not "decline" to do anything, the argument evaporates. It is only the students of the science who can "decline," and they are not banded together to repress any species of inquiry. Each investigator does what in him lies; and declines to do a thousand things most pertinent to the subject. To call a branch of an inquiry "metaphysical" is merely a mode of objurgation, which signifies nothing but the author's personal distaste for that part of his subject. It does not in the least prove that considerations of that sort can throw no light on the questions he has to consider. Indeed, we suspect it might be difficult to show in any way that any two branches of knowledge should be allowed to throw no light on one another. Far less can calling one question scientific and another metaphysical warrant Prof. James in "consequently *rejecting*" certain conclusions, against which he has nothing better to object. Nor is it in the least true that physicists confine themselves to such a "strictly positivistic point of view." Students of heat are not deterred by the impossibility of directly observing molecules from considering and accepting the kinetical theory; students of light do not brand speculations on the luminiferous ether as metaphysical; and the substantiality of matter itself is called in question in the vortex theory, which is nevertheless considered as perfectly germane to physics. All these are "attempts to explain phenomenally given elements as products of deeper-lying entities." In fact, this phrase describes, as well as loose language can, the general character of scientific hypotheses.

Remark, too, that it is not merely nor chiefly the "soul" and the "transcendental ego," for which incomprehensibles he has some tenderness, that Prof. James proposes to banish from psychology, but especially *ideas* which their adherents maintain are direct data of consciousness. In short, not only does he propose, by the simple expedient of declaring certain inquiries extra-psychological, to reverse the conclusions of the science upon many important points, but also by the same negative means to decide upon the character of its data. Indeed, when we come to examine the book, we find it is precisely this which is the main use the author makes of his new principle. The notion that the natural sciences accept their data *uncritically* we hold to be a serious mistake. It is true, scientific men do not subject their observations to the kind of criticism practised by the high-flying philosophers, because they do not believe that method of criticism sound. If they really believed in idealism, they would bring it to bear upon physics as much as possible. But in fact they find it a wordy doctrine, not susceptible of any scientific applications. When, however, a physicist has to investigate, say, such a subject as the scintillation of the stars, the first thing he does is to subject the phenomena to rigid criticism to find whether these phenomena are objective or subjective, whether they are in the light itself, or arise in the eye, or in original principles of mental action, or in idiosyncrasies of the imagination, etc. The principle of the uncritical acceptance of data, to which Prof. James clings, practically amounts to a claim to a new kind of liberty of thought, which would make a complete rupture with accepted methods of psychology and of science in general. The truth of this is seen in the chief application that has been made of the new method, in the author's theory of space-perception. And into the enterprise of thus revolutionizing scientific method he enters with a light heart, without any exhaustive scrutiny of his new logic in its generality, relying only on the resources of the moment. He distinctly discourages a separate study of the method. "No rules can be laid down in advance. Comparative observations, to be definite, must usually be made to test some preëxisting hypothesis; and the only thing then is to use as much sagacity as you possess, and to be as candid as you can."

We have no space for any analysis of the contents of this work, nor is that necessary, for everybody interested in the subject must and will read the book. It discusses most of the topics of psychology in an extremely unequal way, but always interesting and always entertaining. We will endeavor to give a fair specimen of the author's critical method (for the work is essentially a criticism and exposition of critical principles), with a running commentary, to aid a judgment. For this purpose we will select a short section entitled "Is Perception Unconscious Inference?" Perception in its most characteristic features is, of course, a matter of association in a wide sense of that term. If two spots of light are thrown upon the wall of a dark room so as to be adjacent, and one of these is made red while the other remains white, the white one will appear greenish by contrast. If they are viewed through a narrow tube, and this is moved so that the red spot goes out of view, still the white one will continue to look green. But if the red light, now unseen, be extinguished and we then remove the tube from the eye, so as to take a new look, as it were, the apparent greenness will suddenly vanish. This is an example of a thousand phenomena which have led several German psychologists to declare that the process of perception is one of reasoning in a generalized sense of that term.

It is possible some of the earlier writers held it to be reasoning, strictly speaking. But most have called it "unconscious inference," and unconscious inference differs essentially from inference in the narrow sense, all our control over which depends upon this, that it involves a conscious, though it may be an indistinct, reference to a genus of arguments. These German writers must also not be understood as meaning that the perceptive process is any more inferential than are the rest of the processes which the English have so long explained by association—a theory which until quite recently played little part in German psychology. The German writers alluded to explain an ordinary suggestion productive of belief, or any cognition tantamount to belief, as inference conscious or unconscious, as a matter of course. As German writers are generally weak in their formal logic, they would be apt to formulate the inference wrongly; but the correct formulation is as follows:

A well-recognized kind of object, M, has for its ordinary predicates P^1, P^2, P^3, etc., indistinctly recognized.

The suggesting object, S, has these same predicates, P^1, P^2, P^3, etc.

Hence, S is of the kind M.

This is hypothetic inference in form. The first premise is not actually thought, though it is in the mind habitually. This, of itself, would not make the inference unconscious. But it is so because it is not recognized as an inference; the conclusion is accepted without our knowing how. In perception, the conclusion has the peculiarity of not being abstractly thought, but actually seen, so that it is not exactly a judgment, though it is tantamount to one. The advantage of this method of explaining the process is conceived to be this: To explain any process not understood is simply to show that it is a special case of a wider description of process which is more intelligible. Now nothing is so intelligible as the reasoning process. This is shown by the fact that all explanation assimilates the process to be explained to reasoning. Hence, the logical method of explaining the process of association is looked upon as the most perfect explanation possible. It certainly does not exclude the materialistic English explanation by a property of the nerves. The monist school, to which the modern psychologists mostly belong, conceives the intellectual process of inference and the process of mechanical causation to be only the inside and outside views of the same process. But the idealistic tendency, which tinctures almost all German thought not very recent, would be to regard the logical explanation as the more perfect, under the assumption that the materialistic explanation requires itself ultimately to be explained in terms of the reasoning process. But Prof. James is naturally averse to the logical explanation. Let us see, then, how he argues the point. His first remark is as follows:

"If every time a present sign suggests an absent reality to our mind, we make an inference; and if every time we make an inference, we reason, then perception is indubitably reasoning."

Of course, every psychological suggestion is regarded as of the general nature of inference, but only in a far more general sense than that in which perception is so called. This should be well known to Prof. James, and he would have dealt more satisfactorily with his readers if he had not kept it back. Namely, perception attains a virtual judgment, it subsumes something under a class, and not only so, but virtually attaches to the proposition the seal of assent—two strong resemblances to inference which are wanting in ordinary suggestions. However, Prof. James admits that the process *is* inference in a broad sense. What, then, has he to object to the theory under consideration?

"Only one sees no room in it for any unconscious part. Both associates, the present sign and the contiguous things which it suggests, are above board, and no intermediary ideas are required."

Here are two errors. In the first place, "unconscious inference" does not, either with other logicians or with the advocates of the theory in question, mean an inference in which any proposition or term of the argument is unconscious, any more than "conscious inference" implies that both premises are conscious. But unconscious inference means inference in which the reasoner is not conscious of making an inference. He may be conscious of the premise, but he is not conscious that his acceptance of the conclusion is inferential. He does not make that side-thought which enters into all inference strictly so called: "and so it would be in every analogous case (or in most cases)." There is no doubt, therefore, that ordinary suggestion, regarded as inference, is of the unconscious variety. But Prof. James further forgets his logic in hinting, what he soon expresses more clearly, that such an inference is to be regarded as a mere "immediate inference," because it has no middle term. We might suppose he had never heard of the *modus ponens*, the form of which, *A* and *B* being any proposition, is

If *A*, then *B*;
But *A*:
Hence, *B*.

Those who think a light is thrown upon the ordinary process of suggestion by assimilating it to reasoning, assimilate it to the *modus ponens*. The proposition "If *A*, then *B*," is represented by the association itself, which is not present to consciousness, but exists in the mind in the form of a habit, as all beliefs and general propositions do. The second premise A is the suggesting idea, the conclusion B is the suggested idea.

Already quite off the track, our author now plunges into the jungle in this fashion:

> "Most of those who have upheld the thesis in question have, however, made a more complex supposition. What they have meant is that perception is a *mediate* inference, and that the middle term is unconscious. When the sensation which I have called 'this' is felt, they think that some process like the following runs through the mind:
>
> 'This' is M;
> but M is A;
> therefore 'this' is A."

Those who have upheld the thesis are not in dispute among themselves, as represented. They make no supposition throughout not admitted by all the world. To represent any process of inference now as a *modus ponens*, now as a syllogism with a middle term, is not necessarily taking antagonistic views. As for the syllogism given, it is the weakest mode of supporting the thesis, far more open to attack than the form first given above. But Prof. James makes no headway, even against this. He says:

> "Now there seems no good grounds for supposing this additional wheelwork in the mind. The classification of '*this*' as M is itself an act of perception, and should, if all perception were inference, require a still earlier syllogism for its performance, and so backwards *ad infinitum*."

Not one of the authors whom we have consulted makes the M entirely unconscious; but Prof. James says they do. If so, when he insists that "this is M" is an act of perception, he must mean some ultra-Leibnitzian *unconscious* perception! Has he ever found the German authors maintaining that that kind of perception is inferential? If not, where is his *regressus ad infinitum*? What those authors do say is that M, and with it the two premises, are thrown into the background and shade of consciousness; that "this is M" is a perception, sometimes in the strict sense, sometimes only in that sense in which perception embraces every sensation. They do not hold sensation to be inferential, and consequently do not suppose a *regressus ad infinitum*. But even if they did, there would be no *reductio ad absurdum*, since it is well known to mathematicians that any finite interval contains an infinite number of finite intervals; so that supposing there is no finite limit to the shortness of time required for an intellectual process, an infinite number of them, each occupying a finite time, may be crowded into any time, however short.

The Professor concludes:

"So far, then, from perception being a species of reasoning, properly so called, both it and reasoning are coördinate varieties of that deeper sort of process known psychologically as the association of ideas, and—"

We break the sentence, which goes on to something else, in order to remark that "a species of reasoning properly so called" must be a slip of the pen. For otherwise there would be an *ignoratio elenchi*; nobody ever having claimed that perception is inference in the strict sense of conscious inference. Instead of "a species of reasoning properly so called," we must read "reasoning in a generalized sense." Remembering also that Prof. James began by insisting on extending the controversy to association in general, we may put association in place of perception, and thus the conclusion will be, "so far from association being reasoning in a generalized sense, reasoning is a special kind of association." Who does not see that to say that perception and reasoning are coördinate varieties of association, is to say something in entire harmony with the thesis which Prof. James is endeavoring to combat? To resume:

"—physiologically as the law of habit in the brain. To call perception unconscious reasoning is thus either a useless metaphor or a positively misleading confusion between two different things."

Here the section ends, and in these last words, for the first time in the whole discussion, the real question at issue is at length touched, and it is dismissed with an *ipse dixit*. There is no room for doubt that perception and, more generally, associative suggestion, may truthfully be considered as inference in a generalized sense; the only question is whether there is any use in so considering them. Had Prof. James succeeded in establishing his *regressus ad infinitum*, he would have refuted himself effectually, since it would then have been shown that an important consequence, not otherwise known, had been drawn from the theory. As it is, he says nothing pertinent either pro or con. But a little before, when an unconscious predication was called perception, was this perception "properly so called"? And if not, was calling it by that name a "useless metaphor," or was it a "positively misleading confusion between two different things"?

14

. . .

Man's Glassy Essence

Monists assert that dualists err in attributing mental phenomena to one substance and material phenomena to another. Rather, say monists, mind and matter are different aspects of one substance. Peirce's monism is clear in this essay. He analyzes late-nineteenth-century understanding of matter in order to show that its behavior is not precisely determined or subject to exact mechanical principles. The qualities of feeling and spontaneity traditionally associated with mind might therefore be an "inward" character of all matter. Conversely, regularity of behavior by matter would be due to a principle—habit—that is usually associated with a low intensity of feeling or mentality. Mind or feeling intensifies when a habit is broken, as is likely to happen easily in chemically unstable material such as protoplasm.

Thus far, there was little that was entirely new in Peirce's argument, for many late-nineteenth-century scientists would have agreed with him that thought is feeling and that feeling has a physiological explanation. But as a logician, Peirce could not stop there. To call thought feeling does not explain how thought achieves meaning. The answer to that question lay not in natural science (in the ordinary sense) but in semiotic. Triadic, interpretive relations among signs (feelings) make possible general ideas, which not only constitute human personality or selfhood but, Peirce here concludes, have personality even when they pertain to organizations and institutions.

Source: *The Monist* 3 (October 1892): 1–22.

In *The Monist* for January, 1891, I tried to show what conceptions ought to form the brick and mortar of a philosophical system. Chief among these was that of absolute chance for which I argued again in last April's number.[1] In July, I applied another fundamental idea, that of continuity, to the law of mind. Next in order, I have to elucidate, from the point of view chosen, the relation between the psychical and physical aspects of a substance.

The first step towards this ought, I think, to be the framing of a molecular theory of protoplasm. But before doing that, it seems indispensable to glance at the constitution of matter, in general. We shall, thus, unavoidably make a long detour; but, after all, our pains will not be wasted, for the problems of the papers that are to follow in the series will call for the consideration of the same question.

All physicists are rightly agreed the evidence is overwhelming which shows all sensible matter is composed of molecules in swift motion and exerting enormous mutual attractions, and perhaps repulsions, too. Even Sir William Thompson, Lord Kelvin, who wishes to explode action at a distance and return to the doctrine of a plenum, not only speaks of molecules, but undertakes to assign definite magnitudes to them. The brilliant Judge Stallo, a man who did not always rightly estimate his own qualities in accepting tasks for himself, declared war upon the atomic theory in a book well worth careful perusal. To the old arguments in favor of atoms which he found in Fechner's monograph, he was able to make replies of considerable force, though they were not sufficient to destroy those arguments. But against modern proofs he made no headway at all. These set out from the mechanical theory of heat. Rumford's experiments showed that heat is not a substance. Joule demonstrated that it was a form of energy. The heating of gases under constant volume, and other facts instanced by Rankine, proved that it could not be an energy of strain. This drove physicists to the conclusion that it was a mode of motion. Then it was remembered that John Bernoulli had shown that the pressure of gases could be accounted for by assuming their molecules to be moving uniformly in rectilinear paths. The same hypothesis was now seen to account for Avogadro's law, that in equal volumes of different kinds of gases exposed to the same pressure and temperature are contained equal numbers of molecules. Shortly after, it was found to account for the laws of diffusion and

---

1. I am rejoiced to find, since my last paper was printed, that a philosopher as subtle and profound as Dr. Edmund Montgomery has long been arguing for the same element in the universe. Other world-renowned thinkers, as M. Renouvier and M. Delboeuf, appear to share this opinion.

viscosity of gases, and for the numerical relation between these properties. Finally, Crookes's radiometer furnished the last link in the strongest chain of evidence which supports any physical hypothesis.

Such being the constitution of gases, liquids must clearly be bodies in which the molecules wander in curvilinear paths, while in solids they move in orbits or quasi-orbits. (See my definition *solid* II, I, in the *Century Dictionary*.)

We see that the resistance to compression and to interpenetration between sensible bodies is, by one of the prime propositions of the molecular theory, due in large measure to the kinetical energy of the particles, which must be supposed to be quite remote from one another, on the average, even in solids. This resistance is no doubt influenced by finite attractions and repulsions between the molecules. All the impenetrability of bodies which we can observe is, therefore, a limited impenetrability due to kinetic and positional energy. This being the case, we have no logical right to suppose that absolute impenetrability or the exclusive occupancy of space, belongs to molecules or to atoms. It is an unwarranted hypothesis, not a *vera causa*.[2] Unless we are to give up the theory of energy, finite positional attractions and repulsions between molecules must be admitted. Absolute impenetrability would amount to an infinite repulsion at a certain distance. No analogy of known phenomena exists to excuse such a wanton violation of the principle of continuity as such a hypothesis is. In short, we are logically bound to adopt the Boscovichian idea that an atom is simply a distribution of component potential energy throughout space, (this distribution being absolutely rigid,) combined with inertia. The potential energy belongs to two molecules, and is to be conceived as different between molecules *A* and *B* from what it is between molecules *A* and *C*. The distribution of energy is not necessarily spherical. Nay, a molecule may conceivably have more than one centre; it may even have a central curve, returning into itself. But I do not think there are any observed facts pointing to such multiple or linear centres. On the other hand, many facts relating to crystals, especially those observed by Voigt,[3] go to show that the distribution of energy is harmonical but not concentric. We can easily calcu-

2. By a *vera causa*, in the logic of science, is meant a state of things known to exist in some cases and supposed to exist in other cases, because it would account for observed phenomena.

3. Wiedemann, *Annalen* [*Annalen der Physik und Chemie*, edited by Gustav Heinrich Wiedemann], 1887–1889.

late the forces which such atoms must exert upon one another by considering[4] that they are equivalent to aggregations of pairs of electrically positive and negative points infinitely near to one another. About such an atom there would be regions of positive and of negative potential, and the number and distribution of such regions would determine the valency of the atom, a number which it is easy to see would in many cases be somewhat indeterminate. I must not dwell further upon this hypothesis, at present. In another paper, its consequences will be further considered.

I cannot assume that the students of philosophy who read this magazine are thoroughly versed in modern molecular physics, and therefore it is proper to mention that the governing principle in this branch of science is Clausius's law of the virial. I will first state the law, and then explain the peculiar terms of the statement. This statement is that the total kinetic energy of the particles of a system in stationary motion is equal to the total virial. By a *system* is here meant a number of particles acting upon one another.[5] Stationary motion is a quasi-orbital motion among a system of particles so that none of them are removed to indefinitely great distances nor acquire indefinitely great velocities. The kinetic energy of a particle is the work which would be required to bring it to rest, independently of any forces which may be acting upon it. The virial of a pair of particles is half the work which the force which actually operates between them would do if, being independent of the distance, it were to bring them together. The equation of the virial is

$$\frac{1}{2}\sum mv^2 = \frac{1}{2}\sum\sum Rr.$$

Here m is the mass of a particle, v its velocity, R is the attraction between two particles, and r is the distance between them. The sign Σ on the left hand side signifies that the values of mv^2 are to be summed for all the particles,

4. See [James Clerk] Maxwell on Spherical Harmonics, in his *Electricity and Magnetism* [Oxford: Clarendon Press, 1892].

5. The word *system* has three peculiar meanings in mathematics. (*A.*) It means an orderly exposition of the truths of astronomy, and hence a theory of the motions of the stars; as the Ptolemaic *system*, the Copernican *system*. This is much like the sense in which we speak of the Calvinistic *system* of theology, the Kantian *system* of philosophy, etc. (*B.*) It means the aggregate of the planets considered as all moving in somewhat the same way, as the solar *system*; and hence any aggregate of particles moving under mutual forces. (*C.*) It means a number of forces acting simultaneously upon a number of particles.

and $\Sigma\Sigma$ on the right hand side signifies that the values of Rr are to be summed for all the pairs of particles. If there is an external pressure P (as from the atmosphere) upon the system, and the volume of vacant space within the boundary of that pressure is V, then the virial must be understood as including $\frac{3}{2}PV$, so that the equation is

$$\frac{1}{2}\Sigma mv^2 = \frac{3}{2}PV + \frac{1}{2}\Sigma\Sigma Rr.$$

There is strong (if not demonstrative) reason for thinking that the temperature of any body above the absolute zero ($-273°$C.), is proportional to the average kinetic energy of its molecules, or say $a\theta$, where a is a constant and θ is the absolute temperature. Hence, we may write the equation

$$a\theta = \frac{1}{2}\overline{mv^2} = \frac{3}{2}\overline{PV} + \frac{1}{2}\Sigma\overline{Rr}$$

where the heavy lines above the different expressions signify that the average values for single molecules are to be taken. In 1872, a student in the University of Leyden, Van der Waals, propounded in his thesis for the doctorate a specialisation of the equation of the virial which has since attracted great attention. Namely, he writes it

$$a\theta = \left(P + \frac{c}{V^2}\right)(V - b).$$

The quantity b is the volume of a molecule, which he supposes to be an impenetrable body, and all the virtue of the equation lies in this term which makes the equation a cubic in V, which is required to account for the shape of certain isothermal curves.[6] But if the idea of an impenetrable atom is illogical, that of an impenetrable molecule is almost absurd. For the kinetical theory of matter teaches us that a molecule is like a solar system or star-cluster in miniature. Unless we suppose that in all heating of gases and vapors internal work is performed upon the molecules, implying that their atoms are at considerable distances, the whole kinetical theory of gases falls to the ground. As for the term added to P, there is no more than a partial and roughly approximate justification for it. Namely, let us imagine two spheres described round a particle as their centre, the radius of the larger being so great as to

6. But, in fact, an inspection of these curves is sufficient to show that they are of a higher degree than the third. For they have the line $V = 0$, or some line V a constant for an asymptote, while for small values of P, the values of $d^2P/(dV)^2$ are positive.

include all the particles whose action upon the centre is sensible, while the radius of the smaller is so large that a good many molecules are included within it. The possibility of describing such a sphere as the outer one implies that the attraction of the particles varies at some distances inversely as some higher power of the distance than the cube, or, to speak more clearly, that the attraction multiplied by the cube of the distance diminishes as the distance increases; for the number of particles at a given distance from any one particle is proportionate to the square of that distance and each of these gives a term of the virial which is the product of the attraction into the distance. Consequently unless the attraction multiplied by the cube of the distance diminished so rapidly with the distance as soon to become insensible, no such outer sphere as is supposed could be described. However, ordinary experience shows that such a sphere is possible; and consequently there must be distances at which the attraction does thus rapidly diminish as the distance increases. The two spheres, then, being so drawn, consider the virial of the central particle due to the particles between them. Let the density of the substance be increased, say, N times. Then, for every term, Rr, of the virial before the condensation, there will be N terms of the same magnitude after the condensation. Hence, the virial of each particle will be proportional to the density, and the equation of the virial becomes

$$a\theta = P\bar{V} + \frac{c}{V}.$$

This omits the virial within the inner sphere, the radius of which is so taken that within that distance the number of particles is not proportional to the number in a large sphere. For Van der Waals this radius is the diameter of his hard molecules, which assumption gives his equation. But it is plain that the attraction between the molecules must to a certain extent modify their distribution, unless some peculiar conditions are fulfilled. The equation of Van der Waals can be approximately true therefore only for a gas. In a solid or liquid condition, in which the removal of a small amount of pressure has little effect on the volume, and where consequently the virial must be much greater than $P\bar{V}$, the virial must increase with the volume. For suppose we had a substance in a critical condition in which an increase of the volume would diminish the virial more than it would increase $\frac{3}{2}P\bar{V}$. If we were forcibly to diminish the volume of such a substance, when the temperature became equalised, the pressure which it could withstand would be less than before, and it would be still further condensed, and this would go on indefinitely until a condition were reached in which an increase of volume would increase $\frac{3}{2}P\bar{V}$ more than it would decrease the virial. In the case of solids, at least, P may be zero; so that the state reached would be one in which the virial increases with the volume, or the attraction between the particles does not increase so fast with a diminution of their distance as it would if the attraction were inversely as the distance.

Almost contemporaneously with Van der Waals's paper, another remarkable thesis for the doctorate was presented at Paris by Amagat. It related to the elasticity and expansion of gases, and to this subject the superb experimenter, its author, has devoted his whole subsequent life. Especially interesting are his observations of the volumes of ethylene and of carbonic acid at temperatures from 20° to 100° and at pressures ranging from an ounce to 5000 pounds to the square inch. As soon as Amagat had obtained these results, he remarked that the "coefficient of expansion at constant volume," as it is absurdly called, that is, the rate of variation of the pressure with the temperature, was very nearly constant for each volume. This accords with the equation of the virial, which gives

$$\frac{dp}{d\theta} = \frac{a}{\bar{V}} - \frac{d\Sigma\overline{Rr}}{d\theta}.$$

Now, the virial must be nearly independent of the temperature, and therefore the last term almost disappears. The virial would not be quite independent of the temperature, because if the temperature (i.e. the square of the velocity of the molecules) is lowered, and the pressure correspondingly lowered, so as to make the volume the same, the attractions of the molecules will have more time to produce their effects, and consequently, the pairs of molecules the closest together will be held together longer and closer; so that the virial will generally be increased by a decrease of temperature. Now, Amagat's experiments do show an excessively minute effect of this sort, at least, when the volumes are not too small. However, the observations are well enough satisfied by assuming the "coefficient of expansion at constant volume" to consist wholly of the first term, $a/\bar{V}$. Thus, Amagat's experiments enable us to determine the values of a and thence to calculate the virial; and this we find varies for carbonic acid gas nearly inversely to $\bar{V}^{0.9}$. There is, thus, a rough approximation to satisfying Van der Waals's equation. But the most interesting result of Amagat's experiments, for our purpose at any rate, is that the quantity a, though nearly constant for any one volume, differs considerably with the volume, nearly doubling when the volume is reduced fivefold. This can only indicate that the mean kinetic energy of a given mass of the gas for a given temperature is greater the more the gas is compressed. But the laws of mechanics appear to enjoin that the mean kinetic energy of a moving particle shall be constant at any given temperature. The only escape from contradiction, then, is to suppose that the mean mass of a moving particle diminishes upon the condensation of the gas. In other words, many of the molecules are dissociated, or broken up into atoms or sub-molecules. The idea that dissociation should be favored by diminishing the volume will be pronounced by physicists, at first blush, as contrary to all our experience. But it must be remembered that the circumstances we are speaking of, that of a gas under fifty or more atmospheres pressure, are also unusual. That the "coefficient of expansion under constant volume" when multiplied by the volumes should increase with a decrement of the volume is also quite contrary to ordinary experience; yet it undoubtedly takes place in all gases under great pressure. Again, the doctrine of Arrhenius[7] is now generally accepted, that the molecular conductivity of an electrolyte is proportional to the dissociation of ions. Now the molecular conductivity of a fused electrolyte is usually superior to that of a solution. Here is a case, then, in which diminution of volume is accompanied by increased dissociation.

The truth is that several different kinds of dissociation have to be distinguished. In the first place, there is the dissociation of a chemical molecule to form chemical molecules under the regular action of chemical laws. This may be a double decomposition, as when iodhydric acid is dissociated, according to the formula

$$HI + HI = HH + II;$$

or, it may be a simple decomposition, as when pentachloride of phosphorus is dissociated according to the formula

$$PCl_5 = PCl_3 + ClCl.$$

All these dissociations require, according to the laws of thermochemistry, an elevated temperature. In the second place, there is the dissociation of a physically polymerous molecule, that is, of several chemical molecules joined by physical attractions. This I am inclined to suppose is a common concomitant of the heating of solids and liquids; for in these bodies there is no increase of compressibility with the temperature at all comparable with the increase of

7. Anticipated by Clausius as long ago as 1857; and by Williamson in 1851.

the expansibility. But, in the third place, there is the dissociation with which we are now concerned, which must be supposed to be a throwing off of un-saturated sub-molecules or atoms from the molecule. The molecule may, as I have said, be roughly likened to a solar system. As such, molecules are able to produce perturbations of one another's internal motions; and in this way a planet, i.e. a sub-molecule, will occasionally get thrown off and wander about by itself, till it finds another unsaturated sub-molecule with which it can unite. Such dissociation by perturbation will naturally be favored by the proximity of the molecules to one another.

Let us now pass to the consideration of that special substance, or rather class of substances, whose properties form the chief subject of botany and of zoölogy, as truly as those of the silicates form the chief subject of mineralogy: I mean the life-slimes, or protoplasm. Let us begin by cataloguing the general characters of these slimes. They one and all exist in two states of aggregation, a solid or nearly solid state and a liquid or nearly liquid state; but they do not pass from the former to the latter by ordinary fusion. They are readily decom-posed by heat, especially in the liquid state; nor will they bear any consider-able degree of cold. All their vital actions take place at temperatures very little below the point of decomposition. This extreme instability is one of numerous facts which demonstrate the chemical complexity of protoplasm. Every chemist will agree that they are far more complicated than the albu-mens. Now, albumen is estimated to contain in each molecule about a thou-sand atoms; so that it is natural to suppose that the protoplasms contain several thousands. We know that while they are chiefly composed of oxygen, hydro-gen, carbon, and nitrogen, a large number of other elements enter into living bodies in small proportions; and it is likely that most of these enter into the composition of protoplasms. Now, since the numbers of chemical varieties increase at an enormous rate with the number of atoms per molecule, so that there are certainly hundreds of thousands of substances whose molecules con-tain twenty atoms or fewer, we may well suppose that the number of proto-plasmic substances runs into the billions or trillions. Professor Cayley has given a mathematical theory of "trees," with a view of throwing a light upon such questions; and in that light the estimate of trillions (in the English sense) seems immoderately moderate. It is true that an opinion has been emitted, and defended among biologists, that there is but one kind of protoplasm; but the observations of biologists, themselves, have almost exploded that hy-pothesis, which from a chemical standpoint appears utterly incredible. The anticipation of the chemist would decidedly be that enough different chemical substances having protoplasmic characters might be formed to account, not only for the differences between nerve-slime and muscle-slime, between whale-slime and lion-slime, but also for those minuter pervasive variations which characterise different breeds and single individuals.

Protoplasm, when quiescent, is, broadly speaking, solid; but when it is disturbed in an appropriate way, or sometimes even spontaneously without external disturbance, it becomes, broadly speaking, liquid. A moner in this state is seen under the microscope to have streams within its matter; a slime-mould slowly flows by force of gravity. The liquefaction starts from the point of disturbance and spreads through the mass. This spreading, however, is not uniform in all directions; on the contrary it takes at one time one course, at another another, through the homogeneous mass, in a manner that seems a little mysterious. The cause of disturbance being removed, these motions gradually (with higher kinds of protoplasm, quickly) cease, and the slime returns to its solid condition.

The liquefaction of protoplasm is accompanied by a mechanical phenomenon. Namely, some kinds exhibit a tendency to draw themselves up into a globular form. This happens particularly with the contents of muscle-cells. The prevalent opinion, founded on some of the most exquisite experimental investigations that the history of science can show, is undoubtedly that the contraction of muscle-cells is due to osmotic pressure; and it must be allowed that that is a factor in producing the effect. But it does not seem to me that it satisfactorily accounts even for the phenomena of muscular contraction; and besides, even naked slimes often draw up in the same way. In this case, we seem to recognize an increase of the surface-tension. In some cases, too, the reverse action takes place, extraordinary pseudopodia being put forth, as if the surface-tension were diminished in spots. Indeed, such a slime always has a sort of skin, due no doubt to surface-tension, and this seems to give way at the point where a pseudopodium is put forth.

Long-continued or frequently repeated liquefaction of the protoplasm results in an obstinate retention of the solid state, which we call fatigue. On the other hand repose in this state, if not too much prolonged, restores the liquefiability. These are both important functions.

The life-slimes have, further, the peculiar property of growing. Crystals also grow; their growth, however, consists merely in attracting matter like their own from the circumambient fluid. To suppose the growth of protoplasm of the same nature, would be to suppose this substance to be spontaneously generated in copious supplies wherever food is in solution. Certainly, it must be granted that protoplasm is but a chemical substance, and that there is no reason why it should not be formed synthetically like any other chemical substance. Indeed, Clifford has clearly shown that we have overwhelming evidence that it is so formed. But to say that such formation is as regular and frequent as the assimilation of food is quite another matter. It is more consonant with the facts of observation to suppose that assimilated protoplasm is formed at the instant of assimilation, under the influence of the protoplasm already present. For each slime in its growth preserves its distinctive characters with wonderful truth, nerve-slime growing nerve-slime and muscle-slime muscle-slime, lion-slime growing lion-slime, and all the varieties of breeds and even individual characters being preserved in the growth. Now it is too much to suppose there are billions of different kinds of protoplasm floating about wherever there is food.

The frequent liquefaction of protoplasm increases its power of assimilating food; so much so, indeed, that it is questionable whether in the solid form it possesses this power.

The life-slime wastes as well as grows; and this too takes place chiefly if not exclusively in its liquid phases.

Closely connected with growth is reproduction; and though in higher forms this is a specialised function, it is universally true that wherever there is protoplasm, there is, will be, or has been a power of reproducing that same kind of protoplasm in a separated organism. Reproduction seems to involve the union of two sexes; though it is not demonstrable that this is always requisite.

Another physical property of protoplasm is that of taking habits. The course which the spread of liquefaction has taken in the past is rendered thereby more likely to be taken in the future; although there is no absolute certainty that the same path will be followed again.

Very extraordinary, certainly, are all these properties of protoplasm; as extraordinary as indubitable. But the one which has next to be mentioned, while equally undeniable, is infinitely more wonderful. It is that protoplasm feels. We have no direct evidence that this is true of protoplasm universally, and certainly some kinds feel far more than others. But there is a fair analogical inference that all protoplasm feels. It not only feels but exercises all the functions of mind.

Such are the properties of protoplasm. The problem is to find a hypothesis of the molecular constitution of this compound which will account for these properties, one and all.

Some of them are obvious results of the excessively complicated constitution of the protoplasm molecule. All very complicated substances are unstable; and plainly a molecule of several thousand atoms may be separated in many ways into two parts in each of which the polar chemical forces are very nearly saturated. In the solid protoplasm, as in other solids, the molecules must be supposed to be moving as it were in orbits, or, at least, so as not to wander indefinitely. But this solid cannot be melted, for the same reason that starch cannot be melted; because an amount of heat insufficient to make the entire molecules wander is sufficient to break them up completely and cause them to form new and simpler molecules. But when one of the molecules is disturbed, even if it be not quite thrown out of its orbit at first, sub-molecules of perhaps several hundred atoms each are thrown off from it. These will soon acquire the same mean kinetic energy as the others, and therefore velocities several times as great. They will naturally begin to wander, and in wandering will perturb a great many other molecules and cause them in their turn to behave like the one originally deranged. So many molecules will thus be broken up, that even those that are intact will no longer be restrained within orbits, but will wander about freely. This is the usual condition of a liquid, as modern chemists understand it; for in all electrolytic liquids there is considerable dissociation.

But this process necessarily chills the substance, not merely on account of the heat of chemical combination, but still more because the number of separate particles being greatly increased, the mean kinetic energy must be less. The substance being a bad conductor, this heat is not at once restored. Now the particles moving more slowly, the attractions between them have time to take effect, and they approach the condition of equilibrium. But their dynamic equilibrium is found in the restoration of the solid condition, which therefore takes place, if the disturbance is not kept up.

When a body is in the solid condition, most of its molecules must be moving at the same rate, or, at least, at certain regular sets of rates; otherwise the orbital motion would not be preserved. The distances of neighboring molecules must always be kept between a certain maximum and a certain minimum value. But if, without absorption of heat, the body be thrown into a liquid condition, the distances of neighboring molecules will be far more unequally distributed, and an effect upon the virial will result. The chilling of protoplasm upon its liquefaction must also be taken into account. The ordinary effect will no doubt be to increase the cohesion and with that the surface-tension, so that the mass will tend to draw itself up. But in special cases, the virial will be increased so much that the surface-tension will be diminished at points where the temperature is first restored. In that case, the outer film will give way and the tension at other places will aid in causing the general fluid to be poured out at those points, forming pseudopodia.

When the protoplasm is in a liquid state, and then only, a solution of food is able to penetrate its mass by diffusion. The protoplasm is then considerably dissociated; and so is the food, like all dissolved matter. If then the separated and unsaturated sub-molecules of the food happen to be of the same chemical species as sub-molecules of the protoplasm, they may unite with other sub-molecules of the protoplasm to form new molecules, in such a fashion that when the solid state is resumed, there may be more molecules of protoplasm than there were at the beginning. It is like the jackknife whose blade and handle, after having been severally lost and replaced, were found and put together to make a new knife.

We have seen that protoplasm is chilled by liquefaction, and that this brings it back to the solid state, when the heat is recovered. This series of operations must be very rapid in the case of nerve-slime and even of muscle-slime, and may account for the unsteady or vibratory character of their action. Of course, if assimilation takes place, the heat of combination, which is probably trifling, is gained. On the other hand, if work is done, whether by nerve or by muscle, loss of energy must take place. In the case of the muscle, the mode by which the instantaneous part of the fatigue is brought about is easily traced out. If when the muscle contracts it be under stress, it will contract less than it otherwise would do, and there will be a loss of heat. It is like an engine which should work by dissolving salt in water and using the contraction during the solution to lift a weight, the salt being recovered afterwards by distillation. But the major part of fatigue has nothing to do with the correlation of forces. A man must labor hard to do in a quarter of an hour the work which draws from him enough heat to cool his body by a single degree. Meantime, he will be getting heated, he will be pouring out extra products of combustion, perspiration, etc., and he will be driving the blood at an accelerated rate through minute tubes at great expense. Yet all this will have little to do with his fatigue. He may sit quietly at his table writing, doing practically no physical work at all, and yet in a few hours be terribly fagged. This seems to be owing to the deranged sub-molecules of the nerve-slime not having had time to settle back into their proper combinations. When such sub-molecules are thrown out, as they must be from time to time, there is so much waste of material.

In order that a sub-molecule of food may be thoroughly and firmly assimilated into a broken molecule of protoplasm, it is necessary not only that it should have precisely the right chemical composition, but also that it should be at precisely the right spot at the right time and should be moving in precisely the right direction with precisely the right velocity. If all these conditions are not fulfilled, it will be more loosely retained than the other parts of the molecule; and every time it comes round into the situation in which it was drawn in, relatively to the other parts of that molecule and to such others as were near enough to be factors in the action, it will be in special danger of being thrown out again. Thus, when a partial liquefaction of the protoplasm takes place many times to about the same extent, it will, each time, be pretty nearly the same molecules that were last drawn in that are now thrown out. They will be thrown out, too, in about the same way, as to position, direction of motion, and velocity, in which they were drawn in; and this will be in about the same course that the ones last before them were thrown out. Not exactly, however; for the very cause of their being thrown off so easily is their not having fulfilled precisely the conditions of stable retention. Thus, the law of habit is accounted for, and with it its peculiar characteristic of not acting with exactitude.

It seems to me that this explanation of habit, aside from the question of its truth or falsity, has a certain value as an addition to our little store of mechanical examples of actions analogous to habit. All the others, so far as I know, are either statical or else involve forces which, taking only the sensible motions into account, violate the law of energy. It is so with the stream that wears its own bed. Here, the sand is carried to its most stable situation and left there. The law of energy forbids this; for when anything reaches a position of stable equilibrium, its momentum will be at a maximum, so that it can according to this law only be left at rest in an unstable situation. In all the statical illustrations, too, things are brought into certain states and left there. A garment receives folds and keeps them; that is, its limit of elasticity is exceeded. This failure to spring back is again an apparent violation of the law of energy; for the substance will not only not spring back of itself (which might be due to an unstable equilibrium being reached) but will not even do so when an impulse that way is applied to it. Accordingly, Professor James says "the phenomena of habit . . . are due to the plasticity of the . . . materials." Now, plasticity of materials means the having of a low limit of elasticity. (See the *Century Dictionary*, under *solid*.) But the hypothetical constitution of protoplasm here proposed involves no forces but attractions and repulsions strictly following the law of energy. The action here, that is, the throwing of an atom out of its orbit in a molecule, and the entering of a new atom into nearly, but not quite the same orbit, is somewhat similar to the molecular actions which may be supposed to take place in a solid strained beyond its limit of elasticity. Namely, in that case certain molecules must be thrown out of their orbits, to settle down again shortly after into new orbits. In short, the plastic solid resembles protoplasm in being partially and temporarily liquefied by a slight mechanical force. But the taking of a set by a solid body has but a moderate resemblance to the taking of a habit, inasmuch as the characteristic feature of the latter, its inexactitude and want of complete determinacy, is not so marked in the former, if it can be said to be present there, at all.

The truth is that though the molecular explanation of habit is pretty vague on the mathematical side, there can be no doubt that systems of atoms having polar forces would act substantially in that manner, and the explanation is even too satisfactory to suit the convenience of an advocate of tychism. For it may fairly be urged that since the phenomena of habit may thus result from a purely mechanical arrangement, it is unnecessary to suppose that habit-taking is a primordial principle of the universe. But one fact remains unexplained mechanically, which concerns not only the facts of habit, but all cases of actions apparently violating the law of energy; it is that all these phenomena depend upon aggregations of trillions of molecules in one and the same condition and neighborhood; and it is by no means clear how they could have all been brought and left in the same place and state by any conservative forces. But let the mechanical explanation be as perfect as it may, the state of things which it supposes presents evidence of a primordial habit-taking tendency. For it shows us like things acting in like ways because they are alike. Now, those who insist on the doctrine of necessity will for the most part insist that the physical world is entirely individual. Yet law involves an element of generality. Now to say that generality is primordial, but generalisation not, is like saying that diversity is primordial but diversification not. It turns logic upside down. At any rate, it is clear that nothing but a principle of habit, itself due to the growth by habit of an infinitesimal chance tendency toward habit-taking, is the only bridge that can span the chasm between the chance-medley of chaos and the cosmos of order and law.

I shall not attempt a molecular explanation of the phenomena of reproduction, because that would require a subsidiary hypothesis, and carry me away from my main object. Such phenomena, universally diffused though they be, appear to depend upon special conditions; and we do not find that all proto-plasm has reproductive powers.

But what is to be said of the property of feeling? If consciousness belongs to all protoplasm, by what mechanical constitution is this to be accounted for? The slime is nothing but a chemical compound. There is no inherent impos-sibility in its being formed synthetically in the laboratory, out of its chemical elements; and if it were so made, it would present all the characters of natural protoplasm. No doubt, then, it would feel. To hesitate to admit this would be puerile and ultra-puerile. By what element of the molecular arrangement, then, would that feeling be caused? This question cannot be evaded or pooh-poohed. Protoplasm certainly does feel; and unless we are to accept a weak dualism, the property must be shown to arise from some peculiarity of the mechanical system. Yet the attempt to deduce it from the three laws of me-chanics, applied to never so ingenious a mechanical contrivance, would ob-viously be futile. It can never be explained, unless we admit that physical events are but degraded or undeveloped forms of psychical events. But once grant that the phenomena of matter are but the result of the sensibly complete sway of habits upon mind, and it only remains to explain why in the proto-plasm these habits are to some slight extent broken up, so that according to the law of mind, in that special clause of it sometimes called the principle of accommodation,[8] feeling becomes intensified. Now the manner in which hab-its generally get broken up is this. Reactions usually terminate in the removal of a stimulus; for the excitation continues as long as the stimulus is present. Accordingly, habits are general ways of behavior which are associated with the removal of stimuli. But when the expected removal of the stimulus fails to occur, the excitation continues and increases, and non-habitual reactions take place; and these tend to weaken the habit. If, then, we suppose that matter never does obey its ideal laws with absolute precision, but that there are almost insensible fortuitous departures from regularity, these will pro-duce, in general, equally minute effects. But protoplasm is in an excessively unstable condition; and it is the characteristic of unstable equilibrium, that near that point excessively minute causes may produce startlingly large ef-

8. "Physiologically, . . . accommodation means the breaking up of a habit. . . . Psychologically, it means reviving consciousness." Baldwin, *Psychology* [James Mark Baldwin, *Handbook of Psychology*, 2 vols. (New York: Henry Holt, 1891)], Part III ch. i., §5.

fects. Here then, the usual departures from regularity will be followed by others that are very great; and the large fortuitous departures from law so produced, will tend still further to break up the laws, supposing that these are of the nature of habits. Now, this breaking up of habit and renewed fortuitous spontaneity will, according to the law of mind, be accompanied by an intensification of feeling. The nerve-protoplasm is, without doubt, in the most unstable condition of any kind of matter; and consequently, there the resulting feeling is the most manifest.

Thus we see that the idealist has no need to dread a mechanical theory of life. On the contrary, such a theory, fully developed, is bound to call in a tychistic idealism as its indispensable adjunct. Wherever chance-spontaneity is found, there, in the same proportion, feeling exists. In fact, chance is but the outward aspect of that which within itself is feeling. I long ago showed that real existence, or thing-ness, consists in regularities. So, that primeval chaos in which there was no regularity was mere nothing, from a physical aspect. Yet it was not a blank zero; for there was an intensity of consciousness there in comparison with which all that we ever feel is but as the struggling of a molecule or two to throw off a little of the force of law to an endless and innumerable diversity of chance utterly unlimited.

But after some atoms of the protoplasm have thus become partially emancipated from law, what happens next to them? To understand this, we have to remember that no mental tendency is so easily strengthened by the action of habit as is the tendency to take habits. Now, in the higher kinds of protoplasm, especially, the atoms in question have not only long belonged to one molecule or another of the particular mass of slime of which they are parts; but before that, they were constituents of food of a protoplasmic constitution. During all this time, they have been liable to lose habits and to recover them again; so that now, when the stimulus is removed, and the foregone habits tend to reassert themselves, they do so in the case of such atoms with great promptness. Indeed, the return is so prompt that there is nothing but the feeling to show conclusively that the bonds of law have ever been relaxed.

In short, diversification is the vestige of chance-spontaneity; and wherever diversity is increasing, there chance must be operative. On the other hand, wherever uniformity is increasing, habit must be operative. But wherever actions take place under an established uniformity, there so much feeling as there may be takes the mode of a sense of reaction. That is the manner in which I am led to define the relation between the fundamental elements of consciousness and their physical equivalents.

It remains to consider the physical relations of general ideas. It may be well here to reflect that if matter has no existence except as a specialisation of mind, it follows that whatever affects matter according to regular laws is itself matter. But all mind is directly or indirectly connected with all matter, and acts in a more or less regular way; so that all mind more or less partakes of the nature of matter. Hence, it would be a mistake to conceive of the psychical and the physical aspects of matter as two aspects absolutely distinct. Viewing a thing from the outside, considering its relations of action and reaction with other things, it appears as matter. Viewing it from the inside, looking at its immediate character as feeling, it appears as consciousness. These two views are combined when we remember that mechanical laws are nothing but acquired habits, like all the regularities of mind, including the tendency to take habits, itself; and that this action of habit is nothing but generalisation, and generalisation is nothing but the spreading of feelings. But the question is, how do general ideas appear in the molecular theory of protoplasm?

The consciousness of a habit involves a general idea. In each action of that habit certain atoms get thrown out of their orbit, and replaced by others. Upon all the different occasions it is different atoms that are thrown off, but they are analogous from a physical point of view, and there is an inward sense of their being analogous. Every time one of the associated feelings recurs, there is a more or less vague sense that there are others, that it has a general character, and of about what this general character is. We ought not, I think, to hold that in protoplasm habit never acts in any other than the particular way suggested above. On the contrary, if habit be a primary property of mind, it must be equally so of matter, as a kind of mind. We can hardly refuse to admit that wherever chance motions have general characters, there is a tendency for this generality to spread and to perfect itself. In that case, a general idea is a certain modification of consciousness which accompanies any regularity or general relation between chance actions.

The consciousness of a general idea has a certain "unity of the ego," in it, which is identical when it passes from one mind to another. It is, therefore, quite analogous to a person; and, indeed, a person is only a particular kind of general idea. Long ago, in the *Journal of Speculative Philosophy* (Vol. II, p. 156) [selection 5 in this volume], I pointed out that a person is nothing but a symbol involving a general idea; but my views were, then, too nominalistic to enable me to see that every general idea has the unified living feeling of a person.

All that is necessary, upon this theory, to the existence of a person is that the feelings out of which he is constructed should be in close enough connection to influence one another. Here we can draw a consequence which it may be possible to submit to experimental test. Namely, if this be the case, there should be something like personal consciousness in bodies of men who are in intimate and intensely sympathetic communion. It is true that when the generalization of feeling has been carried so far as to include all within a person, a stopping-place, in a certain sense, has been attained; and further generalization will have a less lively character. But we must not think it will cease. Esprit de corps, national sentiment, sym-pathy, are no mere metaphors. None of us can fully realize what the minds of corporations are, any more than one of my brain-cells can know what the whole brain is thinking. But the law of mind clearly points to the existence of such personalities, and there are many ordinary observations which, if they were critically examined and supplemented by special experiments, might, as first appearances promise, give evidence of the influence of such greater persons upon individuals. It is often remarked that on one day half a dozen people, strangers to one another, will take it into their heads to do one and the same strange deed, whether it be a physical experiment, a crime, or an act of virtue. When the thirty thousand young people of the society for Christian Endeavor were in New York, there seemed to me to be some mysterious diffusion of sweetness and light. If such a fact is capable of being made out anywhere, it should be in the church. The Christians have always been ready to risk their lives for the sake of having prayers in common, of getting together and praying simultaneously with great energy, and especially for their common body, for "the whole state of Christ's church militant here in earth," as one of the missals has it. This practice they have been keeping up everywhere, weekly, for many centuries. Surely, a personality ought to have developed in that church, in that "bride of Christ," as they call it, or else there is a strange break in the action of mind, and I shall have to acknowledge my views are much mistaken. Would not the societies for psychical research be more likely to break through the clouds, in seeking evidences of such corporate personality, than in seeking evidences of telepathy, which, upon the same theory, should be a far weaker phenomenon?

15

. . .

Minute Logic

Peirce considered semiotic and logic, in the broad sense, to be synonymous terms, as is evident in the following excerpts from a lengthy 1901 manuscript on logic, the first chapter of a projected book to have been entitled *Minute Logic*. If, as Peirce held, all thinking is inference from signs and every sign relation possesses a quality of mentality or thirdness, then logic—the science of sound thinking—is the science of sign relations. When Peirce argues that human reasoning is analogous to the action of a calculating machine, he is not arguing as Hobbes does for the materiality of the self but is simply denying that logicality is exclusively human or cerebral. Logic should therefore not be premised upon either psychological or supposedly introspective knowledge of the nature of mental operations but upon the logicality of nature—that is, upon a logical quality in external reality. This implies the objective reality not only of the sign relation but also of truth (a point of difference between Peirce and some semioticians of our day). He therefore outlines an argument for thirdness as a mode of Being, which explains how there may be such a thing as a "life in Signs."

Source: MS 425A.

. . . when we have finished a process of thinking, and come to the logical criticism of it, the first question we ask ourselves is "What did I conclude?" To that we answer with some *form of words*, probably. Yet we had probably not been thinking in any such form;—certainly not, if our thought amounted to anything. Our whole logical criticism consists in investigating whether or not to one portion of knowledge, expressed presumably in a very different form from that in which it was thought, we can, without serious danger of error, attach a certain addition. What the process of thinking may have been, has nothing to do with this question. There may, for aught we know or care, be a hundred ways of thinking in passing from such a premiss to such a conclusion. But the question is, whether, granting that there be such a thing as truth, which can be ascertained at all, such a way of adding conclusion to premiss, as that under examination, would lead to the ascertainment of the truth by the speediest path, or not. The whole logical inquiry relates to the *truth*; now the very idea of truth is that it is quite independent of what you or I may think it to be. How we think, therefore, is utterly irrelevant to logical inquiry.

I must be excused for dwelling on this point, for no other in all logic, although it is a science of subtleties, is so hard to see. The confusion is embedded in language, leaving no words available to epigrammatize the error. Now it is not of fools exclusively, but of the greater part of the thinking world that words are the money. A celebrated treatise [by Hobbes] is entitled 'Logic, or Computation,' and although not all reasoning is computation, it is certainly true that numerical computation is reasoning. But calculating machines are in everyday use; and Babbage's analytical engine would perform considerable feats in mathematics. Other logical machines have been constructed. All those instruments perform inferences; and those inferences are subject to the rules of logic. If from true premisses they always yield true conclusions, what more could be desired? Yet those machines have no souls that we know of. They do not appear to think, at all, in any psychical sense; and even if we should discover that they do so, it would be a fact altogether without bearing upon the logical correctness of their operations, which we should still have to assure ourselves of in the same way we do now.

The idea I am endeavoring to convey is difficult to seize. It cannot be seized by a reader who, instead of trying to seize it, puts himself into a resolutely hostile posture of mind toward it. Does he wish to know what I mean? If so, let him postpone criticism until he clearly apprehends what it is that is to be criticized. There are many minds who will be so occupied with a certain objection, that it will quite eclipse the sense of what I have been saying. They will urge that those machines do not perform any inference, at all; that it is, on the contrary, we, who, knowing how they are constructed (be it in detail or in a general way, by testimony), infer that the number which is exhibited at the end of the process must be in a certain arithmetical relation to the numbers which determined the setting and working of the machine.

It will further be urged that if those machines were to be regarded as reasoning, there are others which would reason in far higher ways. For the calculating machines only execute variations upon $1 + 1 = 2$, while there are machines which may, with as much justice, be said to resolve problems before which generations of able mathematicians have fallen back, repulsed. Such, for example, are the solids of different shapes which yacht-designers drag through the water, and thereby come to the knowledge of arcana of hydrodynamics. Blocks of wood should seem, then, on my principles, to be better reasoners than the brains of Gauss and Stokes. And why stop here? Any apparatus whatever used for experimentation would be, on the same principle, a logical machine. A steam-engine would be working out, at every revolution, its problem in thermodynamics; a simple match, scratched on a box, a question that we are unequal so much as to the formulating of it.

This sounds crushing. What have I to say to it all? Simply that it is absolutely just. A logical machine differs from any other machine merely in working upon an excessively simple principle which is applied in a manifold and complex way, instead of upon an occult principle applied in a monotonous way. If anybody wishes me to acknowledge that a logical machine reasons no more than any other machine, I do not know why I should not gratify him. That seems to me a matter of words. The result which the logical machine turns out has a relation to the data with which it was fed, which relation may be considered from the point of view of whether the former could be false so long as the latter are true. That is all there is in the facts of the case; and whether it is called reasoning or not I do not care. All that I insist upon is, that, in like manner, a man may be regarded as a machine which turns out, let us say, a written sentence expressing a conclusion, the man-machine having been fed with a written statement of fact, as premiss. Since this performance is no more than a machine might go through, it has no essential relation to the circumstance that the machine happens to work by geared wheels, while a man happens to work by an ill-understood arrangement of brain-cells; and if there be room for less, still less to the circumstance that a man thinks. Say, if you like, that thinking has everything to do with the life of reasoning; I still insist that it has nothing to do with the logical criticism, which is equally applicable to the machine's performances and to the man's. This is simply the question of whether or not the conclusion can be false while the premiss is true, together with modifications of this question. Were it a question of whether man *can* reason ill, it might be well to examine the process and mechanism of his thinking. But there is no question that he often does reason ill; and that is the reason why we criticize reasoning and why we inquire whether or not a given way of proceeding from premiss to conclusion is conducive to the ascertainment of truth or the reverse. . . .

Logic is obliged to suppose (it need not assert) that there is knowledge embodied in some form, and that there is inference, in the sense that one embodiment of knowledge affects another. It is not obliged even so much as to *suppose* that there is consciousness. Descartes was of opinion that animals were unconscious automata. He might as well have thought that all men but himself were unconscious. To suppose them so does not annul the rules of logic. It still remains true that such and such a habit of determining one virtual store of knowledge by another will result in the concentration of actions so as to bring about definite ends. The essence of rationality lies in the fact the rational being *will* act so as to attain certain ends. Prevent his doing so in one way, and he will act in some utterly different way which will produce the same result. Rationality is being governed by final causes. Consciousness, the feeling of the passing instant, has, as such, no room for rationality. The notion that logic is in any way concerned with it is a fallacy closely allied to hedonism in ethics. . . .

At this point, I interpose a psychological chapter, not for the purpose of introducing psychological matter into logic, but for the purpose of making its irrelevancy quite clear. All our thoughts are signs, and I here consider how they are so, and show that it is in their character as signs that logic is applicable to them. Further, logic is applicable to all signs whether they are directly mental or not. . . .

But now we have to examine whether there be a doctrine of signs corresponding to Hegel's objective logic; that is to say, whether there be a life in Signs, so that,—the requisite vehicle being present,—they will go through a certain order of development, and if so, whether this development be merely of such a nature that the same round of changes of form is described over and over again whatever be the matter of the thought or whether, in addition to such a repetitive order, there be also a greater life-history that every symbol furnished with a vehicle of life goes through, and what is the nature of it. There are minds who will pooh-pooh an idea of this sort, much as they would pooh-pooh a theory involving fairies. I have no objection [to] the pooh-poohing of fairies, provided it be critical pooh-pooh-ing; but I wish I had the leisure to place before those gentlemen a work to be entitled The History of Pooh-pooh-ing. I think it would do them good; and make room in their minds for an essay upon the Logic of Pooh-pooh-ing. Mind, that if some forenoon, while I was in the midst of one of the most valuable of the chapters of my 'Minute Logic,' a rap should come at my outer door, and if, upon going to the door, I were to find two men who proposed to come in and discuss with me the principles of Mormonism or Christian Science, I should promptly recommend them to apply elsewhere. This I should do upon the same grounds upon which I declined to join the American Psychical Research Society when it was started; namely, that I thought that [to] do so would be to sanction a probable great waste of time, together with the placing of some men in a compromising position. In like manner, if a reader who has thought it worth while to listen to what I have had to say upon normative logic finds objective logic too remote from his interests to care to listen to any discussion of it, I shall fully approve of his allowing the leaves of my chapter upon this subject to remain uncut. But my own position is different. It lies directly in the path of my duty to consider the question critically.

The first question, then, which I have to ask is, Supposing such a thing to be true, what is the kind of proof which I ought to demand to satisfy me of its truth? Am I simply to go through the actual process of development of symbols with my own thoughts, which are symbols, and am I to find in the sense of necessity and evidence of the following of one thought upon another an adequate assurance that the course followed is the necessary line of thought's development? That is the way the question has usually been put, hitherto, both by Hegelians and by Anti-Hegelians. But even if I were to find that the sequence of conceptions in Hegel's logic carried my mind irresistibly along its current, that would not suffice to convince me of its universal validity. Nor, on the other hand, does the mere fact that I do not find a single step of Hegel's logic or any substitutes for it that I have met with either convincing or persuasive, give me any assurance whatever that there is no such life-history. It seems to me natural to suppose that it would be far easier satisfactorily to answer the question of whether there is such a thing than to find out what particular form that life-history would take if it were a reality;—and not only natural to suppose so, but made as certain by solid reasons as any such anticipation in regard to proofs could well be.

I am not one of those transcendental apothecaries, as I call them, they are so skillful in making up a bill, who call for a quantity of big admissions, as indispensible *Voraussetzungen* of logic. I am not so indulgent as [Moliere's] Argan, to suppose that they can seriously expect as much as half their demands to be allowed. I reduce the indispensibility of their postulates far more than that, namely, all the way from universality to the single case that happens to have come up; and even then, I do not admit that indispensibility is any ground of belief. It may be indispensible that I should have $500 in the bank; because I have given checks to that amount. But I have never found that the indispensibility directly affected my balance, in the least. When a hand at whist has reached the point at which each player has but three cards left, the one who has to lead often goes on the assumption that the cards are distributed in a certain way, because it is only on that assumption that the odd trick can be saved. This is indisputably logical; and on a more critical analogous occasion there might be some *psychological* excuse, or even warrant, for a "will to believe" that such was really the case. But all that logic warrants is a *hope*, and not a belief. It must be admitted, however, that such hopes play a considerable part in logic. For example, when we discuss a vexed question, we *hope* that there is some ascertainable truth about it, and that the discussion is not to go on forever and to no purpose. A transcendentalist would claim that it is an indispensible "presupposition" that there is an ascertainable true answer to every intelligible question. I used to talk like that, myself; for when I was a babe in philosophy, my bottle was filled from the udders of Kant. But by this time, I have come to want something more substantial.

But whatever be the kind and degree of our logical assurance that there is any real world, external or internal, that same kind and degree of assurance we certainly have that there not only may be a living symbol, realizing the full idea of a symbol, but even that there actually is one.

I examine the question from this point of view. It certainly seems as if the mere hypothesis of such a thing as a symbol sufficed to demonstrate such a life-history. Still, a fallacy is to be suspected. How can a mere hypothesis prove so much as this seems to prove, if it proves anything? I call in the data of experience,—not exactly the every-minute experience which has hitherto been enough, but the experience of most men, together with the history of thought. The conclusion seems the same. Yet still, the evidence is unsatisfactory. The truth is that the hypothesis involves the idea of a different mode of being from that of existential fact. This mode of being seems to claim immediate recognition as evident in the mere idea of it. One asks whether there is not a fallacy in using the ordinary processes of logic either to support it or to refute it.

Aristotelianism admitted two modes of being. This position was attacked by William Ockham, on the ground that one kind sufficed to account for all the phenomena. The hosts of modern philosophers, to the very Hegels, have sided with Ockham in this matter. But now the question comes before us for reëxamination, What are the modes of being? One might antecedently expect that the cenopythagorean categories would require three modes of being. But a little examination will show us that they could be brought into fairly presentable accordance with [the] theory that there were only two, or even only one. The question cannot be decided in that way. Besides, it would be illogical to rely upon the categories to decide so fundamental a question. The only safe way is to make an entirely fresh investigation. But by what method are we to pursue it? In such abstract questions, as we shall have already found, the first step, often more than half the battle, is to ascertain what we mean by the question,—what we possibly *can* mean by it? We know already how we must proceed in order to determine what the meaning of the question is. Our sole guide must be the consideration of the use to which the answer is to be put,—not necessarily the practical application, but in what way it is to subserve the *summum bonum*. Within this principle is wrapped up the answer to the question, what being is, and what, therefore, its modes must be. It is absolutely impossible that the word 'Being' should bear any meaning whatever except with reference to the *summum bonum*. This is true of any word. But that which is true of one word in one respect, of another in another, of every word in some or another respect, that is precisely what the word 'being' aims to express. There are other ways of conceiving Being,—that it is that which manifests itself, that it is that which produces effects,—which have to be considered; and their relations ascertained.

Having thus worked out a tolerable conception of Being, we turn to modes of being. But these are metaphysical conceptions. Let us first inquire how the validity of *any* metaphysical conception is to be determined. For this purpose, we have only to apply the principles of speculative rhetoric. We sketch out the method and apply it to a few metaphysical conceptions, such as Reality, Necessity, etc. In the process of doing this, we discover that all such metaphysical conceptions are but determinations of the categories, and consequently form a regular system. We also find that they can be held as valid only in approximative and imperfect senses.

But this seems to be in conflict with our conception of Being, particularly as derived from the notion of a symbol; which, however, is solidly founded, too. We now begin to see the sense of talking of modes of being. They are elements of cooperation toward the *summum bonum*. The categories now come in to aid us materially, and we clearly make out three modes, or factors, of being, which we proceed to make clear to ourselves.

Arrived at this point, we can construct a *Weltanschauung*. From this platform, ethics acquires a new significance, as will be shown. Logic, too, shines forth with all its native nobility. Common men carry this *Weltanschauung* in their breasts; and perhaps the pimp, the looting missionary, the Jay Gould, may, through the shadows of their degradation, catch now and then a purer glimpse of it, than the most earnest of citizens, the Curtises, the Emersons, the Bishop Myriels. It is beautifully universal; and one must acknowledge that there is something healthy in the philosophy of faith, with its resentment at logic as an impertinence. Only, it is very infantile. Our final view of logic will exhibit it (on one side of it) as faith come to years of discretion.

16

Sign

There are scores of definitions of "sign" in Peirce's writings. This one is representative, especially in its reference to thirdness as "intelligent consciousness."

Source: *Dictionary of Philosophy and Psychology*,
edited by James Mark Baldwin, 3 vols.
(New York: Macmillan, 1901–5), 2:527.

Sign [Lat. *signum*, a mark, a token]: Ger. *Zeichen*; Fr. *signe*; Ital. *segno*. (I) Anything which determines something else (its *interpretant*) to refer to an object to which itself refers (its *object*) in the same way, the interpretant becoming in turn a sign, and so on *ad infinitum*.

No doubt, intelligent consciousness must enter into the series. If the series of successive interpretants comes to an end, the sign is thereby rendered imperfect, at least. If, an interpretant idea having been determined in an individual consciousness, it determines no outward sign, but that consciousness becomes annihilated, or otherwise loses all memory or other significant effect of the sign, it becomes absolutely undiscoverable that there ever was such an idea in that consciousness; and in that case it is difficult to see how it could have any meaning to say that that consciousness ever had that idea, since the saying so would be an interpretant of that idea.

A sign is either an *icon*, an *index*, or a *symbol*. An *icon* is a sign which would possess the character which renders it significant, even though its object had no existence; such as a lead-pencil streak as representing a geometrical line. An *index* is a sign which would, at once, lose the character which makes it a sign if its object were removed, but would not lose that character if there were no interpretant. Such, for instance, is a piece of mould with a bullet-hole in it as sign of a shot; for without the shot there would have been no hole; but there is a hole there, whether anybody has the sense to attribute it to a shot or not. A *symbol* is a sign which would lose the character which renders it a sign if there were no interpretant. Such is any utterance of speech which signifies what it does only by virtue of its being understood to have that signification.

17

■ ■ ■

Lectures on Pragmatism

In the latter part of the selection from his "Minute Logic," Peirce argued for the reality of the sign relation, or thirdness, by insisting that our ability to form the hypothesis of its reality is also its proof. A year and a half later, in 1903, Peirce was a guest speaker at Harvard, where he gave a series of lectures on pragmatism from which the following selection is extracted. Here he again took up the question of the reality of thirdness, this time adopting a different, though not contradictory, argument, which was that we have many objective examples of the operation of thirdness as a real force in the world. Natural laws, for example, are not merely descriptions of dyadic relations but are themselves real triadic relations operating in nature. That knowledge of natural law facilitates prediction of future behavior of natural objects shows that to some degree natural law governs nature. Or again, the power of words to produce physical effects can scarcely be explained in terms of dyadic relations. Surely the physical difference between the sound waves of an insult and a compliment does not alone explain why one produces a scowl and the other a smile. Rather, the different facial (physical) effects are due to the fact that words are signs, or thirds, representing a first person's meaning to a second person. Peirce's example of the potential effect of Patrick Henry's speech is rendered less idiosyncratic if one remembers that in 1903 the United States was militarily subduing an independence movement in the Philippines.

Source: MS 309.

I proceed to argue that *Thirdness* is operative in Nature.

Suppose we attack the question experimentally. Here is a stone. Now I place that stone where there will be no obstacle between it and the floor, and

I will predict with confidence that as soon as I let go my hold upon the stone it will fall to the floor. I will prove that I can make a correct prediction by actual trial if you like. But I see by your faces that you all think it will be a very silly experiment. Why so? Because you all know very well that I can predict what will happen, and that the fact will verify my prediction.

But *how can* I know what is going to happen? You certainly do not think that it is by clairvoyance, as if the future event by its existential reactiveness could affect me directly, as in an *experience* of it, as an event scarcely past might affect me. You know very well that there is nothing of the sort in this case. Still, it remains true that I *do know* that that stone will drop, as a *fact*, as soon as I let go my hold. If I *truly know* anything, that which I know must be *real*. It would be quite absurd to say that I could be enabled to know how events are going to be determined over which I can exercise no more control than I shall be able to exercise over this stone after it shall have left my hand, that I can so peer in the future merely on the strength of any acquaintance with any pure fiction.

I know that this stone will fall if it [is] let go, because experience has convinced me that objects of this kind always do fall; and if anyone present has any doubt on the subject, I should be happy to try the experiment, and I will bet him a hundred to one on the result.

But the general proposition that all solid bodies fall in the absence of any upward forces or pressure, this formula I say, is of the nature of a representation. Our nominalistic friends would be the last to dispute that. They will go so far as to say that it is a *mere* representation,—the word *mere* meaning that to be represented and really to be are two very different things; and that this formula has no being except a being represented. It certainly is of the nature of a representation. That is undeniable, I grant. And it is equally undeniable that that which is of the nature of a representation is not *ipso facto* real. In that respect there is a great contrast between an object of reaction and an object of representation. Whatever reacts is *ipso facto* real. But an object of representation is not *ipso facto* real. If I were to predict that on my letting go of the stone it would fly up in the air, that would be mere fiction; and the proof that it was so would be obtained by simply trying the experiment. That is clear. On the other hand, and by the same token, the fact that I *know* that this stone will fall to the floor when I let it go, as you all must confess, if you are not blinded by theory, that I *do* know,—and you none of you care to take up my bet, I notice,—is the proof that the formula, or uniformity, as furnishing a safe basis for prediction, is, or if you like it better, *corresponds to*, a reality.

Possibly at this point somebody may raise an objection, and say: You admit, that [it] is one thing really to be and another to be represented; and you further admit that it is of the nature of the law of nature to be represented. Then it follows that it has not the mode of being of a reality. My answer to this would be that it rests upon an ambiguity. When I say that the general proposition as to what will happen whenever a certain condition may be fulfilled is of the nature of a representation I mean that it refers to experiences *in futuro* which I do not know are all of them experienced and never can know have been all experienced. But when I say that really to be is different from being represented, I mean that what really is ultimately consists in what shall be forced upon us in experience, that there is an element of brute compulsion in fact and that fact is not a mere question of reasonableness. Thus, if I say, "I shall wind up my watch every day as long as I live," I never can have a positive experience which *certainly* covers all that is here promised, because I never shall know for certain that my last day has come. But what the real fact will be does not depend upon what I represent, but upon what the experiential reactions shall be. My assertion that I shall wind up my watch every day of my life may turn out to accord with facts, even though I be the most irregular of persons, by my dying before nightfall.

If we call that being true by chance, here is a case of a *general proposition* being entirely true in all its generality by chance.

Every general proposition is limited to a finite number of occasions in which it might conceivably be falsified, supposing that it is an assertion confined to what human beings may experience; and consequently it is conceivable that, although it should be true without exception, it should still only be by chance that it turns out true.

But if I see a man who is very regular in his habits and am led to offer to wager that that man will not miss winding his watch for the next month, you have your choice between two alternative hypotheses only

1st, you may suppose that some *principle* or *cause* is *really* operative to *make* him wind his watch daily, which *active principle* may have more or less strength; or

2nd, you may suppose that it is mere chance that his actions have hitherto been regular; and in that case, that regularity in the past affords you not the slightest reason for expecting its continuance in the future, any more than if he had thrown sixes three times running *that* event would render it either more or less likely that his next throw would show sixes.

It is the same with the operations of nature. With overwhelming uniformity, in our past experience, direct and indirect, stones left free to fall have fallen. Thereupon two hypotheses only are open to us. Either

1st, the uniformity with which those stones have fallen has been due to mere chance and affords no ground whatever, not the slightest for any expectation that the next stone that shall be let go will fall; or

2nd, the uniformity with which stones have fallen has been due to some *active general principle* in which case it would be a strange coincidence that it should cease to act at the moment my prediction was based upon it.

That position, gentlemen, will sustain criticism. It is irrefragable.

Of course, every sane man will adopt the latter hypothesis. If he could doubt it in the case of the stone,—which he can't—and I may as well drop the stone once for all,—I told you so!—if anybody doubts this still a thousand other such inductive predictions are getting verified every day, and he will have to suppose every one of them to be merely fortuitous in order reasonably to escape the conclusion that

General principles are really operative in nature. That is the doctrine of scholastic realism.

III

You may, perhaps, ask me how I connect generality with thirdness. . . .

Now Thirdness is nothing but the character of an object which embodies Betweenness or Mediation in its simplest and most rudimentary form; and I use it as the name of that element of the phenomenon which is predominant wherever Mediation is predominant, and which reaches its fullness in Representation.

Thirdness as I use the term is only a synonym for Representation, to which I prefer the less colored term because its suggestions are not so narrow and special as those of the word Representation. Now it is proper to say that a general principle that is operative in the real world is of the essential nature of a Representation and of a Symbol because its *modus operandi* is the same as that by which *words* produce physical effects. Nobody can deny that words do produce such effects. Take, for example, that sentence of Patrick Henry which, at the time of our revolution, was repeated by every man to his neighbor

Three millions of people, armed in the holy cause of Liberty, and in such a country as we possess, are invincible against any force that the enemy can bring against us.

Those words present this character of the general law of nature, [that] they might have produced effects indefinitely transcending any that circumstances allowed them to produce. It might, for example, have happened that some American schoolboy, sailing as a passenger in the Pacific Ocean, should have idly written down those words on a slip of paper. The paper might have been tossed overboard and might have been picked up by some Tagala on a beach of the island of Luzon; and if he had had them translated to him they might easily have passed from mouth to mouth there as they did in this country, and with similar effect.

Words then do produce physical effects. It is madness to deny it. The very denial of it involves a belief in it; and nobody can consistently fail to acknowledge it until he sinks to a complete mental paresis.

18

■ ■ ■

["Pragmatism" Defined]

The following definition is from Peirce's twenty-two-page manuscript review of Herbert Nichols's *Treatise on Cosmology* (1904). With masterful succinctness Peirce explains that pragmatism is not a philosophy of practical results but a method in logic. Based on the proposition that the sign relation is the essence of thinking, pragmatism tends to promote a realist rather than nominalist acceptance of the world of everyday, commonsense experience.

Source: MS 1476.

No criticism of such a book, no characterization of it, not even as slight a one as that here to be attempted, can have any meaning until the standpoint of the critic's observations be recognized. Our standpoint will be pragmatism; but this word has been so loosely used, that a partial explanation of its nature is needful, with some indications of the intricate process by which those who hold it become assured of its truth. If philosophy is ever to become a sound science, its students must submit themselves to that same ethics of terminology that students of chemistry and taxonomic biology observe; and when a word has been invented for the declared purpose of conveying a precisely defined meaning, they must give up their habit of using it for every other purpose that may happen to hit their fancy at the moment. The word *pragmatism* was invented to express a certain maxim of logic, which, as was shown at its first enouncement, involves a whole system of philosophy. The maxim is intended to furnish a method for the analysis of concepts. A concept is something having the mode of being of a general type which is, or may be made, the rational part of the purport of a word. A more precise or fuller definition cannot here be attempted. The method prescribed in the maxim is to trace out in the imagination the conceivable practical consequences,—that

is, the consequences for deliberate, self-controlled conduct,—of the affirma-
tion or denial of the concept; and the assertion of the maxim is that herein lies
the *whole* of the purport of the word, the *entire* concept. The sedulous exclu-
sion from this statement of all reference to sensation is specially to be remarked. Such a distinction as that between red and blue is held to form no
part of the concept. This maxim is put forth neither as a handy tool to serve
so far as it may be found serviceable, nor as a self-evident truth, but as a far-
reaching theorem solidly grounded upon an elaborate study of the nature of
signs. Every thought, or cognitive representation, is of the nature of a sign.
"Representation" and "sign" are synonyms. The whole purpose of a sign is
that it shall be interpreted in another sign; and its whole purport lies in the
special character which it imparts to that interpretation. When a sign determines an interpretation of itself in another sign, it produces an effect external
to itself, a physical effect, though the sign producing the effect may itself be
not an existent object but merely a type. It produces this effect, not in this or
that metaphysical sense, but in an indisputable sense. As to this, it is to be
remarked that actions beyond the reach of self-control are not subjects of
blame. Thinking is a kind of action, and reasoning is a kind of deliberate
action; and to call an argument illogical, or a proposition false, is a special
kind of moral judgment, and as such is inapplicable to what we cannot help.
This does not deny that what cannot be conceived today may be conceivable
tomorrow. But just as long as we cannot help adopting a mode of thought, so
long it must be thoroughly accepted as true. Any doubt of it is idle make-
believe and irredeemable paper. Now we all do regard, and cannot help regarding, signs as *affecting* their interpretant signs. It is by a patient examination of the various modes (some of them quite disparate) of interpretations of
signs, and of the connections between these (an exploration in which one
ought, if possible, to provide himself with a guide, or, if that cannot be, to
prepare his courage to see one conception that will have to be mastered peering over the head of another, and soon another peering over that, and so on,
until he shall begin to think there is to be no end of it, or that life will not be
long enough to complete the study) that the pragmatist has at length, to his
great astonishment, emerged from the disheartening labyrinth with this simple
maxim in his hand. In distrust of so surprising a result he has searched for
some flaw in its method, and for some case in which it should break down,
but after every deep-laid plot for disproving it that long-working ingenuity
could devise has recoiled upon his own head, and all doubts he could start
have been exhausted, he has been forced at last to acknowledge its truth. This

maxim once accepted,—intelligently accepted, in the light of the evidence of its truth,—speedily sweeps all metaphysical rubbish out of one's house. Each abstraction is either pronounced to be gibberish or is provided with a plain, practical definition. The general leaning of the results is toward what the idealists call the naïve, toward common sense, toward anthropomorphism. Thus, for example, the *real* becomes that which is such as it is regardless of what you or I or any of our folks may think it to be. The *external* becomes that element which is such as it is regardless of what somebody thinks, feels, or does, whether about that external object or about anything else. Accordingly, the external is necessarily real, while the real may or may not be external; nor is anything absolutely external nor absolutely devoid of externality. Every assertory proposition refers to something external, and even a dream withstands us sufficiently for one description to be true of it and another not. The *existent* is that which reacts against other things. Consequently, the external world, (that is, the world that is comparatively external) does not consist of existent objects merely, nor merely of these and their reactions; but on the contrary, its most important reals have the mode of being of what the nominalist calls "mere" words, that is, general types and would-bes. The nominalist is right in saying that they are substantially of the nature of words; but his "mere" reveals a complete misunderstanding of what our everyday world consists of.

Prolegomena to an
Apology for Pragmaticism

The following is from the last of a series of three articles on pragmatism that Peirce published in 1905 and 1906. In the passage printed here he argued that syllogisms can be represented and studied in diagrams, for logic is concerned chiefly with forms. Diagrams are forms, or icons, of possible relations. Moreover, he maintained that diagrams (there is not space to include his many examples) not only may represent logical truths but are existential instances of them, thus demonstrating that logic is present "throughout the purely physical world."

In this selection, except in the footnote, words in brackets are Peirce's.

Source: *The Monist* 16 (January 1906): 492–97.

Come on, my Reader, and let us construct a diagram to illustrate the general course of thought; I mean a System of diagrammatization by means of which any course of thought can be represented with exactitude.

"But why do that, when the thought itself is present to us?" Such, substantially, has been the interrogative objection raised by more than one or two superior intelligences, among whom I single out an eminent and glorious General.

Recluse that I am, I was not ready with the counter-question, which should have run, "General, you make use of maps during a campaign, I believe. But why should you do so, when the country they represent is right there?" Thereupon, had he replied that he found details in the maps that were so far from being "right there," that they were within the enemy's lines, I ought to have pressed the question, "Am I right, then, in understanding that, if you were thoroughly and perfectly familiar with the country, as, for example, if it lay just about the scenes of your childhood, no map of it would then be of the smallest use to you in laying out your detailed plans?" To that he could only have rejoined, "No, I do not say that, since I might probably desire the maps to stick pins into, so as to mark each anticipated day's change in the situations of the two armies." To that again, my sur-rejoinder should have been, "Well, General, that precisely corresponds to the advantages of a diagram of the course of a discussion. Indeed, just there, where you have so clearly pointed it out, lies the advantage of diagrams in general. Namely, if I may try to state the matter after you, one can make exact experiments upon uniform diagrams; and when one does so, one must keep a bright lookout for unintended and unexpected changes thereby brought about in the relations of different signifi- cant parts of the diagram to one another. Such operations upon diagrams, whether external or imaginary, take the place of the experiments upon real things that one performs in chemical and physical research. Chemists have ere now, I need not say, described experimentation as the putting of questions to Nature. Just so, experiments upon diagrams are questions put to the Nature of the relations concerned." The General would here, may be, have suggested (if I may emulate illustrious warriors in reviewing my encounters in after- thought,) that there is a good deal of difference between experiments like the chemist's, which are trials made upon the very substance whose behaviour is in question, and experiments made upon diagrams, these latter having no physical connection with the things they represent. The proper response to that, and the only proper one, making a point that a novice in logic would be apt to miss, would be this: "You are entirely right in saying that the chemist experiments upon the very object of investigation, albeit, after the experiment is made, the particular sample he operated upon could very well be thrown away, as having no further interest. For it was not the particular sample that the chemist was investigating; it was the molecular *structure*. Now he was long ago in possession of overwhelming proof that all samples of the same molecular structure react chemically in exactly the same way; so that one sample is all one with another. But the object of the chemist's research, that upon which he experiments, and to which the question he puts to Nature relates, is the Molecular Structure, which in all his samples has as complete an identity as it is in the nature of Molecular Structure ever to possess. Ac- cordingly, he does, as you say, experiment upon the Very Object under inves- tigation. But if you stop a moment to consider it, you will acknowledge, I think, that you slipped in implying that it is otherwise with experiments made upon diagrams. For what is there the Object of Investigation? It is the *form of a relation*. Now this Form of Relation is the very form of the relation between the two corresponding parts of the diagram. . . ."

Not only is it true that by experimentation upon some diagram an experimental proof can be obtained of every necessary conclusion from any given Copulate of Premisses, but, what is more, no "necessary" conclusion is any more apodictic than inductive reasoning becomes from the moment when experimentation can be multiplied *ad libitum* at no more cost than a summons before the imagination. I might furnish a regular proof of this, and am dissuaded from doing so now and here only by the exigency of space. . . . Under these circumstances, I will content myself with a rapid sketch of my proof. First, an analysis of the essence of a sign, (stretching that word to its widest limits, as *anything which, being determined by an object, determines an interpretation to determination, through it, by the same object,*) leads to a proof that every sign is determined by its object, either first, by partaking in the characters of the object, when I call the sign an *Icon*; secondly, by being really and in its individual existence connected with the individual object, when I call the sign an *Index*; thirdly, by more or less approximate certainty that it will be interpreted as denoting the object, in consequence of a habit [which term I use as including a natural disposition], when I call the sign a *Symbol*.[1] I next examine into the different efficiencies and inefficiencies of these three kinds of signs in aiding the ascertainment of truth. A Symbol incorporates a habit, and is indispensable to the application of any intellectual habit, at least. Moreover, Symbols afford the means of thinking about thoughts in ways in which we could not otherwise think of them. They enable us, for example, to create Abstractions, without which we should lack a great engine of discovery. These enable us to count, they teach us that collections are individuals [individual = individual object], and in many respects they are the very warp of reason. But since symbols rest exclusively on habits already definitely formed but not furnishing any observation even of themselves, and since knowledge is habit, they do not enable us to add to our knowledge even so much as a necessary consequent, unless by means of definite preformed habit. Indices, on the other hand, furnish positive assurance of the reality and the nearness of their Objects. But with the assurance there

---

1. In the original publication of this division, in 1867 [in selection 3 of this volume], the term "representamen" was employed in the sense of a sign in general, while "sign" was taken as a synonym of *index*, and an *Icon* was termed a "likeness."

goes no insight into the nature of those Objects. The same Perceptible may, however, function doubly as a Sign. That footprint that Robinson Crusoe found in the sand, and which has been stamped in the granite of fame, was an Index to him that some creature was on his island, and at the same time, as a Symbol, called up the idea of a man. Each *Icon* partakes of some more or less overt character of its object. They, one and all, partake of the most overt character of all lies and deceptions,—their Overtness. Yet they have more to do with the living character of truth than have either Symbols or Indices. The Icon does not stand unequivocally for this or that existing thing, as the Index does. Its Object may be a pure fiction, as to its existence. Much less is its Object necessarily a thing of a sort habitually met with. But there is one assurance that the Icon does afford in the highest degree. Namely, that which is displayed before the mind's gaze—the Form of the Icon, which is also its object,—must be *logically possible*. . . . That which we can learn from this division is of what sort a Sign must be to represent the sort of Object that reasoning is concerned with. Now reasoning has to make its conclusion manifest. Therefore, it must be chiefly concerned with forms, which are the chief objects of rational insight. Accordingly, Icons are specially requisite for reasoning. A Diagram is mainly an Icon, and an Icon of intelligible relations. It is true that what must be is not to be learned by simple inspection of anything. But when we talk of deductive reasoning being necessary, we do not mean, of course, that it is infallible. But precisely what we do mean is that the conclusion follows from the form of the relations set forth in the premiss. Now since a diagram, though it will ordinarily have Symbolide Features, as well as features approaching the nature of Indices, is nevertheless in the main an Icon of the forms of relations in the constitution of its Object, the appropriateness of it for the representation of necessary inference is easily seen. . . .

Thought is not necessarily connected with a brain. It appears in the work of bees, of crystals, and throughout the purely physical world; and one can no more deny that it is really there, than that the colors, the shapes, etc. of objects are really there. Consistently adhere to that unwarrantable denial, and you will be driven to some form of idealistic nominalism akin to Fichte's. Not only is thought in the organic world, but it develops there. But as there cannot be a General without Instances embodying it, so there cannot be thought without Signs. We must here give "Sign" a very wide sense, no doubt, but not too wide a sense to come within our definition.

The Basis of Pragmaticism

In a number of selections in this volume, Peirce speaks of the object as determining the sign, and in the Introduction it was emphasized that unlike some
contemporary semioticians, he was no believer in the arbitrariness of all meaning. Yet he was an indeterminist, as he shows in the following extract from a
long manuscript of 1906. In the triadic sign relation

OBJECT   SIGN   INTERPRETANT

the object determines the sign. But the sign does not determine the interpretant. Rather, the interpretant joins the object in determining the meaning of
the sign. The at least partial indeterminacy of the interpretant (or meaning
of the sign) makes the sign relation a powerful instrument of logical discovery,
contrary to "the dull and lazy brood of modern logicians" in the Cartesian
tradition, who held that only ideas immediately present (unrepresented) in the
mind were a reliable guide to truth.

Source: MS 283.

Mr. Ferdinand C. S. Schiller informs us that he and [William] James have
made up their minds that the true is simply the satisfactory. No doubt; but to
say "satisfactory" is not to complete any predicate whatever. Satisfactory to
what end?

That truth is the correspondence of a representation with its object is, as
Kant says, merely the nominal definition of it. Truth belongs exclusively to
propositions. A proposition has a subject (or set of subjects) and a predicate.
The subject is a sign; the predicate is a sign; and the proposition is a sign that
the predicate is a sign of that of which the subject is a sign. If it be so, it is
true. But what does this correspondence or reference of the sign, to its object,

consist in? The pragmaticist answers this question as follows. Suppose, he says, that the angel Gabriel were to descend and communicate to me the answer to this riddle from the breast of omniscience. Is this supposable; or does it involve an essential absurdity to suppose the answer to be brought to human intelligence? In the latter case, "truth," in this sense, is a useless word, which never can express a human thought. It is real, if you will; it belongs to that universe entirely disconnected from human intelligence which we know as the world of utter nonsense. Having no use for this meaning of the word "truth," we had better use the word in another sense presently to be described. But if, on the other hand, it be conceivable that the secret should be disclosed to human intelligence, it will be something that thought can compass. Now thought is of the nature of a sign. In that case, then, if we can find out the right method of thinking and can follow it out—the right method of transforming signs—then truth can be nothing more nor less than the last result to which the following out of this method would ultimately carry us. In that case, that to which the representation should conform, is itself something in the nature of a representation, or sign—something noumenal, intelligible, conceivable, and utterly unlike a thing-in-itself.

Truth is the conformity of a representamen to its object, *its* object, ITS object, mind you. The International Dictionary at the writer's elbow, the Century Dictionary which he daily studies, the Standard which he would be glad sometimes to consult, all contain the word *yes*; but that word is not true simply because he is going to ask on this eighth of January 1906, in Pike County, Pennsylvania, whether it is snowing. There must be an action of the object upon the sign to render the latter true. Without that, the object is not the representamen's object. If a colonel hands a paper to an orderly and says, "You will go immediately and deliver this to Captain Hanno," and if the orderly does so, we do not say the colonel told the truth; we say the orderly was obedient, since it was not the orderly's conduct which determined the colonel to say what he did, but the colonel's speech which determined the orderly's action. Here is a view of the writer's house: what makes that house to be the object of the view? Surely not the similarity of appearance. There are ten thousand others in the country just like it. No, but the photographer set up the film in such a way that according to the laws of optics, the film was forced to receive an image of this house. What the sign virtually has to do in order to indicate its object—and make it its—all it has to do is just to seize its interpreter's eyes and forcibly turn them upon the object meant: it is what a knock at the door does, or an alarum or other bell, or a whistle, a cannon-shot, etc. It is pure physiological compulsion; nothing else.

So, then, a sign, in order to fulfill its office, to actualize its potency, must be compelled by its object. This is evidently the reason of the dichotomy of the true and the false. For it takes two to make a quarrel, and a compulsion involves as large a dose of quarrel as is requisite to make it quite impossible that there should be compulsion without resistance.

It appears that there are certain mummified pedants who have never waked to the truth that the act of knowing a real object alters it. They are curious specimens of humanity, and as I am one of them, it may be amusing to see how I think. . . .

What is a sign? . . . We all have a ragged-outlined notion of what we call a sign. We wish to replace that by a well-defined concept, which may exclude some things ordinarily called signs and will almost certainly include some things not ordinarily so called. . . . Now a sign as ordinarily understood is an implement of intercommunication. . . . The reader will perhaps have noted that the phrase "medium of communication" is broader than the noun "sign," embracing for example a sentence in the imperative mood, which would be characterized as a "signal" rather than as a "sign."

. . . two separate minds are not requisite for the operation of a sign. Thus the premisses of an argument are a sign of the truth of the conclusion; yet it is essential to argument that the same mind that thinks the conclusion *as such* should also think the premisses. Indeed, two minds in communication are, in so far, "at one," that is, are properly one mind in that part of them. That being understood, the answer to the question [whether every sign is connected with two minds] will go on to recognize that every sign,—or, at any rate, nearly every one,—is a determination of something of the general nature of a mind, which we may call the "quasi-mind."

. . . It seems best to regard a sign as a determination of a quasi-mind; for if we regard it as an outward object, and as addressing itself to a human mind, that mind must first apprehend it as an object in itself, and only after that consider it in its significance: and the like must happen if the sign addresses itself to any quasi-mind. It must begin by forming a determination of that quasi-mind, and nothing will be lost by regarding that determination as the sign.

So, then, it is a determination that really acts upon that of which it is a determination, although *genuine* action is of one thing or another. This perplexes us, and an example of an analogous phenomenon will do good service here. . . .

Let a community of quasi-minds consist of liquid in a number of bottles which are in intimate connexion by tubes filled with the liquid. This liquid is of complex and somewhat unstable, mixed chemical composition. It also has so strong a cohesion and consequent surface-tension that the contents of each bottle take on a self-determined form.

Accident may cause one or another kind of decomposition to start at a point of one bottle producing a molecule of peculiar form, and this action may spread through a tube to another bottle. This new molecule will be a determination of the contents of the first bottle's contents which will thus act upon the contents of the second bottle by continuity. The new molecule produced by decomposition may then act chemically upon the original contents or upon some molecule produced by some other kind of decomposition, and thus we shall have a determination of the contents that actively operates upon that of which it is a determination, including another determination of the same subject.

But it is high time we insured ourselves against snares by determining the precise sense which we are to attach to the term *determination*, and to set in order the terminology of its mental vicinity. A few pages were given to this work in last October's *Monist* (Vol. XV, pp. 487–490) ["Issues of Pragmaticism"]; but those remarks require supplementation. Determination, in general, was not defined at all; and the attempt at defining the determination of a subject with respect to a character only covered (or seemed only to cover) explicit propositional determination. An incidental remark (p. 488) to the effect that words whose meaning should be determinate would leave "no latitude of interpretation" was more satisfactory, since the context made it plain that there must be no such latitude either for the interpreter or for the utterer. The explicitness of the words would leave the utterer no room for explanations of his meaning. This definition has the advantage of being applicable to a command, to a purpose, to a medieval substantial form; in short to anything capable of indeterminacy.[1] Even a future event can only be determinate in so

1. That everything indeterminate is of the nature of a sign can be proved inductively by imagining and analyzing instances of the surdest description. Thus, the indetermination of an event which should happen by pure chance without cause, *sua sponte*, as the Romans mythologically said, *spontanément* in French (as if what was done of one's own motion were sure to be irrational), does not belong to the event,—say, an explosion,—*per se*, or as explosion. Neither is [it] by virtue of any real relation; it is by

far as it is a consequent. Now the concept of a consequent is a logical concept. It is derived from the concept of the conclusion of an argument. But an argument is a sign of the truth of its conclusion; its conclusion is the rational *interpretation* of the sign. This is in the spirit of the Kantian doctrine that metaphysical concepts are logical concepts applied somewhat differently from their logical application. The difference, however, is not really as great as Kant represents it to be, and as he was obliged to represent it to be, owing to his mistaking the logical and metaphysical correspondents in almost every case.

Another advantage of this definition is that it saves us from the blunder of thinking that a sign is indeterminate simply because there is much to which it makes no reference; that, for example, to say, "C. S. Peirce wrote this article," is indeterminate because it does not say what the color of the ink used was, who made the ink, how old the father of the ink-maker [was] when his son was born, nor what the aspect of the planets was when that father was born. By making the definition turn upon the interpretation, all that is cut off.

At the same time, it is tolerably evident that the definition, as it stands, is not sufficiently explicit, and further, that at the present stage of our inquiry cannot be made altogether satisfactory. For what is the interpretation alluded to? To answer that convincingly would be either to establish or to refute the doctrine of pragmaticism. Still some explanations may be made. Every sign has a single object, though this single object may be a single set or a single continuum of objects. No general description can identify an object. But the common sense of the interpreter of the sign will assure him that the object must be one of a limited collection of objects. Suppose, for example, two Englishmen to meet in a continental railway carriage. The total number of subjects of which there is any appreciable probability that one will speak to the other perhaps does not exceed a million; and each will have perhaps half that million not far below the surface of consciousness, so that each unit of it is ready to suggest itself. If one mentions Charles the Second, the other need not consider what possible Charles the Second is meant. It is no doubt the English Charles Second. Charles the Second of England was quite a different man on different days; and it might be said that without further specification the subject is not identified. But the two Englishmen have no purpose of splitting hairs in their talk; and the latitude of interpretation which constitutes

---

virtue of a relation of reason. Now what is true by virtue of a relation of reason is representative, that is, is of the nature of a sign. A similar consideration applies to the indiscriminate shots and blows of a Kentucky free fight.

the indeterminacy of a sign must be understood as a latitude which might affect the achievement of a purpose. For two signs whose meanings are for all possible purposes equivalent are absolutely equivalent. This, to be sure, is rank pragmaticism; for a purpose is an affection of action.

What has been said of subjects is as true of predicates. Suppose the chat of our pair of Englishmen had fallen upon the color of Charles II's hair. Now that colors are seen quite differently by different retinas is known. That the chromatic sense is much more varied than it is positively known to be is quite likely. It is very unlikely that either of the travelers is trained to observe colors or is a master of their nomenclature. But if one says that Charles II had dark auburn hair, the other will understand him quite precisely enough for all their possible purposes; and it will be a determinate predication.

The October remarks made the proper distinction between the two kinds of indeterminacy, viz.: indefiniteness and generality, of which the former consists in the sign's not sufficiently expressing itself to allow of an indubitable determinate interpretation, while the latter turns over to the interpreter the right to complete the determination as he please. It seems a strange thing, when one comes to ponder over it, that a sign should leave its interpreter to supply a part of its meaning; but the explanation of the phenomenon lies in the fact that the entire universe,—not merely the universe of existents, but all that wider universe, embracing the universe of existents as a part, the universe which we are all accustomed to refer to as "the truth,"—that all this universe is perfused with signs, if it is not composed exclusively of signs. Let us note this in passing as having a bearing upon the question of pragmaticism.

The October remarks, with a view to brevity, omitted to mention that both indefiniteness and generality might primarily affect either the logical breadth or the logical depth of the sign to which it belongs. It now becomes pertinent to notice this. When we speak of the depth, or signification, of a sign we are resorting to hypostatic abstraction, that process whereby we regard a thought as a thing, make an interpretant sign the object of a sign. It has been a butt of ridicule since Molière's dying week, and the depth of a writer on philosophy can conveniently be sounded by his disposition to make fun of the basis of voluntary inhibition, which is the chief characteristic of mankind. For cautious thinkers will not be in haste to deride a kind of thinking that is evidently founded upon observation,—namely, upon observation of a sign. At any rate, whenever we speak of a predicate we are representing a thought as a thing, as a *substantia*, since the concepts of *substance* and *subject* are one, its concomitants only being different in the two cases. It is needful to remark this in the present connexion, because, were it not for hypostatic abstraction, there could be no generality of a predicate, since a sign which should make its interpreter its deputy to determine its signification at his pleasure would not signify anything, unless *nothing* be its significate. But hypostatic abstraction (the product of which may be termed a *hypostasis*) renders general classes of predicates possible, and classes of those classes, and so on, in a manner which the dull and lazy brood of modern logicians has failed to investigate sufficiently, not to say altogether. Oh, it maddens one to think how ignorant,—and in many respects, doubtless, far worse than ignorant,—their criminal neglect has left us. Only think, what legions of good-for-nothing bummers have written logic-books without bestirring themselves to repay their debt to the Greeks and to the medieval doctors by adding a single sentence of new truth to the science!

21

■ ■ ■

A Neglected Argument
for the Reality of God

Religiously, Peirce was a lifelong believer of a more or less pantheistic sort, as is suggested by the following essay, in which he argues that the interrelatedness of things is an argument for God's reality. By the three "Universes," as he calls them here, Peirce refers to his three categories of firstness, secondness, and thirdness. By "Musing" in spontaneous thought or "Pure Play" on their interrelatedness, one may come to believe in the reality of thirdness, or mentality. The fact that there can be no thirds without firsts (say, brain cells) and seconds (say, physical, or dyadic, relations between brain cells), scarcely proves that there are no thirds. Rather, the ability of signs (say, words) to affect firsts and seconds indicates the reality of thirdness, or spirit. God is the ultimate sign, the final third or general idea relating every phenomenon, be it first, second, or third. Even if not "Actual," God is still "Real."

As qualification for the special position of concluding essay, this piece has the advantage of including a retrospective glance at some of Peirce's earlier writings. The complexity of his terminology and the large shifts in denotation that he accorded to some terms have resulted in charges of inconsistency in his philosophy as it developed over the course of his life. He admitted to numerous changes of opinion and no doubt failed to recognize many others. Yet that Peirce's late philosophy of "pragmaticism" was a fundamentally consistent evolution of his earlier views can be ascertained by comparing his distinction between "real" and "actual" in this essay with what he said of reality in his 1871 review of Fraser's edition of Berkeley's *Works* and in "How to Make Our Ideas Clear" (1878)—selections 7 and 10 of this volume.

A final advantage of this essay as a closing selection is that it reminds us of what it has been impossible sufficiently to emphasize in a one-volume col-

lection—that Peirce's semiotic is a logical proposition: the validity of inference—whether deductive, inductive, or hypothetical ("Retroductive")—can be
established on entirely objective grounds, without reference to any supposedly
unrepresented or immediate self-knowledge by the mind.

Source: *Hibbert Journal* 7 (October 1908): 90–112.

I

The word "God," so "capitalised" (as we Americans say), is *the* definable
proper name, signifying *Ens necessarium*; in my belief Really creator of all
three Universes of Experience.

Some words shall herein be capitalised when used, not as vernacular, but
as terms defined. Thus an "idea" is the substance of an actual unitary thought
or fancy; but "Idea," nearer Plato's idea of ἰδέα, denotes anything whose
Being consists in its mere capacity for getting fully represented, regardless of
any person's faculty or impotence to represent it.

"Real" is a word invented in the thirteenth century to signify having Properties, *i.e.* characters sufficing to identify their subject, and possessing these
whether they be anywise attributed to it by any single man or group of men,
or not. Thus, the substance of a dream is not Real, since it was such as it was,
merely in that a dreamer so dreamed it; but the fact of the dream is Real, if it
was dreamed; since if so, its date, the name of the dreamer, etc., make up a
set of circumstances sufficient to distinguish it from all other events; and these
belong to it, *i.e.* would be true if predicated of it, whether A, B, or C Actually
ascertains them or not. The "Actual" is that which is met with in the past,
present, or future.

An "Experience" is a brutally produced conscious effect that contributes
to a habit, self-controlled, yet so satisfying, on deliberation, as to be destruc-
tible by no positive exercise of internal vigour. I use the word "self-controlled" for "controlled by the thinker's self," and not for "uncontrolled"
except in its own spontaneous, *i.e.* automatic, self-development, as Professor
J. M. Baldwin uses the word. Take for illustration the sensation undergone by
a child that puts its forefinger into a flame with the acquisition of a habit of
keeping all its members out of all flames. A compulsion is "Brute," whose
immediate efficacy nowise consists in conformity to rule or reason.

Of the three Universes of Experience familiar to us all, the first comprises all mere Ideas, those airy nothings to which the mind of poet, pure mathematician, or another *might* give local habitation and a name within that mind. Their very airy-nothingness, the fact that their Being consists in mere capability of getting thought, not in anybody's Actually thinking them, saves their Reality. The second Universe is that of the Brute Actuality of things and facts. I am confident that their Being consists in reactions against Brute forces, notwithstanding objections redoubtable until they are fairly and closely examined. The third Universe comprises everything whose being consists in active power to establish connections between different objects, especially between objects in different Universes. Such is everything which is essentially a Sign—not the mere body of the Sign, which is not essentially such, but, so to speak, the Sign's Soul, which has its Being in its power of serving as intermediary between its Object and a Mind. Such, too, is a living consciousness, and such the life, the power of growth, of a plant. Such is a living constitution—a daily newspaper, a great fortune, a social "movement."

An "Argument" is any process of thought reasonably tending to produce a definite belief. An "Argumentation" is an Argument proceeding upon definitely formulated premises.

If God Really be, and be benign, then, in view of the generally conceded truth that religion, were it but proved, would be a good outweighing all others, we should naturally expect that there would be some Argument for His Reality that should be obvious to all minds, high and low alike, that should earnestly strive to find the truth of the matter; and further, that this Argument should present its conclusion, not as a proposition of metaphysical theology, but in a form directly applicable to the conduct of life, and full of nutrition for man's highest growth. What I shall refer to as the N.A.—the Neglected Argument—seems to me best to fulfil this condition, and I should not wonder if the majority of those whose own reflections have harvested belief in God must bless the radiance of the N.A. for that wealth. Its persuasiveness is no less than extraordinary; while it is not unknown to anybody. Nevertheless, of all those theologians (within my little range of reading) who, with commendable assiduity, scrape together all the sound reasons they can find or concoct to prove the first proposition of theology, few mention this one, and they most briefly. They probably share those current notions of logic which recognise no other Arguments than Argumentations.

There is a certain agreeable occupation of mind which, from its having no distinctive name, I infer is not as commonly practised as it deserves to be; for indulged in moderately—say through some five to six per cent of one's waking time, perhaps during a stroll—it is refreshing enough more than to repay the expenditure. Because it involves no purpose save that of casting aside all serious purpose, I have sometimes been half-inclined to call it reverie, with some qualification; but for a frame of mind so antipodal to vacancy and dreaminess such a designation would be too excruciating a misfit. In fact, it is Pure Play. Now, Play, we all know, is a lively exercise of one's powers. Pure Play has no rules, except this very law of liberty. It bloweth where it listeth. It has no purpose, unless recreation. The particular occupation I mean—a *petite bouchée* with the Universes—may take either the form of esthetic contemplation, or that of distant castle-building (whether in Spain or within one's own moral training), or that of considering some wonder in one of the Universes, or some connection between two of the three, with speculation concerning its cause. It is this last kind—I will call it "Musement" on the whole—that I particularly recommend, because it will in time flower into the N.A. One who sits down with the purpose of becoming convinced of the truth of religion is plainly not inquiring in scientific singleness of heart, and must always suspect himself of reasoning unfairly. So he can never attain the entirety even of a physicist's belief in electrons, although this is avowedly but provisional. But let religious meditation be allowed to grow up spontaneously out of Pure Play without any breach of continuity, and the Muser will retain the perfect candour proper to Musement.

If one who had determined to make trial of Musement as a favourite recreation were to ask me for advice, I should reply as follows: The dawn and the gloaming most invite one to Musement; but I have found no watch of the nychthemeron that has not its own advantages for the pursuit. It begins passively enough with drinking in the impression of some nook in one of the three Universes. But impression soon passes into attentive observation, observation into musing, musing into a lively give-and-take of communion between self and self. If one's observations and reflections are allowed to specialise themselves too much, the Play will be converted into scientific study; and that cannot be pursued in odd half-hours.

I should add: adhere to the one ordinance of Play, the law of liberty. I can testify that the last half century, at least, has never lacked tribes of Sir Oracles, colporting brocards to bar off one or another roadway of inquiry; and a Rabelais would be needed to bring out all the fun that has been packed in their airs of infallibility. Auguste Comte, notwithstanding his having apparently produced some unquestionably genuine thinking, was long the chief of such a band. The vogue of each particular maxim of theirs was necessarily brief. For what distinction can be gained by repeating saws heard from all mouths? No bygone fashion seems more grotesque than a *panache* of obsolete wisdom. I remember the days when a pronouncement all the rage was that no science must borrow the methods of another; the geologist must not use a microscope, nor the astronomer a spectroscope. Optics must not meddle with electricity, nor logic with algebra. But twenty years later, if you aspired to pass for a commanding intellect, you would have to pull a long face and declare that "It is not the business of science to search for origins." This maxim was a masterpiece, since no timid soul, in dread of being thought naïve, would dare inquire what "origins" were, albeit the secret confessor within his breast compelled the awful self-acknowledgment of his having no idea into what else than "origins" of phenomena (in some sense of that indefinite word) man can inquire. That human reason can comprehend some causes is past denial, and once we are forced to recognise a given element in experience, it is reasonable to await positive evidence before we complicate our acknowledgment with qualifications. Otherwise, why venture beyond direct observation? Illustrations of this principle abound in physical science. Since, then, it is certain that man is able to understand the laws and the causes of some phenomena, it is reasonable to assume, in regard to any given problem, that it would get rightly solved by man, if a sufficiency of time and attention were devoted to it. Moreover, those problems that at first blush appear utterly insoluble receive, in that very circumstance, as Edgar Poe remarked in his *The Murders in the Rue Morgue*, their smoothly-fitting keys. This particularly adapts them to the Play of Musement.

Forty or fifty minutes of vigorous and unslackened analytic thought bestowed upon one of them usually suffices to educe from it all there is to educe, its general solution. There is no kind of reasoning that I should wish to discourage in Musement; and I should lament to find anybody confining it to a method of such moderate fertility as logical analysis. Only, the Player should bear in mind that the higher weapons in the arsenal of thought are not playthings but edge-tools. In any mere Play they can be used by way of exercise alone; while logical analysis can be put to its full efficiency in Musement. So, continuing the counsels that had been asked of me, I should say, "Enter your skiff of Musement, push off into the lake of thought, and leave the breath of heaven to swell your sail. With your eyes open, awake to what is about or within you, and open conversation with yourself; for such is all meditation." It is, however, not a conversation in words alone, but is illustrated, like a lecture, with diagrams and with experiments.

Different people have such wonderfully different ways of thinking, that it would be far beyond my competence to say what courses Musements might not take; but a brain endowed with automatic control, as man's indirectly is, is so naturally and rightly interested in its own faculties that some psychological and semi-psychological questions would doubtless get touched; such, in the latter class, as this: Darwinians, with truly surprising ingenuity, have concocted, and with still more astonishing confidence have accepted as proved, one explanation for the diverse and delicate beauties of flowers, another for those of butterflies, and so on; but why is all nature—the forms of trees, the compositions of sunsets—suffused with such beauties throughout, and not nature only, but the other two Universes as well? Among more purely psychological questions, the nature of pleasure and pain will be likely to attract attention. Are they mere qualities of feeling, or are they rather motor instincts attracting us to some feelings and repelling others? Have pleasure and pain the same sort of constitution, or are they contrasted in this respect, pleasure arising upon the formation or strengthening of an association by resemblance, and pain upon the weakening or disruption of such a habit or conception?

Psychological speculations will naturally lead on to musings upon metaphysical problems proper, good exercise for a mind with a turn for exact thought. It is here that one finds those questions that at first seem to offer no handle for reason's clutch, but which readily yield to logical analysis. But problems of metaphysics will inevitably present themselves that logical analysis will not suffice to solve. Some of the best will be motived by a desire to comprehend universe-wide aggregates of unformulated but partly experienced phenomena. I would suggest that the Muser be not too impatient to analyse these, lest some significant ingredient be lost in the process; but that he begin by pondering them from every point of view, until he seems to read some truth beneath the phenomena.

At this point a trained mind will demand that an examination be made of the truth of the interpretation; and the first step in such examination must be a logical analysis of the theory. But strict examination would be a task a little too serious for the Musement of hour-fractions, and if it is postponed there will be ample remuneration even in the suggestions that there is not time to examine; especially since a few of them will appeal to reason as all but certain.

Let the Muser, for example, after well appreciating, in its breadth and depth, the unspeakable variety of each Universe, turn to those phenomena that are of the nature of homogeneities of connectedness in each; and what a spectacle will unroll itself! As a mere hint of them I may point out that every small part of space, however remote, is bounded by just such neighbouring parts as every other, without a single exception throughout immensity. The matter of Nature is in every star of the same elementary kinds, and (except for variations of circumstance) what is more wonderful still, throughout the whole visible universe, about the same proportions of the different chemical elements prevail. Though the mere catalogue of known carbon-compounds alone would fill an unwieldy volume, and perhaps, if the truth were known, the number of amido-acids alone is greater, yet it is unlikely that there are in all more than about 600 elements, of which 500 dart through space too swiftly to be held down by the earth's gravitation, coronium being the slowest-moving of these. This small number bespeaks comparative simplicity of structure. Yet no mathematician but will confess the present hopelessness of attempting to comprehend the constitution of the hydrogen-atom, the simplest of the elements that can be held to earth.

From speculations on the homogeneities of each Universe, the Muser will naturally pass to the consideration of homogeneities and connections between two different Universes, or all three. Especially in them all we find one type of occurrence, that of growth, itself consisting in the homogeneities of small parts. This is evident in the growth of motion into displacement, and the growth of force into motion. In growth, too, we find that the three Universes conspire; and a universal feature of it is provision for later stages in earlier ones. This is a specimen of certain lines of reflection which will inevitably suggest the hypothesis of God's Reality. It is not that such phenomena might not be capable of being accounted for, in one sense, by the action of chance with the smallest conceivable dose of a higher element; for if by God be meant the *Ens necessarium*, that very hypothesis requires that such should be the case. But the point is that that sort of explanation leaves a mental explanation just as needful as before. Tell me, upon sufficient authority, that all cerebration depends upon movements of neurites that strictly obey certain physical laws, and that thus all expressions of thought, both external and internal, receive a physical explanation, and I shall be ready to believe you. But if you go on to say that this explodes the theory that my neighbour and myself are governed by reason, and are thinking beings, I must frankly say that it will not give me a high opinion of your intelligence. But however that may be, in the Pure Play of Musement the idea of God's Reality will be sure sooner or later to be found an attractive fancy, which the Muser will develop in various ways. The more he ponders it, the more it will find response in every part of his mind, for its beauty, for its supplying an ideal of life, and for its thoroughly satisfactory explanation of his whole threefold environment.

II

The hypothesis of God is a peculiar one, in that it supposes an infinitely incomprehensible object, although every hypothesis, as such, supposes its object to be truly conceived in the hypothesis. This leaves the hypothesis but one way of understanding itself; namely, as vague yet as true so far as it is definite, and as continually tending to define itself more and more, and without limit. The hypothesis, being thus itself inevitably subject to the law of growth, appears in its vagueness to represent God as so, albeit this is directly contradicted in the hypothesis from its very first phase. But this apparent attribution of growth to God, since it is ineradicable from the hypothesis, cannot, according to the hypothesis, be flatly false. Its implications concerning the Universes will be maintained in the hypothesis, while its implications concerning God will be partly disavowed, and yet held to be less false than their denial would be. Thus the hypothesis will lead to our thinking of features of each Universe as purposed; and this will stand or fall with the hypothesis. Yet a purpose essentially involves growth, and so cannot be attributed to God. Still it will, according to the hypothesis, be less false to speak so than to represent God as purposeless.

Assured as I am from my own personal experience that every man capable of so controlling his attention as to perform a little exact thinking will, if he examines Zeno's argument about Achilles and the tortoise, come to think, as I do, that it is nothing but a contemptible catch, I do not think that I either am or ought to be less assured, from what I know of the effects of Musement on myself and others, that any normal man who considers the three Universes in the light of the hypothesis of God's Reality, and pursues that line of reflection in scientific singleness of heart, will come to be stirred to the depths of his nature by the beauty of the idea and by its august practicality, even to the point of earnestly loving and adoring his strictly hypothetical God, and to that of desiring above all things to shape the whole conduct of life and all the springs of action into conformity with that hypothesis. Now to be deliberately and thoroughly prepared to shape one's conduct into conformity with a proposition is neither more nor less than the state of mind called Believing that proposition, however long the conscious classification of it under that head be postponed.

III

There is my poor sketch of the Neglected Argument, greatly cut down to bring it within the limits assigned to this article. Next should come the discussion of its logicality; but nothing readable at a sitting could possibly bring home to readers my full proof of the principal points of such an examination. I can only hope to make the residue of this paper a sort of table of contents, from which some may possibly guess what I have to say; or to lay down a series of plausible points through which the reader will have to construct the continuous line of reasoning for himself. In my own mind the proof is elaborated, and I am exerting my energies to getting it submitted to public censure. My present abstract will divide itself into three unequal parts. The first shall give the headings of the different steps of every well-conducted and complete inquiry, without noticing possible divergencies from the norm. I shall have to mention some steps which have nothing to do with the Neglected Argument in order to show that they add no jot nor tittle to the truth which is invariably brought just as the Neglected Argument brings it. The second part shall very briefly state, without argument (for which there is no room), just wherein lies the logical validity of the reasoning characteristic of each of the main stages of inquiry. The third part shall indicate the place of the Neglected Argument in a complete inquiry into the Reality of God, and shall show how well it would fill that place, and what its logical value is supposing the inquiry to be limited to this; and I shall add a few words to show how it might be supplemented.

Every inquiry whatsoever takes its rise in the observation, in one or another of the three Universes, of some surprising phenomenon, some experience which either disappoints an expectation, or breaks in upon some habit of expectation of the *inquisiturus*; and each apparent exception to this rule only confirms it. There are obvious distinctions between the objects of surprise in different cases; but throughout this slight sketch of inquiry such details will be unnoticed, especially since it is upon such that the logic-books descant. The inquiry begins with pondering these phenomena in all their aspects, in the search of some point of view whence the wonder shall be resolved. At length a conjecture arises that furnishes a possible Explanation, by which I mean a syllogism exhibiting the surprising fact as necessarily consequent upon the circumstances of its occurrence together with the truth of the credible conjecture, as premises. On account of this Explanation, the inquirer is led to regard his conjecture, or hypothesis, with favour. As I phrase it, he provisionally holds it to be "Plausible"; this acceptance ranges in different cases—and reasonably so—from a mere expression of it in the interrogative mood, as a question meriting attention and reply, up through all appraisals of Plausibility, to uncontrollable inclination to believe. The whole series of mental performances between the notice of the wonderful phenomenon and the acceptance of the hypothesis, during which the usually docile understanding seems to hold the bit between its teeth and to have us at its mercy—the search for pertinent circumstances and the laying hold of them, sometimes without our cognisance, the scrutiny of them, the dark labouring, the bursting out of the startling conjecture, the remarking of its smooth fitting to the anomaly, as it is turned back and forth like a key in a lock, and the final estimation of its Plausibility, I reckon as composing the First Stage of Inquiry. Its characteristic formula of reasoning I term Retroduction, *i.e.* reasoning from consequent to antecedent. In one respect the designation seems inappropriate; for in most instances where conjecture mounts the high peaks of Plausibility—and is *really* most worthy of confidence—the inquirer is unable definitely to formulate just what the explained wonder is; or can only do so in the iight of the hypothesis. In short, it is a form of Argument rather than of Argumentation.

Retroduction does not afford security. The hypothesis must be tested.

This testing, to be logically valid, must honestly start, not as Retroduction starts, with scrutiny of the phenomena, but with examination of the hypothesis, and a muster of all sorts of conditional experiential consequences which would follow from its truth. This constitutes the Second Stage of Inquiry. For its characteristic form of reasoning our language has, for two centuries, been happily provided with the name Deduction.

Deduction has two parts. For its first step must be by logical analysis to Explicate the hypothesis, *i.e.* to render it as perfectly distinct as possible. This process, like Retroduction, is Argument that is not Argumentation. But unlike Retroduction, it cannot go wrong from lack of experience, but so long as it proceeds rightly must reach a true conclusion. Explication is followed by Demonstration, or Deductive Argumentation. Its procedure is best learned from Book I. of Euclid's *Elements*, a masterpiece which in real insight is far superior to Aristotle's *Analytics*; and its numerous fallacies render it all the more instructive to a close student. It invariably requires something of the nature of a diagram; that is, an "Icon," or Sign that represents its Object in resembling it. It usually, too, needs "Indices," or Signs that represent their Objects by being actually connected with them. But it is mainly composed of "Symbols," or Signs that represent their Objects essentially because they will be so interpreted. Demonstration should be Corollarial when it can. An accurate definition of Corollarial Demonstration would require a long explanation; but it will suffice to say that it limits itself to considerations already introduced or else involved in the Explication of its conclusion; while *Theorematic* Demonstration resorts to a more complicated process of thought.

The purpose of Deduction, that of collecting consequents of the hypothesis, having been sufficiently carried out, the inquiry enters upon its Third Stage, that of ascertaining how far those consequents accord with Experience, and of judging accordingly whether the hypothesis is sensibly correct, or requires some inessential modification, or must be entirely rejected. Its characteristic way of reasoning is Induction. This stage has three parts. For it must begin with Classification, which is an Inductive Non-argumentational kind of Argument, by which general Ideas are attached to objects of Experience; or rather by which the latter are subordinated to the former. Following this will come the testing-argumentations, the Probations; and the whole inquiry will be wound up with the Sentential part of the Third Stage, which, by Inductive reasonings, appraises the different Probations singly, then their combinations, then makes self-appraisal of these very appraisals themselves, and passes final judgment on the whole result.

The Probations, or direct Inductive Argumentations, are of two kinds. The first is that which Bacon ill described as "*inductio illa quæ procedit per enumerationem simplicem.*" So at least he has been understood. For an enumeration of instances is not essential to the argument that, for example, there are no such beings as fairies, or no such events as miracles. The point is that there is no well-established instance of such a thing. I call this Crude Induction. It is the only Induction which concludes a logically Universal Proposition. It is the weakest of arguments, being liable to be demolished in a moment, as happened toward the end of the eighteenth century to the opinion of the scientific world that no stones fall from the sky. The other kind is Gradual Induction, which makes a new estimate of the proportion of truth in the hypothesis with every new instance; and given any degree of error there will *sometime* be an estimate (or would be, if the probation were persisted in) which will be absolutely the last to be infected with so much falsity. Gradual Induction is either Qualitative or Quantitative, and the latter either depends on measurements, or on statistics, or on countings.

IV

Concerning the question of the nature of the logical validity possessed by Deduction, Induction, and Retroduction, which is still an arena of controversy, I shall confine myself to stating the opinions which I am prepared to defend by positive proofs. The validity of Deduction was correctly, if not very clearly, analysed by Kant. This kind of reasoning deals exclusively with Pure Ideas attaching primarily to Symbols and derivatively to other Signs of our own creation; and the fact that man has a power of Explicating his own meaning renders Deduction valid. Induction is a kind of reasoning that may lead us into error; but that it follows a method which, sufficiently persisted in, will be Inductively Certain (the sort of certainty we have that a perfect coin, pitched up often enough, will *sometime* turn up heads) to diminish the error below any predesignate degree, is assured by man's power of perceiving Inductive Certainty. In all this I am inviting the reader to peep through the big end of the telescope; there is a wealth of pertinent detail that must here be passed over.

Finally comes the bottom question of logical Critic, What sort of validity can be attributed to the First Stage of inquiry? Observe that neither Deduction nor Induction contributes the smallest positive item to the final conclusion of the inquiry. They render the indefinite definite; Deduction Explicates; Induction evaluates: that is all. Over the chasm that yawns between the ultimate goal of science and such ideas of Man's environment as, coming over him during his primeval wanderings in the forest, while yet his very notion of error was of the vaguest, he managed to communicate to some fellow, we are building a cantilever bridge of induction, held together by scientific struts and ties. Yet every plank of its advance is first laid by Retroduction alone, that is to say, by the spontaneous conjectures of instinctive reason; and neither Deduction nor Induction contributes a single new concept to the structure. Nor is this less true or less important for those inquiries that self-interest prompts.

The first answer we naturally give to this question is that we cannot help accepting the conjecture at such a valuation as that at which we do accept it; whether as a simple interrogation, or as more or less Plausible, or, occasionally, as an irresistible belief. But far from constituting, by itself, a logical justification such as it becomes a rational being to put forth, this pleading, that we *cannot help* yielding to the suggestion, amounts to nothing more than a confession of having failed to train ourselves to control our thoughts. It is more to the purpose, however, to urge that the strength of the impulse is a symptom of its being instinctive. Animals of all races rise far above the general level of their intelligence in those performances that are their proper function, such as flying and nest-building for ordinary birds; and what is man's proper function if it be not to embody general ideas in art-creations, in utilities, and above all in theoretical cognition? To give the lie to his own consciousness of divining the reasons of phenomena would be as silly in a man as it would be in a fledgling bird to refuse to trust to its wings and leave the nest, because the poor little thing had read Babinet, and judged aerostation to be impossible on hydrodynamical grounds. Yes; it must be confessed that *if we knew* that the impulse to prefer one hypothesis to another really were analogous to the instincts of birds and wasps, it would be foolish not to give it play, within the bounds of reason; especially since we must entertain some hypothesis, or else forego all further knowledge than that which we have already gained by that very means. But is it a fact that man possesses this magical faculty? Not, I reply, to the extent of guessing right the first time, nor perhaps the second; but that the well-prepared mind has wonderfully soon guessed each secret of nature, is historical truth. All the theories of science have been so obtained. But may they not have come fortuitously, or by some such modification of chance as the Darwinian supposes? I answer that three or four independent methods of computation show that it would be ridiculous to suppose our science to have so come to pass. Nevertheless, suppose that it can be so "explained," just as that any purposed act of mine is supposed by materialistic necessitarians to have come about. Still, what of it? Does that materialistic explanation, supposing it granted, show that reason has nothing to do with my actions? Even the parallelists will admit that the one explanation leaves the same need of the other that there was before it was given; and this is certainly sound logic. There is a reason, an interpretation, a logic, in the course of scientific advance, and this indisputably proves to him who has perceptions of rational or significant relations, that man's mind must have been attuned to the truth of things in order to discover what he has discovered. It is the very bed-rock of logical truth.

Modern science has been builded after the model of Galileo, who founded it on *il lume naturale*. That truly inspired prophet had said that, of two hypotheses, the *simpler* is to be preferred; but I was formerly one of those who, in our dull self-conceit fancying ourselves more sly than he, twisted the maxim to mean the *logically* simpler, the one that adds the least to what has been observed, in spite of three obvious objections: first, that so there was no support for any hypothesis; secondly, that by the same token we ought to content ourselves with simply formulating the special observations actually made; and thirdly, that every advance of science that further opens the truth to our view discloses a world of unexpected complications. It was not until long experience forced me to realise that subsequent discoveries were every time showing I had been wrong, while those who understood the maxim as Galileo had done, early unlocked the secret, that the scales fell from my eyes and my mind awoke to the broad and flaming daylight that it is the simpler Hypothesis in the sense of the more facile and natural, the one that instinct suggests, that must be preferred; for the reason that unless man have a natural bent in accordance with nature's, he has no chance of understanding nature at all. Many tests of this principal and positive fact, relating as well to my own studies as to the researches of others, have confirmed me in this opinion; and when I shall come to set them forth in a book, their array will convince everybody. Oh no! I am forgetting that armour, impenetrable by accurate thought, in which the rank and file of minds are clad! They may, for example, get the notion that my proposition involves a denial of the rigidity of the laws of association: it would be quite on a par with much that is current. I do not mean that logical simplicity is a consideration of no value at all, but only that its value is badly secondary to that of simplicity in the other sense.

If, however, the maxim is correct in Galileo's sense, whence it follows that man has, in some degree, a divinitory power, primary or derived, like that of a wasp or a bird, then instances swarm to show that a certain altogether peculiar confidence in a hypothesis, not to be confounded with rash cocksureness, has a very appreciable value as a sign of the truth of the hypothesis. I regret I cannot give an account of certain interesting and almost convincing cases. The N.A. excites this peculiar confidence in the very highest degree.

V

We have now to apply these principles to the evaluation of the N.A. Had I space I would put this into the shape of imagining how it is likely to be esteemed by three types of men: the first of small instruction with corresponding natural breadth, intimately acquainted with the N.A., but to whom logic is all Greek; the second, inflated with current notions of logic, but prodigiously informed about the N.A.; the third, a trained man of science who, in the modern spirit, has added to his specialty an exact theoretical and practical study of reasoning and the elements of thought, so that psychologists account him a sort of psychologist, and mathematicians a sort of mathematician.

I should, then, show how the first would have learned that nothing has any kind of value in itself—whether esthetic, moral, or scientific—but only in its place in the whole production to which it appertains; and that an individual soul with its petty agitations and calamities is a zero except as filling its infinitesimal place, and accepting his little futility as his entire treasure. He will see that though his God would not *really* (in a certain sense) adapt means to ends, it is nevertheless quite true that there are relations among phenomena which finite intelligence must interpret, and truly interpret, as such adaptations; and he will macarise himself for his own bitterest griefs, and bless God for the law of growth with all the fighting it imposes upon him—Evil, *i.e.* what it is man's duty to fight, being one of the major perfections of the Universe. In that fight he will endeavour to perform just the duty laid upon him and no more. Though his desperate struggles should issue in the horrors of his rout, and he should see the innocents who are dearest to his heart exposed to torments, frenzy and despair, destined to be smirched with filth, and stunted in their intelligence, still he may hope that it be best *for them*, and will tell himself that in any case the secret design of God will be perfected through their agency; and even while still hot from the battle, will submit with adoration to His Holy will. He will not worry because the Universes were not constructed to suit the scheme of some silly scold.

The context of this I must leave the reader to imagine. I will only add that the third man, considering the complex process of self-control, will see that the hypothesis, irresistible though it be to first intention, yet needs Probation; and that though an infinite being is not tied down to any consistency, yet man, like any other animal, is gifted with power of understanding sufficient for the conduct of life. This brings him, for testing the hypothesis, to taking his stand upon Pragmaticism, which implies faith in common sense and in instinct, though only as they issue from the cupel-furnace of measured criticism. In short, he will say that the N.A. is the First Stage of a scientific inquiry, resulting in a hypothesis of the very highest Plausibility, whose ultimate test must lie in its value in the self-controlled growth of man's conduct of life.

Since I have employed the word *Pragmaticism*, and shall have occasion to use it once more, it may perhaps be well to explain it. About forty years ago, my studies of Berkeley, Kant, and others led me, after convincing myself that all thinking is performed in Signs, and that meditation takes the form of a dialogue, so that it is proper to speak of the "meaning" of a concept, to conclude that to acquire full mastery of that meaning it is requisite, in the first place, to learn to recognise the concept under every disguise, through extensive familiarity with instances of it. But this, after all, does not imply any true understanding of it; so that it is further requisite that we should make an abstract logical analysis of it into its ultimate elements, or as complete an analysis as we can compass. But, even so, we may still be without any living comprehension of it; and the only way to complete our knowledge of its nature is to discover and recognise just what general habits of conduct a belief in the truth of the concept (of any conceivable subject, and under any conceivable circumstances) would reasonably develop; that is to say, what habits would ultimately result from a sufficient consideration of such truth. It is necessary to understand the word "conduct," here, in the broadest sense. If, for example, the predication of a given concept were to lead to our admitting that a given form of reasoning concerning the subject of which it was affirmed was valid, when it would not otherwise be valid, the recognition of that effect in our reasoning would decidedly be a habit of conduct.

In 1873, in a Metaphysical Club in Cambridge, Mass., I used to preach this principle as a sort of logical gospel, representing the unformulated method followed by Berkeley, and in conversation about it I called it "Pragmatism." In December 1877 and January 1878 I set forth the doctrine in the *Popular Science Monthly*; and the two parts of my essay were printed in French in the *Revue Philosophique*, volumes vi. and vii. Of course, the doctrine attracted no particular attention, for, as I had remarked in my opening sentence, very few people care for logic. But in 1897 Professor James remodelled the matter, and transmogrified it into a doctrine of philosophy, some parts of which I highly approved, while other and more prominent parts I regarded, and still regard, as opposed to sound logic. About the time Professor Papirie discovered, to the delight of the Pragmatist school, that this doctrine was incapable of definition, which would certainly seem to distinguish it from every other doctrine in whatever branch of science, I was coming to the conclusion that my poor little maxim should be called by another name; and accordingly, in April 1905, I renamed it *Pragmaticism*. I had never before dignified it by any name in print, except that, at Professor Baldwin's request,

I wrote a definition of it for his *Dictionary of Psychology and Philosophy*. I did not insert the word in the *Century Dictionary*, though I had charge of the philosophical definitions of that work; for I have a perhaps exaggerated dislike of *réclame*.

It is that course of meditation upon the three Universes which gives birth to the hypothesis and ultimately to the belief that they, or at any rate two of the three, have a Creator independent of them, that I have throughout this article called the N.A., because I think the theologians ought to have recognised it as a line of thought reasonably productive of belief. This is the "humble" argument, the innermost of the nest. In the mind of a metaphysician it will have a metaphysical tinge; but that seems to me rather to detract from its force than to add anything to it. It is just as good an argument, if not better, in the form it takes in the mind of the clodhopper.

The theologians could not have *presented* the N.A.; because that is a living course of thought of very various forms. But they might and ought to have *described* it, and should have defended it, too, as far as they could, without going into original logical researches, which could not be justly expected of them. They are accustomed to make use of the principle that that which convinces a normal man must be presumed to be sound reasoning; and therefore they ought to say whatever can truly be advanced to show that the N.A., if sufficiently developed, will convince any normal man. Unfortunately, it happens that there is very little established fact to show that this is the case. I have not pretended to have any other ground for my belief that it is so than my assumption, which each one of us makes, that my own intellectual disposition is normal. I am forced to confess that no pessimist will agree with me. I do not admit that pessimists are, at the same time, thoroughly sane, and in addition are endowed in normal measure with intellectual vigour; and my reasons for thinking so are two. The first is, that the difference between a pessimistic and an optimistic mind is of such controlling importance in regard to every intellectual function, and especially for the conduct of life, that it is out of the question to admit that both are normal, and the great majority of mankind are naturally optimistic. Now, the majority of every race depart but little from the norm of that race. In order to present my other reason, I am obliged to recognise three types of pessimists. The first type is often found in exquisite and noble natures of great force of original intellect whose own lives are dreadful histories of torment due to some physical malady. Leopardi is a famous example. We cannot but believe, against their earnest protests, that if such men had had ordinary health, life would have worn for them the same colour as for the rest of us. Meantime, one meets too few pessimists of this type to affect the present question. The second is the misanthropical type, the type that makes itself heard. It suffices to call to mind the conduct of the famous pessimists of this kind, Diogenes the Cynic, Schopenhauer, Carlyle, and their kin with Shakespeare's Timon of Athens, to recognize them as diseased minds. The third is the philanthropical type, people whose lively sympathies, easily excited, become roused to anger at what they consider the stupid injustices of life. Being easily interested in everything, without being overloaded with exact thought of any kind, they are excellent raw material for *littérateurs*: witness Voltaire. No individual remotely approaching the calibre of a Leibniz is to be found among them.

The third argument, enclosing and defending the other two, consists in the development of those principles of logic according to which the humble argument is the first stage of a scientific inquiry into the origin of the three Universes, but of an inquiry which produces, not merely scientific belief, which is always provisional, but also a living, practical belief, logically justified in crossing the Rubicon with all the freightage of eternity. The presentation of this argument would require the establishment of several principles of logic that the logicians have hardly dreamed of, and particularly a strict proof of the correctness of the maxim of Pragmaticism. My original essay, having been written for a popular monthly, assumes, for no better reason than that real inquiry cannot begin until a state of real doubt arises and ends as soon as Belief is attained, that "a settlement of Belief," or, in other words, a state of *satisfaction*, is all that Truth, or the aim of inquiry, consists in. The reason I gave for this was so flimsy, while the inference was so nearly the gist of Pragmaticism, that I must confess the argument of that essay might with some justice be said to beg the question. The first part of the essay, however, is occupied with showing that, if Truth consists in satisfaction, it cannot be any *actual* satisfaction, but must be the satisfaction which *would* ultimately be found if the inquiry were pushed to its ultimate and indefeasible issue. This, I beg to point out, is a very different position from that of Mr. Schiller and the pragmatists of to-day. I trust I shall be believed when I say that it is only a desire to avoid being misunderstood in consequence of my relations with pragmatism, and by no means as arrogating any superior immunity from error which I have too good reason to know that I do not enjoy, that leads me to express my personal sentiments about their tenets. Their avowedly undefinable position, if it be not capable of logical characterisation, seems to me to be characterised by an angry hatred of strict logic, and even some disposition to rate any exact thought which interferes with their doctrines as all humbug. At the same time, it seems to me clear that their approximate acceptance of the Pragmaticist principle, and even that very casting aside of difficult distinctions (although I cannot approve of it), has helped them to a mightily clear discernment of some fundamental truths that other philosophers have seen but through a mist, and most of them not at all. Among such truths—all of them old, of course, yet acknowledged by few—I reckon their denial of necessitarianism; their rejection of any "consciousness" different from a visceral or other external sensation; their acknowledgment that there are, in a Pragmatistical sense, Real habits (which Really *would* produce effects, under circumstances that may not happen to get actualised, and are thus Real generals); and their insistence upon interpreting all hypostatic abstractions in terms of what they *would* or *might* (not actually *will*) come to in the concrete. It seems to me a pity they should allow a philosophy so instinct with life to become infected with seeds of death in such notions as that of the unreality of all ideas of infinity and that of the mutability of truth, and in such confusions of thought as that of active willing (willing to control thought, to doubt, and to weigh reasons) with willing not to exert the will (willing to believe).

Bibliography

■ ■ ■

For further writings by Peirce the reader should turn, as is indicated in the Introduction, to *Collected Papers of Charles Sanders Peirce*, 8 vols., edited by Charles Hartshorne and Paul Weiss (vols. 1–6) and by Arthur Burks (vols. 7–8) (Cambridge: Harvard University Press, 1931–58), and, better still, to the *Writings of Charles S. Peirce: A Chronological Edition*, 5 vols. to date (Bloomington: Indiana University Press, 1982–).

Some suggested further readings on Peirce and on semiotic are offered here. Because there is a voluminous body of writing about Peirce's thought and a vast literature on semiotic, no attempt has been made at comprehensiveness. Studies listed here are simply those that have proven useful in one respect or another to the editor of this volume and that are judged of possible usefulness to others interested in Peirce and semiotic.

Beginners interested in a general overview of Peirce's thought might do well to begin with Hookway. Interesting details of Peirce's life and suggestions as to his immense range and achievements are in Fisch. For a broader introduction that locates Peirce's place in the history of semiotic, Deely is highly recommended.

Apel, Karl-Otto. *Charles S. Peirce: From Pragmatism to Pragmaticism.* Amherst: University of Massachusetts Press, 1981.

Buchler, Justus. *Charles Peirce's Empiricism.* New York: Harcourt, Brace, 1939.

Colapietro, Vincent. *Peirce's Approach to the Self: A Semiotic Perspective on Human Subjectivity.* Albany: State University of New York Press, 1989.

Conkin, Paul. *Puritans and Pragmatists: Eight Eminent American Thinkers.* New York: Dodd, Mead, 1968.

Culler, Jonathan. *The Pursuit of Signs—Semiotics, Literature, Deconstruction.* Ithaca: Cornell University Press, 1981.

Deely, John N. *Introducing Semiotic: Its History and Doctrine.* Bloomington: Indiana University Press, 1982.

Derrida, Jacques. *Of Grammatology.* Translated by Gayatri Chakravorty Spivak. Baltimore: Johns Hopkins University Press, 1976.

Eco, Umberto. *The Role of the Reader: Explorations in the Semiotics of Texts*. Bloomington: Indiana University Press, 1979.

——. *Semiotics and the Philosophy of Language*. Bloomington: Indiana University Press, 1984.

——. *A Theory of Semiotics*. Bloomington: Indiana University Press, 1976.

Fisch, Max. *Peirce, Semeiotic, and Pragmatism: Essays*. Edited by Kenneth Laine Ketner and Christian J. W. Kloesel. Bloomington: Indiana University Press, 1986.

Freeman, Eugene, ed. *The Relevance of Charles Peirce*. La Salle, Ill.: Hegler Institute, 1983.

Gallie, W. B. *Peirce and Pragmatism*. Harmondsworth, Middlesex: Penguin Books, 1952.

Goudge, Thomas A. *The Thought of C. S. Peirce*. New York: Dover Publications, 1969.

Hardwick, Charles S., ed. *Semiotic and Significs: The Correspondence between Charles S. Peirce and Lady Victoria Welby*. Bloomington: Indiana University Press, 1977.

Hookway, Christopher. *Peirce*. London: Routledge and Kegan Paul, 1985.

Hoopes, James. *Consciousness in New England: From Puritanism and Ideas to Psychoanalysis and Semiotic*. Baltimore: Johns Hopkins University Press, 1989.

John of St. Thomas. *Tractatus de Signis: The Semiotic of John Poinsot*. Translated and presented by John N. Deely in consultation with Ralph Austin Powell. Berkeley: University of California Press, 1985.

Ketner, Kenneth Laine. *A Comprehensive Bibliography of the Published Works of Charles Sanders Peirce, with a Bibliography of Secondary Studies*. Bowling Green, Ohio: Bowling Green State University, Philosophy Documentation Center, 1986.

Kuklick, Bruce. *The Rise of American Philosophy: Cambridge, Massachusetts, 1860–1930*. New Haven: Yale University Press, 1977.

Moore, Edward C., and Richard S. Robin, eds. *Studies in the Philosophy of Charles Sanders Peirce*. Second Series. Amherst: University of Massachusetts Press, 1964.

Morris, Charles William. *Foundations of the Theory of Signs*. Chicago: University of Chicago Press, 1938.

Murphey, Murray G. *The Development of Peirce's Philosophy*. Cambridge: Harvard University Press, 1961.

Savan, David. *An Introduction to C. S. Peirce's Semiotics*. Toronto: Toronto Semiotic Circle, 1988.

Sebeok, Thomas Albert. *The Sign and Its Masters*. Austin: University of Texas Press, 1979.

Thompson, Manley. *The Pragmatic Philosophy of C. S. Peirce*. Chicago: University of Chicago Press, 1953.

Wiener, Philip H., and Frederick H. Young, eds. *Studies in the Philosophy of Charles Sanders Peirce*. Cambridge: Harvard University Press, 1952.

Index

■ ■ ■